Jason Cowley is a widely published journalist. Formerly editor of the award-winning *Observer Sport Monthly*, and *Granta magazine*, he is now editor of the *New Statesman* and a columnist on the London *Evening Standard*.

Further praise for *The Last Game*:
'This book is certainly not just for Arsenal or Liverpool fans but for all who want to reflect on the huge changes which have taken place in the culture of football over the past 20 years. It is particularly timely to read this book, with all the media coverage of the recent 20th anniversary commemorations of the Hillsborough tragedy. Those who only vaguely recall this terrible event will learn a great deal more from this book. They may also understand the hold football can have on an individual's life and relationships within a family . . . Very moving' Kate Hoey, *The Spectator*

'Elegant. Cowley handles the subject with grace . . . Beautifully touching. There is much more to this book than football. In the age of Cristiano Ronaldo and Ashley Cole it is a sign that football has not quite lost its soul – if it can inspire a book as lucid, moving and emotionally literate as this' Dominic Sandbrook, *Prospect*

'A personal history and a societal epoch . . . Cowley marks his narrative with extensive, well-sketched reminiscences and in-depth interviews with key actors from the Arsenal v Liverpool drama. He recreates the game on the page with great vigour . . . Profoundly moving, lovingly crafted and well executed . . . Cowley is indisputably a good writer' *Observer*

'Jason Cowley, in his nimble, affecting new book, uses a single game – Liverpool vs Arsenal, the climax of the 1988/89 season – as the springboard for an analysis of Britain at the tail-end of Thatcherism, an elegy for football as it was, and a memoir of his father' *Times Literary Supplement*

'Cowley is a renaissance man. A devotion to football is at the heart of his compelling new book, which skilfully weaves together a memoir of his suburban youth with an account of the nerve-shredding climax to the 1988–89 season. There was always a danger that Cowley's book might fall under the shadow of Hornby's masterpiece. Through the quality of his writing and his thought-provoking material, Cowley triumphantly avoids such a fate. He is excellent on the match itself, his descriptions of the game enlivened by first-hand testimony from many of the players he interviewed. The book has so much more than just football. There are reflections on racism, first romance, indie music and England's addiction to social status . . . But by far the strongest theme is the author's close relationship with his father and some of the most poignant scenes cover his father's last brooding months. The book ends, not just as a tribute to a famous Arsenal victory, but also as an elegy to his departed father and a vanished footballing tradition' Leo McKinstry, *Sunday Telegraph*

'Cowley's exploration of these cultural and historical matters is fine, discursive journalism. But his writing finds fresh legs in the book's other dimension . . . *The Last Game* is also a memoir centring on the relationship between Cowley and his complex and charismatic father . . . poignant, revelatory' *Guardian*

'Since Nick Hornby's *Fever Pitch* in 1992, it has been hard, perhaps impossible, to write a memoir that takes the journey from adolescence to adulthood through the landscape of English football without merely retracing its steps. Even harder, if the story is about Arsenal. Almost two decades later, Jason Cowley, gingerly but bravely, takes us on the same journey but with a very different itinerary because he chooses to read that landscape politically. To judge *The Last Game* on political grounds alone is to do it a disservice. Cowley's own journey, and his relationship with his father, are engagingly written and sweetly entwined with the football . . . Touching' David Goldblatt, *Independent*

'Beautifully nuanced ... Jason Cowley has done a bold thing with this book: he has pinpointed the cusp, the day the game's Berlin Wall crumbled. Cowley tells the story of that game poignantly, using eyewitness accounts. And perhaps, he argues, given the horrors of Hillsborough, the bloated, self-important game we have now isn't all that bad' *Daily Telegraph*

'For Cowley, as for most fans, football is a very personal love affair. *The Last Game* is also an honest and moving memoir about Cowley's relationship with his West Ham-supporting working class dad ... It is in fact the personal story which stands out ... Cowley's telling of the game itself is masterful and his pen portraits of the Arsenal players involved are well drawn. There are too few books which attempt to put our national obsession into a political context ... A highly readable and at times very moving exploration of a period of football that has now gone forever' *Tribune*

'An enjoyable book, pacily written and well researched. The actual game is brilliantly described in a lyrical match report which makes what we already know seem fantastically new. The tracts of the memoir are almost unbearably poignant' *Metro*

'A neat summary of all that has changed about English football over the past two decades' *FourFourTwo*

'*The Last Game* has the power to spark debate for several more seasons to come' *When Saturday Comes Magazine*

'A fascinating look back at a time when football changed forever' *Irish Daily Star on Sunday*

'What gives *The Last Game* its edge are the glimpses into a 1970s childhood lived out in the Essex hinterlands with an elusive father ... unexpectedly poignant' DJ Taylor, *Waterstone's Books Quarterly*

'Further confirmation that football reads aren't all staid stats and premature biographies. Cowley's page-turner details Arsenal's unlikely last-gasp 1988/89 title victory. It also packs in plenty for non-sports nuts, too, juxtaposing current affairs and fond anecdotes of a time before the Premier League came to town' *Short List*

'Much more than "Gooner" triumphalism' Liverpool *Daily Post*

'*The Last Game* is biographical, anecdotal, factual and emotional, changing tack constantly. It's much the richer for it, too. Always informative, considered and interesting. With a single football match at its core, Cowley has produced a genuinely fascinating book about life and death: in football, in history and, just as significantly, as individuals' Robin Hackett, Setanta.com

'The match is expertly recreated. Reading Cowley's account it is hard to argue with his analysis. The book is required reading' Jim White, *Eurosport*

'Intriguing, the most talked-about soccer book this year' *Soccerphile*

'Where Cowley succeeds is in diligently exploring the characters and context that make the story so absorbing, not least the profoundly different landscape of Hillsborough-era footballers in the late 1980s. Interviews with players, eye-witnesses, officials and journalists provide illuminating vignettes ... A rewarding and often poignant portrait' *City A.M.*

THE LAST GAME

Love, Death and Football

Jason Cowley

POCKET
BOOKS

LONDON • SYDNEY • NEW YORK • TORONTO

First published in Great Britain in 2009 by Simon & Schuster UK Ltd
This edition first published by Pocket Books, 2010
An imprint of Simon & Schuster UK Ltd
A CBS COMPANY

1 3 5 7 9 10 8 6 4 2

Simon & Schuster UK Ltd
1st Floor
222 Gray's Inn Road
London
WC1X 8HB

www.simonandschuster.co.uk

Simon & Schuster Australia
Sydney

Pictures courtesy of the author and © Corbis

A CIP catalogue for this book is available
from the British Library.

ISBN 978-1-84739-218-3

Typeset in Palatino by M Rules
Printed by CPI Cox & Wyman, Reading, Berkshire RG1 8EX

The Imagination is always at the end of an era
Wallace Stevens

This book is dedicated to my mother

Contents

Prologue: At Highbury   1

Part One: Before the Game

One: Out of Time   11

Two: Claret and Blue   27

Three: A Little Bit of Beckenbauer   54

Four: A Moment of Pause   68

Five: North and South   86

Six: This is Anfield   109

Part Two: The Last Game

Seven: The First Half   129

Eight: The Second Half   144

Nine: Outside the Cage   160

Part Three: After the Game

Ten: World in Motion   171

Eleven: Things Happen   198

Twelve: The Big Sleep   238

Epilogue: At the Emirates   266

Author's Note   277

Bibliography   278

Prologue: At Highbury

Who can deny that these things to come are not yet?
Yet already there is in the mind an expectation
Of things to come

St Augustine

Saturday 15 April 1989

In the spring of 1989 I was in my final year at Southampton University, studying English and philosophy and living with friends in a rented house on an estate on which all the roads were named after flowers. Our house was on Honeysuckle Road, and was a three-bedroom, brick-built, semi-detached former council property owned by an Iranian businessman named Ali Mohammad. He had once been a science teacher in Tehran and had come to live in England to escape the terror of Ayatollah Khomeini's Islamic revolution – that was how he told it – only to embrace another kind of revolution: the Thatcher revolution. He had become a property entrepreneur and now owned numerous houses in Southampton, most of which were rented out to students. In rudimentary English he told us that although we were paying 'bad rent' (a weekly £13, negotiated down from about £20), we were 'good students' – presumably because we always paid on time. We paid on time because three of us in the house received housing benefit, which took care of most of the rent. This was the high noon of Thatcherite free market fundamentalism, when taxes were being reduced (at the 1987 budget the top rate of income tax was cut from sixty to forty per cent) and the old nationalised utilities were being privatised as the Tories sought to break from the quasi-socialist consensus politics of the postwar decades. There were widespread and punitive cuts in public spending and services as Britain moved towards becoming a 'market economy'. In spite of the so-called rolling back of the welfare state, students still received housing benefit and government maintenance grants as well as being able to claim unemployment benefit during vacations, even the short five-week Easter break. We were indulged by the state in ways that must seem grotesquely unfair to today's harassed and debt-burdened students with their loans and tuition fees.

It felt like a good time to be a student but I often wondered if I was really making the best of it. I certainly didn't feel much like doing any work that weekend, though I was soon to begin my final exams. So I took the train to London and went to see a football match instead: Arsenal versus Newcastle at Highbury. No forward planning, no ticket required; you just turned up, paid at the gate and stood on the terraces in the place where you always tried to stand.

The crowd of 38,000 that afternoon was smaller than I'd expected: Highbury's capacity before the advent of all-seater stadiums was 55,000 and at this point, after more than a decade and a half of drift, Arsenal were in contention to win the First Division title for the first time since 1971. But perhaps the crowd was actually better than it should have been: it's hard for people who don't know what English football was like in the late seventies or much of the eighties to understand not only how different it seemed then but also how intractable, indeed insoluble, its problems were believed to be. English football wasn't exactly a dying game, but it was withered and sickly. It was, like the old pre-Blair Labour Party, riven by factionalism, in thrall to the past, especially unattractive to women, and urgently requiring a consensus-breaking transformation. But of what kind no one quite knew.

For the Newcastle game that afternoon there was space enough for our group – me, my close friend Matthew and my younger sister Victoria's boyfriend – to move freely on the North Bank terrace, and we all shared the same terrific sense of restless anticipation. The match of the day, however, was the FA Cup semi-final between Liverpool and Nottingham Forest being played more than 150 miles away at the Hillsborough stadium in Sheffield.

Not long into the game at Highbury it was announced over the public-address system that the match at Hillsborough had been abandoned because of 'crowd trouble'. The reply from the Highbury crowd was instantaneous: *We hate Scousers/We hate Scousers*, a chant with which I idiotically joined in. The announcer responded: there had been 'fatalities' at the game. This time there was no Highbury reply; only sudden silence then ripples of whispered unease. This being before mobile phones and the text message, before the Internet and the BlackBerry; we had only the public announcements and those few among the crowd with pocket transistor radios to communicate the news from Sheffield. We knew that the game had been abandoned and that people had died, but we had little idea as to exactly why or how.

Arsenal went on to win a subdued game 1–0 to remain well positioned for the title. *We are top-o-th-league/We are top-o-th-league*, we chanted as we left the stadium, but our usual happy conviction was seemingly absent. From Highbury I went back to see my younger sister at the family home in Hertfordshire, where I intended to spend the rest of the weekend.

Ninety-six people were crushed to death on the terraces at Hillsborough that afternoon; the American novelist Don DeLillo described their suffering in his novel *Mao II* as being like a scene from a great religious painting, 'a crowded twisted vision of a rush to death as only a master of the age could paint it'. But that isn't right. The crush on the Leppings Lane terrace at Hillsborough followed the opening of an exit gate and the consequent surge of many hundreds, perhaps even thousands, of people into the stadium, some with tickets, some without, just before the start of the game. The fans who found themselves trapped were not rushing. How could they rush when they had nowhere to go, when they could scarcely put one foot in front of the other? Many died on their feet that day as the very breath of life was squeezed out of them.

The Hillsborough tragedy came at a critical moment in the history of English football. By 1989 the sport and its attitudes had become an embarrassment to a nation that had throughout the decade striven aggressively to remake itself, both economically and culturally. Through all the wider changes and convulsions of the long tumultuous years of the Thatcher government, as the prime minister sought to haul Britain from the path it had followed for sixty years, football had remained largely unreformed and unreconstructed, stubbornly apart.

Mrs Thatcher and her advisors had little understanding of its culture and history and thus considered measures that would achieve little but the stigmatisation of the fans – the introduction of compulsory identity cards, for example. For a period it was even considered that matches might be played behind closed doors, without crowds.

In 1989 English football was as reviled and isolated as it has ever been, our club sides banned from European competitions. The ban was enacted after a rampage by Liverpool supporters before the start of the 1985 European Cup Final at the decrepit Heysel Stadium in Belgium led to the collapse of a wall inside. Thirty-nine Juventus fans died and many hundreds more were injured. The match was, astonishingly, still played, with dead bodies piled up at one end of the ground and rubble from the collapsed wall scattered across the running track that enclosed the pitch.

Yet, after Heysel, as millions of people turned in disgust away from football, I found myself turning towards it, being re-engaged by it. Attendances may have been dropping to record postwar lows, but I started going to games again, falling in love once more with a sport that had defined my boyhood and mid-teenage years. I'd become interested in music, fashion and politics in the early eighties, and it was around then that I'd stopped going to football. I'd accepted the false dichotomy between the so-called highbrow and lowbrow and had concluded that you couldn't be both a book man and a sports man – that the two cultures were separate, with no connecting bridge between them. A choice had to be made: books or games, music or sport, exercise or nightclubbing. And football was bound up in complicated ways with my Essex boyhood, from which I'd been in confused retreat, and with the East End heritage of my father, with which, in middle age, he was suddenly and quite bewilderingly seeking to reconnect.

The 1988–89 season was the Football League's centenary, but there was little to celebrate. Hillsborough was the final act in a decade of misfortune, the last in a chain of calamities and woes that included Heysel and the Bradford fire disaster, also in 1985, when a blaze which started during a Third Division match between Bradford City and Lincoln City devastated the home side's seventy-seven-year-old wooden main stand and killed fifty-six people.

The morning after Hillsborough, after I'd read the newspaper reports, studied the front-page photographs of those crushed against the fences – the sad, sickening, bloated faces of the dying – and watched and listened to the various news reports on TV and radio, I felt the need to speak to my father, who had introduced me to football many years before and who, in recent times, had inspired my reconnection with the game. The trouble was that I didn't know how to reach him in Hong Kong, where he was on business. Where he stayed while he was away, whom he saw: these details didn't matter to me then. In the event, he called me; it was early evening in Hong Kong and he wanted to know the mood in England. He and my mother had been at a dinner party together in Kowloon, he said; the game had been on in another room – the host was, like my father, a football fan. During the dinner party someone had gone to check the score and there it was, the tragedy of Hillsborough unfolding on the screen. Everyone left the table and gathered around the television. They watched the injured and dying being carried away on the advertising hoardings that were being used as emergency stretchers; watched people trying to scale the security fences to reach the safety of the pitch only to be beaten back by police who didn't fully understand what was happening; watched the stunned, aghast faces of those people trapped behind the fences.

'How can the season continue after this?' I asked. 'It obviously can't,' my father said. 'It's over.'

'What?' I said, unsure if I'd heard him properly, since there was the inevitable, irritating delay on the line.

'It's over,' he said again.

When I heard him say this I was surprised by my own instant feelings of disappointment. I hadn't wanted him to agree that it was over. I'd wanted him to call for continuity. He'd done a bit of acting; he knew the rules of the stage and that no matter what happened the show must go on. *How can it be over?* I thought. *We're top of the League. After waiting so long, after all these years, this is our season.*

But I said: 'I agree, it's over.' I heard my voice return as a sombre echo.

'What happened up there,' he continued, 'could've happened to any of us, anywhere, at any time. The whole infrastructure of the game is corrupt.'

As I waited for him to speak again I thought of him all that distance away and tried to picture the expression on his face. Then he said: 'I'm finished with football.'

It was announced the next day that the season would be suspended for two weeks to allow for a period of mourning and for the government and other authorities to prepare their appalled and urgent responses.

Part One: Before the Game

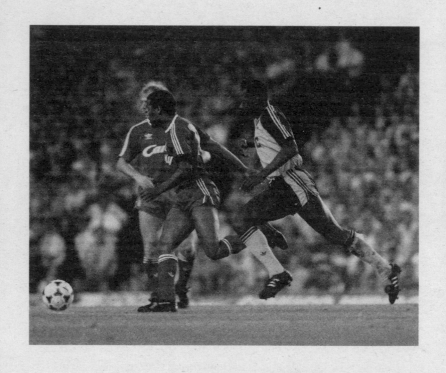

One: Out of Time

Six weeks later

The clock is running down – beyond ninety minutes now.
The floodlights are hard and bright against the night sky.
The ball is with the Arsenal goalkeeper. For once, he doesn't
launch it high upfield but throws it out instead to his right-
back, Lee Dixon. These are the closing moments of the last
game of the last full football season of the eighties. Nothing
is resolved. Dixon plays the ball long and accurately, and it is
collected by the tall striker Alan Smith, scorer of Arsenal's
disputed first goal. He receives the pass and with his usual
unostentatious economy of movement turns to play the ball
through to Michael Thomas, rushing forward from midfield,
just as he has, tirelessly and without reward, throughout
the match.

Unmarked and sprinting deep into Liverpool territory,
Thomas miscontrols Smith's pass; the ball spins away,
bounces against a Liverpool defender and then, improbably,
back to Thomas. He accepts his gift as calmly as though
he were expecting it. Sensing danger the Liverpool goalkeeper, Bruce Grobbelaar, moves towards Thomas just as
he reaches the edge of the penalty box. Red-shirted Liverpool

defenders are pursuing Thomas as if he's just made off with someone's wallet: *Help, stop that man!* As many as 42,000 spectators are watching inside the ground and many millions more on television, all of them suspended at a point of heightened crisis. It's all happening so fast, yet there's also something hallucinatory about what's unfolding, as if time itself is being slowed. Too little time, too much time.

Brian Moore, on commentary duty for ITV, describes the action with characteristic authority.

'Arsenal come streaming forward now in surely what will be their last attack.'

His voice is resolute against the sound of the crowd.

'A good ball by Dixon finding Smith.'

His tone is expectant, quickening.

'To Thomas, charging through the midfield. Thomas.'

He sounds incredulous.

'It's up for grabs now . . .'

Here he comes, Thomas, free – lost to the moment, as he would later describe it. He must know that the defenders are closing on him, must feel the hot rush and strain of their exertion. He has the ball and is moving towards the penalty spot. The goalkeeper is coming towards him, narrowing the space. Thomas has the ball. He is waiting for the goalkeeper to commit, just waiting.

'Thomas' – Moore is almost shouting – 'right at the end.'

At around nine o'clock on the morning of Friday 26 May 1989 the Arsenal players began gathering at their London Colney training ground, just off junction 22 of the M25 in the monotonous flatlands of this part of Hertfordshire. It was another warm day for London in the spring: the temperature would reach sixty-eight degrees and there would be thirteen hours of continuous sunshine in Liverpool. Arsenal had, nine days earlier, drawn at home to Wimbledon, a failure that was widely accepted to have led to their relinquishing a chance to win a title that not long before had seemed theirs to win as and when they chose. Since then, the Arsenal players had spent their time in an antechamber of uncertainty. For every club other than Arsenal and Liverpool the season was over. The FA Cup Final, traditionally the grand finale of the season, had been and gone, having been won the previous Saturday by Liverpool. But there was still one more game to play. Arsenal's visit to Anfield was originally scheduled for Sunday 23 April but, after Hillsborough and the suspension of the season, was rescheduled most unusually for the evening of 26 May. Unusual because 26 May that year fell on a Friday, a day on which top-flight League football was seldom played. Arsenal were going into the last game three points behind Liverpool and with an inferior goal difference, having been top of the table for most of the second half of the season and overhauled by a resurgent Liverpool only at the last. To be champions they had to win at Anfield by two goals against a team unbeaten since 2 January.

Liverpool had won the title six times in the eighties; Arsenal's last title win was in 1971. And they hadn't won a match at Anfield since 1974. 'Arsenal's journey to the North-West tonight promises to end as dishearteningly as it did thirty-seven years ago,' wrote Stuart Jones in *The Times* on the morning of the match. 'Then, on the last day of the season, they went to Old Trafford needing to beat Manchester United by seven clear goals to win the title.

They lost 6–1 . . . It would be astonishing if Liverpool failed to claim their tenth title in thirteen years.'

The bookmakers had Arsenal at odds of 16–1 to win 2–0; Perry Groves, manager George Graham's first signing at the club in 1986 and one of two substitutes that night at Anfield, was asked before the game if Arsenal had any chance of winning. 'We've got two,' he said. 'Slim and no.'

The weather, especially in the south of England, had been warm and untypically settled. It was so warm during my finals that I took several of them wearing only a careless T-shirt and shorts. This irritated my tutor, a philosophy professor. He was an inscrutable blue-nosed existentialist with a Max Wall haircut who'd been an undergraduate at Oxford just after the war and worn a formal gown during his finals – even though, he said, his voice betraying his disapproval, 'it was hotter that summer than it is for you now'.

The players were wearing their club tracksuits as they boarded the coach that would take them north. Their Scottish manager, George Graham, always fastidious and self-consciously smart, was by contrast wearing a stiffly starched white shirt, a blazer and club tie. No one personified the spirit of the Arsenal side of 1989 more than their twenty-two-year-old captain, Tony Adams. He was, like the team itself, young, raw and unsophisticated. He was also fanatically determined.

The Arsenal directors had been long reluctant to support their managers in the transfer market by paying high fees and wages for players, which meant that the club were especially dependent on the excellence of their scouting and youth networks. On the rare occasions when, against character and expectation, the board gambled by sanctioning a major singing – such as when Charlie Nicholas, then the most coveted player in Britain, joined from Celtic for £800,000 in June 1983 – they invariably came to regret what they regarded as their profligacy. (In the summer of 1995, when Arsenal paid a then club record £7.5million to sign Denis Bergkamp from Internazionale on an estimated salary of £15,000 per week, chairman Peter Hill-Wood, sitting alongside Bergkamp at the press conference to welcome him, eccentrically described the fee and salary as 'complete madness'. In the event Bergkamp excelled; he has since been voted by the fans on the club's official website as the second-greatest player in Arsenal history. His original salary now seems modest in the era of the £120,000-per-week player.)

When Graham, a former Arsenal player himself, arrived at Highbury as manager from Millwall on a £60,000-a-year contract in the summer of 1986, succeeding the sacked Don Howe, he was determined to effect a radical transformation. The club was not exactly in disarray but aspirations were diminished, expectations low, attendances falling. The players were not unified, together. 'I had done my homework before talking to the players, and I knew that I had a lot of weeding out to do,' he wrote in *The Glory and the Grief: The Life of George Graham*. 'My aim was to quickly break the three cliques that had been allowed to build up. There were the prima donnas who wanted the star treatment without earning it, and there were two pools of former youth-team players who had grown up together from their apprenticeship days and were distinctive by their colour, on the one side white players and the other side black. There was no racial tension, but they went their separate ways. I was determined to have them all pulling together in one direction.'

Graham wanted his players to share his restlessness for change: before his first season had begun he acted decisively by allowing ageing England internationals Tony Woodcock and Paul Mariner to leave. They would soon afterwards be followed out by Graham Rix, Steve Williams, Stewart Robson, Viv Anderson and Kenny Sansom – all England internationals, all unwanted. Graham knew what he was doing by letting these players go, knew that he'd been fortunate in having inherited an exceptional group of young homegrown players led by Adams. There was also the centre-back Martin Keown (who would soon join Aston Villa following a pay dispute; Graham brought him back to the club in 1993), the free-running forward Paul Merson, the black Londoners Paul Davis, David Rocastle and Michael Thomas, and the squad members Martin Hayes and Niall Quinn. Graham was prepared to promote them, to discover if they were as good as many at the club believed.

'George was lucky to inherit a lot of good young players who were emerging at the same time,' I was told by David O'Leary, who played a club record of 722 games for Arsenal. 'The same thing happened to me at Leeds [from 1998–2002 O'Leary was manager there]. The brave thing is to play them. Those young players, especially Adams, were very confident. I remember when Tony was an apprentice, he'd be down there in the boot-room. You'd go past and he'd say hello and ask if you'd had a good weekend with the wife and kids. In his position, I'd never have had the confidence to address a senior player like that.'

When Graham did make signings they were shrewd. The striker Alan Smith joined from Leicester in 1987; left-back

Nigel Winterburn was bought from Second Division Wimbledon, and defenders Lee Dixon and Steve Bould joined from another Second Division club, Stoke City. None of them was an international or had experience of playing at a big city club or in European club competitions, yet each adapted well and would feature prominently throughout the 1988–89 season and far beyond.

What Graham wanted to re-create was the spirit of Arsenal's Double-winning team of 1971, of which he himself was part. 'We had then arguably a limited team, talent-wise,' he said, 'but what we lacked in talent we made up for in organisation, application and, most of all, wonderful camaraderie among the players.'

Prior to becoming manager of Arsenal, Graham was already both a fan and historian of the club; one room in his house in Hampstead, in North-West London, was dedicated to an extensive collection of Arsenal memorabilia. He knew the history of the club, understood its grand pseudo-aristocratic traditions, its culture of benign paternalism. He knew how the role of chairman had been passed through one family of Old Etonians, the Hill-Woods, former cotton-mill owners from the Peak District, from grandfather (Samuel) to father (Denis) to son (Peter, the current chairman), in a line of direct descent extending into the present. Graham would use the phrase 'this is the Arsenal way', if he approved of something, or 'this isn't the Arsenal way', if he disapproved. He knew that Arsenal – originally called Woolwich Arsenal – were the Football League's first London club and that under their present name had never been relegated; he admired the great visionary manager Herbert Chapman, who helped to transform the fortunes of the club in the 1930s, a decade during which they won the title five times and the Art Deco West Stand at Highbury was opened.

Graham wanted his players to feel as he did about the club, to feel as if they had something to prove to him and to themselves; he loathed complacency and self-regard. 'When I signed for Arsenal,' Lee Dixon told me, 'I thought: *How did that happen?* So perhaps I was always trying to prove to myself that I belonged, that I was good enough. Maybe that's why I kept improving. I remember once, in my second-last season – I can't remember the exact game – Tony Adams turned to me, after I'd got him out of trouble, and said: "You're one hell of a footballer, do you know that?" I remember thinking, *Wow! He said that to me.* And that was right at the end of my career.'

Dixon played 458 games for Arsenal, excelling under Graham but also under the more progressive, scientific-cerebral and attack-orientated coaching of Arsène Wenger. However, he told me that he never really 'believed that I belonged. I lacked confidence. As a boy I used to play up front for my Sunday team. I was a striker. I was, like, the third- or fourth-best player. I signed pro for Burnley at eighteen, and then, after one season, I was released. I joined Chester, who had just finished ninety-second in the League. The next season, we finished ninety-first. My dad was a pro, a goalkeeper for Manchester City in the fifties, and none of this was good for my ego or confidence. Yet I was always determined to make the most of whatever talent I had. That came from in there –' he punched his chest – 'that's a heart thing, a reluctance to fail, if you like. Even so, I was always waiting for that game in which I'd be found out.'

Graham would have approved of and might even have

encouraged Dixon's insecurity as well as his quest for self-improvement. His team of 1989 was characterised above all else by its reluctance to fail. He didn't want his players to feel quite at ease; what he demanded of them was absolute commitment to the ethic of the team. His was a philosophy of sweat and ferocious exertion; in return, he wanted to be respected by his players – and he relished being feared.

'George was an authoritarian, remote,' Alan Smith says now. 'He wasn't an arms-round-the-shoulder type of coach; we had Theo Foley [Graham's assistant from 1986 to 1990] to do that. George was so demanding and fierce in training. When you saw him walking up to the pitch everyone made sure they were trying that little bit harder. On match days he wouldn't go absolutely ballistic too often; he would reserve that for special occasions. But you didn't answer him back. If someone did, we'd all be surprised. Towards the end it became more common to answer him back when the team was disintegrating. He'd said it all; we'd heard it all. There were rumours that he was going to be sacked; and the rollickings were becoming more personal and vitriolic. He was on the way out. He knew what was coming.'

George Graham was born on 30 November 1944 – St Andrew's Day – in the former pit village of Bargeddie, about eight miles from Glasgow in what is today north Lanarkshire. He was three weeks old when his father, a steelworker named Robert Graham, died from tuberculosis on Christmas Day. (His eldest sister died from the same disease at the age of nineteen.) His early years were difficult and impoverished: when Graham was born his soon-to-be-widowed mother was thirty-six, and he was her seventh child. The family home was, as he remembers it, 'small and cramped'. His mother supported her children by working as a potato-picker on local farmland. It was dour work: eight hours a day, hands scrambling in the soil, broken fingernails behind which dirt would become thickly wedged; sometimes a sprained or dislocated finger; stiff joints and knees, a continuous dull ache in the lower back.

Football offered Graham a way out of poverty and a route south: aged fifteen he signed for Aston Villa, and later went on to play for Chelsea, Arsenal (227 games), Manchester United, Portsmouth and Crystal Palace. Graham was a languid presence in midfield. He passed and moved so gracefully that he was known variously as the Stroller, the Ringmaster and the Peacock. 'I had a quick brain but a slow body,' he has said. 'I needed time, which is not available in the English game today.'

With his dark hair and dark skin the young Graham could have been mistaken as someone from the Mediterranean south. He was debonair and self-possessed. He liked metropolitan life – the nightclubs and hotel bars, the restaurants and parties, the women who made themselves available to him. He dressed with care and flamboyance, the self-styled Beau Brummell of Bargeddie. He was articulate and urbane and, according to journalist Ken Dyer, 'his party piece was a perfectly respectable version of "Nice and Easy Does It" by his favourite singer, Frank Sinatra'.

Graham was no dilettante, however: he knew what he wanted from his post-playing career and how to go about getting it. He didn't want to become another unfulfilled playboy, adrift without the routine and rituals of the game.

The final years of his playing career, once he left Arsenal, were disappointing. From Manchester United to Portsmouth to Crystal Palace he was never again in contention for the highest honours. What he sought from management was longevity and consistent achievement – and good money, the kind of money he never earned as a player. He demanded discipline of himself and expected the same of those who worked with or for him. He knew that if he could succeed as a manager the wealth and security for which he'd yearned since childhood would follow. And so began a process of self-reinvention during the second act of his career in management as the Stroller became if not exactly the Ayatollah (as he was called by some of those who played under him at Arsenal) then a manager of unbreakable and singular determination. 'George is a good-looking guy who dresses well and has style,' Don Howe said. 'But that's not his real image. He's a strong man. A professional who wants to win. If he gets anyone trying to challenge him, George will have them out.'

As a young coach, given his first opportunity by his old friend and former Chelsea team-mate Terry Venables at Crystal Palace and also at Queens Park Rangers, and then, later, as a manager in his own right at Millwall and Arsenal, Graham showed just how strong he could be. There's a story I was told of how one afternoon while at Millwall he was giving one of his players a lift home after training when the player broke wind. Graham was outraged; he stopped the car and ordered the player out. He then drove slowly away, leaving the baffled and humiliated player at the roadside.

Sports journalist Ken Jones, who knew Graham well

during his playing days, has written of how management 'hardened' him, and of how there were times during his early years at Arsenal 'when he was more remote than I ever thought he could be'.

Graham did not like strollers or peacocks: the footballer as egoist or exhibitionist. He preferred grafters, such as Kevin Richardson, who was brought in on a small fee from Everton and ended up playing thirty-two games in midfield during the 1988–89 season. Graham demanded toil and labour from his players and coaching staff. His Arsenal team of the late eighties were a fast, direct, hard-running and tackling side; they compressed space through masterful manipulation of the offside trap, and invariably played the ball long from the back, by-passing the midfield as they sought out Smith, the central striker who was accomplished at holding up the ball or laying it off or fighting for it in the air. Because they continuously hit balls long, much of their play depended largely on chance: the fortuitous knock-down, the ricochet, the lucky bounce, the scramble following a corner. Theirs was a new style of power football during a period when the long-ball game had intellectual exponents at the Football Association; the intensity was relentless as they pressed and harried and tracked down and forced. 'Pressure, pressure, pressure,' Graham used to say.

In both of Graham's first two seasons Arsenal had periods during which they were the top of the League. And on both occasion they faltered, finishing fourth in 1987 and sixth in 1988.

'George knew what he wanted from the moment he arrived,' Paul Davis told me. 'He cleared out a lot of the older players – Mariner, Woodcock, and ultimately Nicholas and Sansom. He went with youth. Our contracts were coming up when he arrived but nobody got any pay rises. It was more: "Let me see what you can do." He wanted us to prove ourselves. This revitalised us. Everyone was trying hard, trying to get that new contract. And we played some exciting football in his early seasons, quick and direct. A great start for us.

'But I eventually fell out with George over the way we played. I wanted to get on the ball and play through midfield. He didn't want us to hold on to the ball and play. He wanted us to get it and give it.'

Davis's disenchantment with his manager and their subsequent disputes – which led to his being excluded from the first team and spending a long, eighteen-month exile training only with the reserve and youth squads – were in the future. That morning as they began to arrive at London Colney in preparation for the journey to Liverpool, the Arsenal squad were youthful, settled, disciplined and determined, a collective expression of their manager's fierce will to power. Each player knew what was expected of him and the role he had to perform, even if that role in some ways violated his natural instincts as a player. Certainly this was so for the more creative players, such as Davis and his fellow midfielders Rocastle and Thomas.

The London Colney training ground is unrecognisable today from how it was at the end of the eighties. Transformed by the wealth of the new game in the era of Sky Sports and our globalised Premier League, and by the exactitude and expertise of longstanding French manager Arsène Wenger, it's a model of high-tech sophistication and impregnable security. It combines the opulence of a luxury gated spa resort with the stark, clinical efficiency of a well-resourced private hospital. Everything takes place behind high security fences, patrolled by uniformed guards, as if high-level government-sanctioned experiments were taking place inside. The surveillance is oppressive; there are cameras monitoring wherever you go. Meanwhile, the improbably wealthy, polyglot, multinational players sweep in and out of the main car park, mere shadows behind the dark windows of their formidable four-wheel-drive vehicles. They are remote and unknowable to the fans waiting at the gates in hope of getting an autograph or even an acknowledgement – *Just let us know that you know we're here*.

There was nothing grand about the London Colney complex at the end of the eighties. Its modesty was consistent with the kind of club Arsenal then were: traditional, rather conservative in aspiration and outlook, but with ambitions that were reawakening after nearly two decades of upper-mid-table ordinariness. The club didn't even own its own training ground; the property and pitches belonged to the University of London.

From winning the League and FA Cup Double in 1971, under manager Bertie Mee and coach Don Howe, to the start of the 1988–89 season, Arsenal had won only the FA Cup against Manchester United, in 1979, and the Littlewoods Cup, in Graham's first season. Fans were used to Arsenal missing out in the transfer market or selling their best home-developed players. Liam Brady, for example, joined Arsenal as a schoolboy and, as Hugh McIlvanney once wrote, had a left foot so delicate he could have used it to lift 'a speck of dust from a baby's eye'. He was sold to Juventus in 1979.

In 1981 the striker Frank Stapleton, who was, like Brady, an Ireland international and a product of the club's youth system, was sold to Manchester United. If the club were prepared to sell their best players to English rivals, it was easy to conclude that the directors were not ambitious for Arsenal once again to become champions of England.

Two: Claret and Blue

When I first became interested in football Liverpool were spoken of by my father with reverence. I was born and grew up in Harlow, in Essex. On the quiet, intimate cul-de-sac where we lived in a brick-built modern open-plan house with a large garden dominated by a mature weeping willow tree there also lived a family from Merseyside, whose four sons all supported Liverpool. Other boys living on our small development, and at school and at the local football team for whom I played, supported Liverpool too. From a young age I was used to being around people who supported Liverpool: Cockney reds. As the years passed it seemed to me that Liverpool, rather than Manchester United, were the closest thing this country had to a national club side, not least because of how successfully they represented the English League in European cup competitions. With many Irish, Scottish and Welsh players their squad seemed also to truly reflect these islands: a British and Irish side, not exclusively English.

There was, too, a quality of special difference about the actual club. If you had any interest in the history of the English League, and in how Liverpool had come to be our pre-eminent club, you soon learnt about Bill Shankly. You learned of how he'd arrived in 1959 from Huddersfield to galvanise both the club and city of Liverpool with his vision of the romantic game; of the famous Spion Kop ('the Kop'), named for the battle between British Lancashire and Boer troops that had been fought in January 1900 on the Spion Kop hillside in Natal, South Africa, and in which many men from Liverpool died; of the fans' anthem 'You'll Never Walk Alone'. I'd seen news pictures and television footage of Shankly that showed him, dressed in a smart red shirt and dark tie beneath a grey suit, celebrating Liverpool's 1973 title win, their third since he became manager, by embracing fans on the Kop in a rapture of mutuality and understanding. (At the end of the following season, having won the FA Cup, Shankly suddenly announced his retirement. Before this, a few days after the Cup Final, he had appeared on the steps of St George's Hall in Liverpool city centre to speak to and receive the adulation of at least 100,000 people gathered before him. It was hard to know who held whom in greater esteem.)

Shankly was a witty aphorist, canny and intelligent, with a distinctively sharp, rasping voice. He knew what he wanted to say and how to say it; he knew how to motivate, when to praise and when to tease or taunt. 'Bill always used to insist that the players changed at Anfield before training and then they were taken out to our training ground at Melwood, a fifteen-minute journey by coach,' says Peter Robinson, who from 1965 to 1990 was first secretary and then chief executive of Liverpool. 'Bill liked the banter on the coach, thought it was good for morale and for bonding. It was the same routine every day. Everyone would return to Anfield to shower and to have lunch.'

Born in 1913 in the Ayrshire mining village of Glenbuck,

Bill Shankly could just as easily have come from the tight terraced streets around Anfield where many of the Liverpool fans themselves lived. 'I was only in the game for the love of football,' he said, 'and I wanted to bring back happiness to the people of Liverpool.' He was a football socialist (before becoming a professional player he had worked for two years as a miner), the moralist of the people's game, even if he was also capable of low cunning to inspire or deflate. 'Our aim at Liverpool was to provide the best entertainment at the cheapest possible price for the fans,' says Peter Robinson. 'Bill would not have had it any other way.'

In 1964 the BBC broadcast a *Panorama* documentary about the Kop. To watch it now is to be profoundly affected by the crowd scenes, by the astonishing sight of so many men – for they are all men – of all ages pressed up against each other, many wearing flat caps, smart shirts and ties. They're all so slim, a reminder of the austerity of those years and of how recent was the scarcity and rationing of the 1950s. They're all pushing and swaying in harmony, and singing pop songs, 'She Loves You' and 'Anyone Who Had a Heart'. It's Liverpool's last home game of the season and the Kop is enchanted as they secure their first championship under Shankly, with a 5–0 victory over none other than Arsenal, described on *Panorama* as the 'poor, sacrificial victims, southerners'. Speaking in the precise, clipped BBC accent of the period – standard Oxford English, as it was once called – the narrator continues in a manner that suggests he was encountering for the first time a rare and exotic tribe. Perhaps he was.

This season over two million people on Merseyside have watched Liverpool or their neighbours Everton, last year's champions. But they don't behave like any other football crowd; especially at one end of the ground, on the Kop. The music the crowd sings is the music that Liverpool has sent echoing around the world. It used to be thought that the Welsh international rugby crowds were the most musical and passionate in the world. But I've never seen anything like this Kop crowd. On the field here the gay and inventive ferocity they show is quite stunning. The Duke of Wellington before the Battle of Waterloo said of his own troops: 'I don't know what they do to the enemy, but by God they frighten me.' And I'm sure some of the players in this match this afternoon must be feeling the same way.

An anthropologist studying this Kop crowd would be introduced into as rich and mystifying a popular culture as in any South Sea island . . . They seem, mysteriously, to be in touch with one another, with Wacka, the Spirit of Scouse.

The presenter goes on, seeking to intellectualise and thus explain what perhaps can never be properly explained or accounted for: the colossal emotional power and drama of crowds. At the time of the *Panorama* film the Liverpool dockers were close to winning a victory for which they had been campaigning for nearly a century: the replacement of casual labour by permanent contracts. Liverpool FC drew much support from the dockers, from the Irish emigrant families who lived in Scotland (Scottie) Road and arrived in the city to work in the docks in the 1880s. When Robbie Fowler (born in Toxteth), after scoring in a European Cup-Winners' Cup quarter-final in March 1997, lifted his shirt to reveal another T-shirt on which was written 'Support the 500 sacked dockers', he was expressing solidarity with

Liverpool dockers and a connection between players, clubs and fans that was once so much part of Shankly's vision of the people's game. Fowler understood the role the docks had played in forming the working culture of the great port city in which he'd grown up. Could the same be said of any Liverpool player in the 2008–09 squad, with the possible exception of the local-born Steven Gerrard and Jamie Carragher?

As a student in the late 1960s, studying for an MA in English, Gérard Houllier lived in Liverpool while writing a thesis on inner-city deprivation, and taught at Alsop comprehensive school, which is in the area of Anfield itself. He recalls standing as a young man on the Kop at Anfield, of being enchanted to find himself amid so much spontaneity and song: 'The noise, the singing, the moving. It was swaying all the time; you could hardly see the game!'

When in 1998 he returned to the city as manager of Liverpool, Houllier was determined to reinvent the club but without violating its traditions. 'Liverpool has a tradition of passing football,' he told John Williams, director of the Centre for Football Research at Leicester University. 'It is linked to the fact that the passing is a language between people – it's a bond between people. Everybody involved in the passing, everybody working for the same aims, and so on. Has this got something to do with tradition? It must appeal to the "imaginary" of the people in Liverpool. All I know is that, having been a technical director in France, it is not the same there and it couldn't be the same. And it has got something to do with the way of living, the culture, the history of Liverpool.'

Houllier knew the history of the club and chose to live close to Sefton Park, in the city proper, rather than in one of the more affluent suburbs such as Formby or in Lancashire or North Wales. (Shankly had lived in a semi-detached house within walking distance of Anfield.) Houllier was a historian of Liverpool. He knew all about Shankly, about how he and each of his four elder brothers were footballers and of how together they used to play five-a-side games in and around the pit village of Glenbuck. He knew how Shankly, assisted by Bob Paisley and Joe Fagan, each of whom would go on to manage the club, had transformed Liverpool from a Second Division club with a broken-down training ground at Melwood and a shabby stadium into a team capable of winning the First Division, a team celebrated for their unusual togetherness and the relentless fluency of their passing game. 'My aim in life,' Shankly said, 'even when you went into the services during the war and got some horrible jobs – working in the cookhouse, where you had to clean 6,000 dishes, or clean out the latrines – well, my aim in life was if I had a job to do, even cleaning the floor, I'd want my floor to be cleaner than yours. Now, if everyone thinks along these lines and does all the small jobs to the best of their abilities, that's honesty. Then the world would be better. And football would be better. So what we want is hard work and honesty. No football club is successful without hard work.'

Shankly's players, like their manager, were extraordinarily hard-working and fitter than most. Their passing game, an expression of their unity and collectivity – the neat, intricate patterns and structures, the ease in possession, the close control, the simple, accurate delivery – was worked on and enhanced in five-a-side games in training, a Shankly innovation. Pass and move, pass and move. Keep working, keep working. Together, together. The politics of togetherness: on and off the field; togetherness, the bond between players, manager and fans; togetherness, the club as an expression of the pride of the wider community.

'I'm a people's man,' Shankly said. 'Only the people matter.'

My first visit to Liverpool was with my father when I was twelve years old. We went to see West Ham play at Anfield and I brought along two friends, Essex-born Sicilian brothers who lived on our road. The elder brother was the same age as me and, like many boys in our west Essex town, a West Ham fan; his younger brother, Salvatore, was an Arsenal fan. We drove up in my father's red Alfa Romeo Alfetta, a car especially admired by my friends because of its association with the country they identified as home, even though they'd lived nowhere but in Essex and visited Italy only on holiday. (It was also the official escort car of Italian prime minister Aldo Moro when he was kidnapped by the Red Brigades the following year – something that amused my father, as if somehow the incident reflected well on the car he drove.)

We had breakfast at a motorway service station and soon afterwards one of the brothers was sick in the car. He was embarrassed and started to cry. My father pulled on to the hard-shoulder and patiently comforted him. He asked us to get out and stand well away from the car while he fastidiously cleaned the back seat, using torn pages from a newspaper, a couple of rags and some distilled water he kept in a plastic container in the boot.

I once asked my father which car he'd choose if he had the free pick of the market. 'A Jowett,' he said without pause. A Jowett Javelin was the car he'd owned as a newly married young man; he often talked about it, about how much he regretted what happened to it. 'We ran out of petrol one day coming back from visiting my parents,' my mother told me. 'We left it overnight at a garage. But that night it was very cold. We didn't have antifreeze in the car. When we returned the next morning the engine block had frozen and split. We had to sell it off for scrap and this broke his heart.'

He once showed me a picture of his Jowett – an odd, bubble-shaped car with a sloping roof. *That's his favourite car!* I remember thinking. Much more interesting to me was how my parents had looked in the photograph – so tall and slim and attractive, like two young movie stars. My father's dark hair was cropped short at the back and sides like a US marine. His expression was one of jaunty hopeful-ness as he leant against the Jowett and stared straight at the camera, wearing a leather jacket and well-polished black leather shoes. He was recognisably my father in that picture but also someone unfamiliar. I wasn't yet born. I wasn't in his life. He was a different person, with different hopes and needs.

What of those needs? The truth was that he never spoke about them. They were hidden needs. As for material pos-sessions . . . With the exception of his Alfas and his clothes, he had very little. For his entire adult life he wore the same simple, unpretentious watch, persevering with it even as it failed to keep reliable time, losing a few minutes each day, even as its once-clear plain face acquired a grubby, faded, buttery-yellow hue. He also wore a blue-faced silver St Christopher pendant, which you would sometimes glimpse, if a few buttons of his shirt were undone, tangled up in his thick reddy-brown chest hair. The pendant was bought for him by my mother on the day he passed his proficiency test on a Lambretta scooter; the watch was a twenty-first birthday gift from his parents. He was never without either. Another of his most valued possessions was a glazed brown pottery shaving mug, on which was inscribed, in a tinted panel, 'When a Man is Tired of Pleasure He is Tired of Life'. This too was a present from my mother. He kept his razor, bristle brush and cream in the mug, and for some reason he cherished it as one might treasure a family heirloom.

Despite what was written on his shaving mug, my father was no idle pleasure-seeker, no epicurean or libertine. He was sociable, he liked parties – and he and my mother hosted many – but everything in his life seemed to be moderated, controlled. He didn't smoke and he drank only modestly – good red wine or occasional cans of Carlsberg Special Brew, which he chilled and then poured into a stainless-steel tankard he kept in a teak cabinet. Any spare money he spent on books, records and clothes for himself, or on my mother and my sisters and me. None of us was indulged but we had most of what we wanted, when we wanted. And in matters of personal style my father was a formalist. He had done some modelling in menswear magazines and liked to wear well-cut shirts, well-made shoes and smart trousers, the clothes he designed himself or bought as samples on his trips to Paris and Milan; never something too casual, never just T-shirts and ragged jeans or beaten-up slacks.

Once we were settled in the car and on our way again to Liverpool, my father entertained us by singing a song:

> What does Harold Wilson eat?
> (Rhubarb, rhubarb)
> What does Harold Wilson eat?
> Rhubarb, rhubarb, rhubarb . . .

It was our role to sing the repeat line – which we did, reluctantly at first but ultimately with huge enthusiasm.

Much of the rest of that afternoon is lost to me now, as are the play-by-play sequences of the game itself. What remains most vivid from the perspective of our seats in what my father described as the 'neutral area' but which seemed very partisan indeed once the match began, is the spectacle of Anfield itself: the reverberations, concussions, echoes and noise inside the stadium, the police patrolling the edges of the pitch, the heaving density of the massed ranks of spectators on the steep banked terraces. I remember how, as Liverpool attacked, pulsing towards goal with a rushing intensity, they seemed to sway and move as one on the Kop, in wave after wave, as if they were being sucked towards the pitch, as if their very momentum would carry them beyond the hoardings and on to the field of play itself. I'd never experienced anything quite as communally intense during my visits with my father to matches in London. I didn't feel frightened or overwhelmed, as I had at the very first game I'd attended five years before. The atmosphere wasn't one of violence or intimidation, in spite of the astonishing noise. This was the home of Liverpool, then European champions, our national club side. Surrounded by narrow streets of tight terraced housing, each one indistinguishable from the one beside it – the homes of the fans – as well as small shops and pubs, the stadium was part of a living neighbourhood. The football club was not apart from but was instead an expression of this community: for these people the love of football was an expression of the love of place. It was a form of secular worship.

'It's not looking good for us,' my father said gloomily as we trudged across Stanley Park after the match to where the car had been left, about a mile from the ground. He was right about that: West Ham had lost 2–0 and would be relegated that season while Liverpool would finish second, behind Brian Clough's Nottingham Forest. I liked the way he said 'us'. I liked the sense of ownership it implied, this sense of an inclusive 'we-ness'. I was on my way to learning the vocabulary and grammar of fandom.

On the journey home I stirred from shallow sleep and, in the seat beside my father, looked on silently as he tapped his wedding band against the wooden steering wheel in time to the music; he was listening to Glen Campbell's 'Wichita Lineman', a song I always associate when I hear it now with that particular journey as we made our own way, like Campbell's lonely travelling lineman, on the long road *that stretched down south*.

A journey seldom passed without my father playing music in the car. Modern jazz, Neil Young (the albums *After the Goldrush* and *Harvest* were favourites), sometimes David Bowie or Roxy Music. On this occasion his window was ajar, the winter breeze disturbing his fine hair, and he seemed lost to the moment, lost even to himself, unreachable.

Is he thinking about the game? I wondered. *Is he depressed by the defeat?* He eventually noticed that I was awake and asked if I was all right, if I wanted anything. His voice was hoarse from all the shouting.

Behind us, on the back seat, the brothers were asleep.

Anthony Frank Cowley – Tony, or TC, to his friends – was born an only child in Upton Park, east London, on 7 September 1934. Having lived in Upton Park for the early years of his life his parents moved out to Forest Gate. Home there was a two-bedroom Victorian brick terraced villa that was heated by an open coal fire, had an outside lavatory, warmed by a paraffin lamp, and no bathroom; my father used to bathe at the West Ham public baths. His father, Frank, was a bus driver in London's West End; his mother, Jane, a fierce, passionate red-haired woman from an Irish family, worked in a brewery. Jane was extraordinarily close to and protective of her son. In many ways she lived vicariously through him. She was political, a member of the Labour Party, and she encouraged her son to become a dedicated reader of newspapers, magazines and books, to speak well, to have ambition, to be, in short, an old-style autodidact for whom the public library was an enchanted island of discovery. 'Always stand up tall,' she told him, 'be clean and polite.' In middle age she wore a brooch in which she kept a photograph of her son as a young man. 'My Tony is everybody's favourite,' she used to say. She wanted her son to leave the East End as soon as he could, to get away, to live a life unlike her own.

My father grew up in a house of deep quiet. Jane disapproved of her husband and seldom spoke to him. She took her teenage son away on holiday, leaving Frank behind. When my mother first began to visit my father at his family home she was unsettled by the odd hush and strange silences inside his house, with poor Frank ostracised and keeping alone as if he'd committed an unpardonable crime. There was, too, everywhere the oppressive, musty smell of mothballs, as if the house was less a living, vibrant family home than it was a mausoleum. She disliked the darkness and narrowness of some of those old East End terraced streets, the feelings of claustrophobia they induced in her. She lived outside London; she was used to air, space and light – as well as laughter and conversation inside the family home.

'I think Jane was embittered,' my mother says now. 'She was ambitious but Frank was happy with his lot. There was no feeling of warmth in their relationship. I remember feeling sorry for Frank and tried to include him in the conversation.'

Frank liked a drink after those long, grinding days working on the buses – who wouldn't? He smoked unfiltered John Player cigarettes; he boxed part-time in the East End pubs. 'He doesn't want to better himself,' Jane used to say of her husband. 'He doesn't want a better life.'

Jane was not satisfied: she burned with frustration. She wanted so much more, if not for herself – she accepted that this would not be possible, with the world as it was and the old class hierarchies as they were – then for her intelligent and good-looking son. Tony told his mother that he wanted to be a journalist. Secretly, he wanted to be an actor and would spend as much time as he could watching American movies at local cinemas that had survived or been rebuilt following the wartime bombing raids. He was seduced by the glamour of America as represented in the films he watched, so remote from his own experiences.

Because of his war-interrupted, war-curtailed education, my father left school at the age of fifteen, determined to find his own way. He was encouraged by his mother to learn a trade, 'to learn any useful skill'. She didn't want him to try his hand at journalism – 'too much risk,' she said – and certainly not at being a bus driver, like his father. As for seeking to become an actor, that was unmentionable. So he became an apprentice shirt-cutter. 'Men will always need to wear shirts,' his mother told him, 'and there'll be regular work for you.'

My parents had met at a dance at the Manor Hall in

Chigwell, Essex. That night my father wore a knitted yellow tie, a starched white shirt and a beige suit; my mother noticed him as soon as she entered the hall. 'He was tall,' she told me, 'so smart, good-looking, poised.' She loitered a while outside the cloakroom as he chatted with two male friends. Later, she felt a hand on her shoulder as she paused after yet another dance; she turned to see the tall, dark-haired man with the yellow tie. He asked her to dance, she accepted and they continued dancing through the rest of the evening.

After they married, my parents lived in a flat on the edges of the Wanstead Flats, the low-lying rough expanse of common land where the old East End begins to thin out and nudge up against Epping Forest, where you are neither of the town nor fully in the country. My father and his young wife, just twenty-two when they married, then moved further north to Harlow new town, where my mother's eldest sister Connie was already living and where land was plentiful and cheap property abundant.

My father didn't end up working as a journalist, as he once might have hoped; he never tried out as a professional actor, though he was a member of several drama groups and regularly appeared in amateur productions of Pinter, Beckett, Osborne and Arthur Miller (*Death of a Salesman* became a particular favourite). He wasn't doing what he'd once dreamed of but he was all right, he was on his way. My mother had encouraged him to go to night school to study, and now he was making a good living in fashion and clothing – the 'rag trade', as he called it – and in time they would buy their modern family house, a house with a garden large enough to accommodate a five-a-side goal (with a net) on the back lawn as well as an area of uncultivated wasteland on which for one charmed summer a goat grazed. No longer simply cutting shirts for others to wear, he was now designing and merchandising them, working for established brand names such as Rael Brook. He was beginning to travel widely – to the United States, India, the Far East, the Middle East – and he felt settled. He liked the way the country was changing, opening up, becoming more meritocratic as it recovered from the deprivations of the immediate postwar years. In many ways Britain was becoming more like America, an emerging consumer society. The East End, with its bombed-out streets and austere, unheated Victorian terraced houses must have seemed so distant now, a lifetime away. 'Once you're out of here,' Jane used to say, 'you'll never come back, because you'll never want to come back.'

But my father did go back, often, to watch West Ham. He'd grown up supporting his local team, which in the way of these things in football families should have been my team as well, *our* team. West Ham United. Except that it didn't work out in that way. When it came to football we were disunited. For my father supporting West Ham was a statement of identity and belonging. I grew up with no similar sense of fixity and rootedness. I was born in a new town, after all, and I was used to nearly everything around me being new, recently built or under construction.

Harlow was built with utopian aspirations and had from the beginning its own distinct local identity. It was centrally planned with model housing estates – many of them constructed using experimental materials and modish techniques – a 'central business district', designated 'green wedges', pubs named after butterflies and roads named after left-wing political heroes (Mandela Avenue, Allende Avenue, and so on). It had a long-established Labour council, a progressive, liberal intelligentsia, which congregated around the excellent local Playhouse, where my father was a member and performed in plays, eight comprehensive schools, a well-funded network of children's playschemes and recreational sports facilities (Glenn Hoddle emerged from the Harlow leagues).

Many of the people who came to live in Harlow were in one way or another in flight from history – from the inner city, from the memories of war – and Harlow offered them a new start, a new life. Growing up in Harlow I had very little sense of history, local or otherwise. The stone steps of my schoolyard were not shaped by the footfalls of centuries of pupils. I was familiar with the names of the old villages that had been erased by or subsumed into the new town – Great Parndon, Latton, Tye Green – but they were old in name only, ancient settlements that had been built on, expanded, developed. In effect, they had been obliterated.

Always so much emphasis on novelty, on newness, on the here and now. One of the consequences of growing up in a new town, even one with a population the size of Harlow's, which was about 70,000 in the mid-seventies, was that we had no local professional football team. To watch professional football you had to go to London, from where most of our parents had come. For me, then, supporting a football team had very little to do with a sense of place, with identity and belonging; it was more an act of choice and of self-positioning – of positioning myself against my friends (all those Spurs and West Ham fans I was at school with) and, above all, against my father.

I can't remember when I first began to call myself an Arsenal fan but I can remember the first game of football I watched on television: the 1971 FA Cup Final, between Arsenal and Liverpool. I was five years old. This was a year before we moved to the house with the weeping willow tree, where I spent most of my childhood and adolescence. Before then we lived in Potter Street, in what had been one of the old villages of this once-rural part of west Essex but was now devoured and swallowed up into the maw of the new town. The family who lived in the house adjacent to ours were named the Bunns and they were exceptionally dedicated Arsenal fans, always gently encouraging me to turn against my father and support the same team as they did.

I didn't watch all of the 1971 Cup Final; at full time, with the score at 1–1, I went with my sister Alison to buy some sweets from a parade of shops about ten minutes' walk from our house. On the way back, with the match stretching into extra time, I passed a house which had all its downstairs windows open – it was a hot, airless afternoon – and from the street I could hear the match. I was curious to know what the score was and so paused to look in through one of the open windows and there I saw a group of men and one woman sitting around the television. The woman, I noticed, was smoking. It was at just this moment that Charlie George struck his long-range winning goal for Arsenal; as the ball hit the back of the net it was as if a bomb had exploded inside the house, scattering bodies. If the windows weren't already open I'd have sworn the sound of the celebrations inside would have blown out the glass; and I experienced a surge of exhilaration and together with my sister I found myself running as hard as I could, running blindly into the heavy heat of the long afternoon.

The next season my father took me to my first game, West Ham versus Derby at Upton Park. It was a 0–0 draw. Having witnessed the celebrations inside that house and then back at the Bunns' on Cup Final day, and having listened beforehand to my father talking about the live experience of match day, I thought I knew what to expect at Upton Park: the aggression and hostility of the terraces, but also the ardour, the camaraderie, the tribalism, the rituals, the rough expressions of love. In truth, though, I was simply too young and ended up being completely overwhelmed by the intensity of the experience. The greatest shock of all – frightening in its way – was to discover just how at ease my father was among the hoards of men on the standing terrace he called the Chicken Run and how easily he seemed to lose himself in the collectivity of song and chant and synchronised movement. He seemed to me to be a completely different man as he locked shoulders with those around him, all swaying as they sang 'We're Forever Blowing Bubbles'; so absorbed was he that it was as if he'd forgotten I was there with him even as I held his hand or tugged at his shirt.

We didn't go to football again for several years, during which time my commitment to Arsenal hardened into firm support. That disorientating first trip to Upton Park, perhaps because it had come too early in my life, perhaps because it had come after the 1971 Cup Final and the Charlie George goal, had left me even more emotionally detached from West Ham, a team I tried hard to love but, for all my father's benign promptings, could not. Our next live game when it came was, in contrast to that first match at Upton Park, dramatic and unforgettable – the 1975 sixth-round FA Cup tie between Arsenal and West Ham. It was a wet Saturday in March and the crowd, according to the official records, was 56,000, by far Arsenal's largest of that season. But it felt as if there were many thousands more inside the ground and I've seldom since experienced an atmosphere quite like it.

We arrived without tickets a couple of hours before kick-off, but the queues outside the gates were already long and impatient. Once inside, my father held on to me tightly to prevent me from being knocked off the wooden stool we'd brought with us from home and on which I was precariously balanced for the whole game. We were standing on the terraces of the lower West Stand, and even behind us, in the seats, where the wealthier and more responsible fans were supposed to be, I remember seeing men fighting before and during the game.

It rained throughout the afternoon; the pitch was saturated, mud-clogged and cutting up. Graham Paddon was playing for West Ham. I remember him: blow-dried, dark-blond bouffant-styled hair, bearded. The atmosphere was ferocious, with a steady flow of fans being led away from the terraces by police around the sides of the pitch. Before the game West Ham fans had en masse infiltrated the North Bank, hardcore Arsenal territory, and, after prolonged fighting, they continued to hold its centre. This was an audacious occupation by enemy fans. For the West Ham hooligans that afternoon it was very much a case of we came, we saw, we conquered Arsenal's North Bank – and my father understood the significance of this and was impressed by it.

He kept saying to me, 'I can't believe this, we've actually taken the North Bank.' I must have looked at him with incomprehension, though I understood something of the magnitude of the afternoon: not only would Arsenal lose the game 2–0, but also their fans would lose the war, humiliatingly evicted from their own patch, their own familiar stretch of terrace, by the firm of hardened raiders from East London. Rather than occupying the very centre of the North Bank, as was their inalienable right as the home supporters, the Arsenal fans had allowed themselves to be pushed to the margins of it, with thick dark lines of police standing between them and the West Ham invaders, preventing any attempt at massed reoccupation.

What a raw and viscerally exciting afternoon it turned out to be – and what an introduction to Highbury! It would be my last visit there for several years, but over the next few seasons I was taken regularly by my father to watch West Ham play at Upton Park. I became familiar with all the players and began to like and admire several of them, notably Billy Bonds and Trevor Brooking, and even today I can still name all the West Ham players from that period. Although I was always pleased to spend the time with my father and I loved football of any kind, I would still sometimes mount my own protests against his quiet refusal to accept that I supported another team, located in a different part of London. (Or perhaps it was less a refusal than it was a stubborn hope that I might be persuaded through sheer familiarity and regularity of attendance at Upton Park to switch allegiance.)

My protests took many forms and included wearing an Arsenal shirt under my jacket to some games or an Arsenal scarf or carrying a red Arsenal bag. My father never complained about any of this and would accept the good-natured jibing from the guys who stood around us on the Chicken Run, some of whom we got to know quite well. 'Well, I've tried my best,' he would say. Or: 'What can you do?' Or: 'He's a stubborn boy.' Or: 'I blame his mother!'

Once I turned up at a West Ham match wearing a West Germany football shirt. This shirt was a legacy of the 1974 World Cup, in the lead-up to which I'd entered a competition organised by DER, a television-rental company. You had to predict the two finalists and the winning score a month before the tournament began. In those days, at the age of eight, football was all I knew. As hosts it was obvious to me that West Germany would be hard to beat and I knew that Bayern Munich and Ajax Amsterdam were among the best club sides in Europe. So, with the deadline approaching, I chose West Germany to beat Holland 2–1 in the Final, and sent off my entry. My memories of the actual tournament are mostly indistinct, though I'm told I watched as many of the games as I could. I recall now the absence of England and the presence of Zaire and Haiti, who were repeatedly thrashed; the technique and creativity of the Netherlands, exponents of a style of play we quickly learned to call Total Football but failed to emulate at whichever level the game was played in England; and I recall a match between East and West Germany in Hamburg, played in unceasing rain, and surprisingly won 1–0 by the team from the wrong side of the Wall, with a seventy-eighth-minute goal by Jürgen Sparwasser. That result was significant: had West Germany won they would have met the Netherlands in the next round.

In the days before the Final I felt isolated. Everyone I knew admired the Dutch side, led and inspired by Johan Cruyff and Johan Neeskens. No one admired the Germans, who in style and performance were considered by many to be the antithesis of that great Dutch side: dour, mechanical, efficient, the embodiment of the new Germany. I watched the Final with my father and my friend Mike Barrett on our newly rented DER colour television. On the morning of the Final my father had, oddly, begun – and I think this was for the first time – telling me about the War; about how, before he was evacuated, bombs from German planes had fallen from the night sky, destroying his school and houses on the road on which he lived, killing acquaintances of his parents. He spoke of the heat and claustrophobia of the air-raid shelter at the end of his road in which he huddled with his mother as the bombs came down, and of the swagger of the American troops he saw passing in open-top trucks, and how gloomily reduced the British troops seemed by comparison – he wrote a poem about this titled 'Don't Cheer Us Girls We're British'. He spoke of how, following one sustained raid, he was left mute for days; of how he used to play among the bombed-out houses and collapsed buildings, fascinated by some of the wildflowers that sprouted defiantly among the ruins: purple willowherb, poppies, Michaelmas daisies, loosestrife, groundsel. He told me of how his own father, Frank, who would eventually die at the age of eighty-nine, never joined the family down in the air-raid shelters or in the tunnels of the Underground. Instead, Frank remained at home, in his own bed, as houses around him were reduced to bomb-rubble. I didn't know why my father was telling me all this now, on the morning of the World Cup Final, but during the match it all became clear: emphatically he did not want the Germans to win. In fact, along with most of the country, he hated them.

The Dutch took the lead with a penalty in the first minute but the Germans equalised midway through the half with a penalty of their own, scored by Paul Breitner. That was too much for my father. He couldn't resist shouting, 'You cheating German swines.' It was obviously an innocent remark but I took it as a statement of disloyalty – to me. To the amusement of Mike, who, like my father, was supporting the Netherlands, I started to cry. I was laughing by the end, however, as West Germany won 2–1, just as I had predicted they would nearly two months before.

The next morning, after we had checked the rules of entry, we discovered what my prize would be: not a television to replace the one we rented, as we all wanted, but a replica black-and-white German kit, which when it eventually arrived in the post I wore at first nervously but later without inhibition, out on the street, at football training and at school. I was still wearing the white V-necked shirt if not the black shorts when, two years later, West Germany played Czechoslovakia in the Final of the 1976 European Championship. We were on holiday staying at a hotel on the Isle of Wight, and I watched the Final with my father and many other men in the hotel's small television room, the air opaque with cigarette smoke. I was alone in supporting Germany, and it was as if I were German, so anxiously absorbed was I by a match that was eventually won by the Czechs following a penalty shootout. The decisive penalty was scored by Antonín Panenka; an audacious, soft-floated chip. Never before had I felt so devastated.

When I began playing football myself my father came along occasionally to watch me train and he was present for my first proper game, an early-season evening friendly. I remember feeling exposed by his presence on the touchline, because I wanted to show just how good I was; and even then I wasn't sure that I was as good as I wanted to be. I played as a second striker and was substituted early in the second half after a timid performance – years later we joked about how I'd run alongside the ball or the player with the ball, rather than trying to intervene or get a touch myself. As I came off I asked sulkily to be taken straight home, but my father persuaded me to stay on to the end, 'to support your mates'; we spent part of the second half desultorily playing table-tennis in a cold, echoing sports hall that overlooked the pitch. He showed me how to hold the bat, how to serve, how to score, and when he saw that I was losing interest he showed me how the Chinese held the bat, in what he called the traditional penhold grip. 'I've played in Hong Kong against guys who use this grip,' he told me. 'The spin they get is amazing. You can just about keep it on the table when hitting returns.'

On the way home, he stopped at a petrol station to buy me some crisps. We didn't talk about the match or my performance but I knew one thing for sure: I didn't want him to watch me play again. In some obscure way I felt that he was to blame for my humiliating substitution, because I knew I could play better than I had. Later in the week I told my mother exactly that, and she said: 'Your dad was proud to see you play the other night, you know he was. But we can't be good at everything, can we?'

So what exactly had he said? I wanted to know. What had he really said about me?

'He said you haven't got it, son,' she said, softening her voice. 'But you'll show him how good you can be.'

My mother didn't like sport – she was something of a bohemian, she painted and sketched, and preferred gardening to watching or playing games – but she was always encouraging and supportive, always prepared to listen when I talked to her about football or cricket. Freud wrote that a 'man who has been the indisputable favourite of his mother keeps for life the feeling of a conqueror, that confidence of success that often induces real success.' But for days after that first match I did not feel much like a conqueror. I was troubled by what my father had said – *You haven't got it, son* – and this, in retrospect, was probably my first understanding of the ambiguous space that exists between objective and subjective perception. My father didn't see me as I saw myself. Did others see me as he did? It's troubling, this moment when you begin to realise that you're not who you imagined yourself to be. You're not who you thought you were. I was in no way bookish as a child. Up until about the age of fourteen, when I studied *Macbeth* and a couple of mediocre novels for my English literature O level, I read nothing much beyond the *Victor* comic, with its boys' own stories of sporting adventure and wartime conquests and heroism, the Tintin books, and the sports pages of the newspapers my parents bought, notably the *Observer*.

I used to amuse my family by reciting entire storylines from each issue of the *Victor* as well as, when challenged, the exact position of every team in the top four divisions of the English football League at any given time, a prodigious feat of memory that was testament to my obsessions. I knew what I was doing on and off the field of play, or so I thought. But soon I found myself lying to compensate for my sporting limitations because, after being substituted in that first match and even when he wasn't present to watch me, I still felt the pressure of my father's expectation. On one occasion I told him I'd scored the winner in an important game when I hadn't; at that point I'd never scored in any game I'd played in. He discovered my lie when he enthusiastically bought the local paper which carried short match reports from our league. His hurt was so profound that it was as if there'd been a death in the family. 'You must always try to tell the truth, son,' he said. 'The truth can be painful but it is the truth, the only reality we have.'

The desire to be better than you are, to be more than you are, to live as intensely as you can: you see a version of this behaviour at the highest level, perhaps most poignantly at the highest level, especially when a great sportsman is approaching the end and seems intent on defying time itself. The greater the sportsman, the less willing he or she can be to accept mortal limits. Who wasn't moved by the sight of an aged Muhammad Ali stumbling abjectly through his final fights against Larry Holmes and Trevor Berbick? Here was a champ devoured by his own greatness who'd stayed too long in the ring. Or who now doesn't feel sorrow at the prospect of Evander Holyfield, once a great warrior champion, a natural light-heavyweight who willed himself to become a heavyweight, fighting on into his mid-forties in pursuit of another futile shot at a world title?

The long, improbably hot summer of 1976 marked the end, to my father's relief, of my support for West Germany. Yet while it lasted I'd rather enjoyed the rivalry it provoked between us. The whole experience was a useful exercise in self-definition, in striking out in my own way, against the expectation of those closest to me. I was beginning to find out more about who I was, and what I wanted, and the role football and sport in general would play in all this.

Three: A Little Bit of Beckenbauer

The Arsenal coach set off from London Colney just before ten a.m. on Friday 26 May at the start of the long Bank Holiday weekend. The players as they settled down in their usual clusters and groupings observed how many more unfamiliar faces there were on the coach. It was as if as many of those connected to the club as possible had negotiated a ride north: fringe and injured players, boardroomers and their guests, backroom bureaucrats, money men. 'The coach was packed with players and directors and vice-presidents and the like,' said Perry Groves. 'We were all pretty jovial as we travelled up. It was almost like a day out, as no one was expecting us to win. There were plenty of cars with Arsenal scarves as we drove up the motorway and lots of the fans gave us the thumbs-up.'

The feeling among the players was that they'd lost the title. At the turn of the year Arsenal's lead over Liverpool had been fifteen points. Since then they'd faltered just as Liverpool began to improve, strengthened by the return of Bruce Grobbelaar, who had missed much of the season because of illness (he had meningitis). Since 2 January Liverpool had won twenty-one of their twenty-four games, scoring sixty and conceding fifteen. Arsenal had won just ten of their previous twenty games, with four defeats. There was now a frenetic, jittery quality to their play, as long balls were hit more in hope than expectation and the defence became brittle.

So unreliable were Arsenal becoming in defence that Graham was forced to experiment by playing five at the back, with O'Leary operating nominally as a sweeper. He was no *libero*, the defender who invents his own idiom, who plays in a manner and at a tempo entirely his own. The great German captain Franz Beckenbauer had over many years demonstrated how a counter-attacking defender could be the most creative player in the team, but O'Leary, reliable as he was strong, was no Beckenbauer. He never called the play as the German did. Nevertheless he was now required to line up alongside Bould and Adams, in a defensive wall of resolution. The three stoppers were flanked by industrious, fast-raiding full-backs, who were encouraged to attack as and when they could. Graham called it the sweeper system. My Arsenal-hating friends called it the donkey system.

Whatever you called it, the system was used first away at Manchester United on 2 April. It worked well enough; Arsenal came away with a 1–1 draw, from a fractious game played in torrential rain, with Adams scoring at both ends. His own-goal – a sliced clearance which spun off his saturated boot and looped up and over the flat-footed goalkeeper – was comically unfortunate, and it came at a time when Adams was the most vilified footballer in England. He was, to rival fans, the 'donkey'. The morning after the Old Trafford draw there appeared on the back page of one of the tabloids a photomontage of him, under the headline 'Eey Ore/Eey Ore', in which he was depicted as a human donkey, with huge floppy ears. *Eey Ore/Eey Ore*: this was a familiar taunt and it had followed him through much of the season, chanted from the terraces whenever he missed a header or thrashed the ball out of play or lunged into a tackle or tripped and fell. Poor Tony. It seemed everyone wanted to wound him, except Arsenal fans.

Born in Romford, Essex, on 10 October 1966, Adams had been an outstanding schoolboy player, as adept at creating as he was at defending. Under Graham's tutelage he became a hugely accomplished defender, though his ball-playing skills were by managerial diktat suppressed to the brutal efficiency of the team. 'George would hammer us on the training ground,' Adams has said. 'We would go through routines of one-on-one, two-on-two, and even five defenders against eight attackers, working on closing down the opposition. Closing and squeezing, tackling and tackling, until it became the mentality.'

Emerging from the youth team, Adams was widely admired for his on-field intelligence, reading of the game, positional sense, leadership and courage. He had the potential, it was said, to become one of the greatest of all English central defenders. 'Tony was always such a leader,' says Kate Hoey, who before her present role as a Labour MP was an educational advisor at Arsenal in the mid-eighties when Adams was coming up from the youth team. 'The influence he had was so important. It's incredible to think of what he achieved at such a young age, becoming Arsenal's youngest-ever captain, at twenty-one, and then staying in the role until he retired. It's almost as though he had his problems later in life because he had to be so mature from so early on.'

Adams was hurried into the England team at the age of twenty, making his debut against Spain at the Bernabeu Stadium, Madrid, in February 1987. But his inexperience and technical limitations would be exposed at the 1988 European Championship in West Germany, when England lost each of their three group games. This included a 3–1 defeat to the eventual champions, Holland, in which Marco Van Basten scored an outstanding hat-trick and humiliated Adams with his turns, feints, positioning, and all-round superiority.

On his return from the European Championship, Adams became a tabloid figure of fun, a comic grotesque, pilloried and ridiculed, as if he were being held solely accountable for England's failure. It did not help that he wasn't a confident speaker and that he was a drinker, a leader of Arsenal's 'Tuesday-Night Club', the group of players who used to go off on long drinking binges in the West End as soon as training ended on Tuesday afternoon (Wednesday was their day off).

The perception of Adams as a crude artisan was not helped by the demands made on him by Graham, who didn't want his defenders to play or create from deep positions, as Wenger did. If they had the ball at their feet, Graham demanded that they hit it long.

It was under Wenger, during the final five seasons of his career, that we discovered just how creative Adams could be as he ceaselessly moved forward to support the attack. I was at Highbury on a luminous Sunday afternoon in May 1998 – I was there with my friend Salvatore, one of the Sicilian brothers who had come with me on that first visit to Anfield – when Arsenal clinched their first Premier League title under Wenger by beating Everton 4–0. The predominantly right-footed Adams scored the fourth goal after he'd run beyond the strikers from deep to collect a finely threaded pass from none other than his old central defensive partner Bould, on as a substitute during his final season at the club and, improbably, playing in central midfield. Adams took the pass on his chest, knocked it down and scored with his left foot in one swift movement; it was the culmination of the kind of sequence of free-flowing creative play that would have been unimaginable during the Graham years. Afterwards, when asked about the goal and Bould's pass, Wenger, breathless with success, replied, 'A little bit of Beckenbauer, no!' Then he smiled.

Graham never ceased to believe in his young captain; in some ways he'd invented him – and he certainly encouraged his rage. In his first two seasons at the club Graham paired Adams in central defence with O'Leary, a regular in the team since his debut as a seventeen-year-old in 1975. Yet from the beginning, according to O'Leary, Graham was suspicious of the Ireland defender's influence at the club. He was the highest-paid player and was earning more than his manager. In his autobiography Graham complains repeatedly of the meanness of the Arsenal board and of how he was never paid what he thought he was worth. This long-nurtured resentment as well as instinctive insecurity no doubt contributed to Graham accepting illegal payments from transfer deals – bungs or backhanders – which resulted in his sacking in 1995.

'I think George was wary of me,' O'Leary says now. 'Wary of how popular I was, of how many people I knew behind the scenes. Maybe he felt I was just too popular, and was a bit of a threat. When he first came he wanted personal meetings with all the players. He asked specifically to have our meeting at my house. It was obvious that he wanted to see my house, where I lived. I had a lovely big place at the time, out at Hadley Wood [near Barnet, in north London]. When he came over he asked to have a look round. He made sure he saw all the rooms.'

O'Leary later worked as Graham's assistant at Leeds. 'I trusted George as a manager, even if I disliked the way he could treat me,' he says. 'He let himself down by the way he acted. He was very aggressive, could be abusive, but he was also constructive. I was shocked by his appointment at Arsenal. He came from Millwall, not a big club. When he came in he really shook the place up. He was a combination of Don Howe and Bertie Mee. Bertie could manage but couldn't coach. It was the opposite with Don; he could coach but couldn't manage. George could do both. He was very standoffish, methodical. Everything was repetitive: how he wanted us to play, the drills we did. Plus there was the fear factor. I wasn't scared of him but the younger players were. As for his actual knowledge of football, he *knew*.'

O'Leary is courteous. He speaks slowly, in a low, deliberate, deep voice, with a strong Irish accent. Persuasive and polite, he takes you into his confidence by using your name repeatedly, as if he were an old friend. But you know that he knows what he wants: he's a tough man. As a player he never failed to defend his own interests and this led him into long and protracted disputes with both Graham, who liked his players to be subservient, and the Ireland national-team coach Jack Charlton.

'George would often talk to me about the game,' O'Leary says. 'He'd ask what I thought of the team and the way we were playing. He'd ask me, in a very roundabout way, whether I thought I could play at right-back or as a holding midfielder. Could I play left-back, if needed? He was always picking my brains like that. It backfired on me in the end. Steve Bould had joined us from Stoke in the summer of 1988. I knew he had a bright future, but didn't think he'd been bought to play, just to keep us on our toes. One Friday evening

[ahead of a home game against West Ham on 1 October 1988]
George called me over for a chat. He told me he was going to
drop Adams. Tony was having a torrid time. He'd struggled
for England at the European Championship; he'd been
destroyed by Van Basten. He was getting abuse from the
crowds. They were calling him a donkey. Terrible things. And
now he was beginning to struggle at Highbury. George
wanted to drop him. "What do you think?" he said. I told him
if he dropped Adams now it would be the final nail in his
coffin. It would destroy him. George listened and nodded.
The next day I arrived for the match to discover that it was me,
not Adams, who was being dropped. I was stunned. I asked
George why. He said: "I took your opinion. But I wanted
Bould to play." That was the end of it. No further explanation.'

O'Leary remained out of the first team for many months
afterwards.

On 27 August 1988, the opening day of the season, Arsenal
beat Wimbledon 5–1, their confidence and authority serving as a declaration of intent: *We're here, we're dangerous, we're
title contenders.* Nine months later, having drawn with
Wimbledon in the return fixture, their final game at
Highbury, the players set off on a traditional end-of-season
lap of honour. They were back on top, just, on goal difference, but Liverpool had a game to play.

'We'd taken the lead twice, but each time Wimbledon
came back,' Alan Smith says. 'As we did our lap of honour,
the crowd was applauding and cheering us. It was as if they
were saying, "Well done, good try" – even if it wasn't quite
good enough. We thought we'd blown it. We expected
Liverpool to win their game in hand against West Ham, and
we didn't think we could win at Anfield in the last game.'

After the Wimbledon draw the players were given an extended break from training and one another. 'I wanted them to get away from football,' Graham said, 'to get over the disappointment of recent games. I didn't want them to spend the next week just fretting about the Liverpool match to come.'

Adams spent the Monday of the final week of the season doing what he liked to do best when liberated from training: he gambled and drank, starting off at Windsor racecourse. Later, he and Niall Quinn moved on to a nightclub in Maidenhead, then on to a hotel at Heathrow, where they stayed the night. He continued drinking with some of his fellow players, including Quinn, right through the next day, and, on what he called a 'right bender', he drank himself into a condition of willed forgetfulness; the Liverpool–West Ham game at Anfield passed by that Tuesday evening without his even being aware of it. Excessive binge-drinking was how Adams sought to escape from Graham, from the responsibility of captaincy, and what he has since described as an innate shyness.

It would be while recovering from another 'bender', and sickened by self-loathing, that Adams began to ask himself some important questions: what is it that I want from my life? What kind of person do I want to be? How can I live better and free from addiction?

On 26 June 1996 England lost a European Championship semi-final to Germany after a penalty shootout at Wembley. The semi-final – one of those unusual occasions of national unity when it seems as if nearly everyone you meet is absorbed by and talking about the football – was watched by a home television audience of more than twenty-four million. It was the culmination of a febrile fortnight during which G. K. Chesterton's secret people wrapped themselves in the flag of St George and rediscovered their patriotic voice.

The defeat that night at Wembley was anguished for all fans who hoped the match against Germany would mark the end of 'thirty years of hurt', as the Baddiel and Skinner song that topped the charts during Euro '96 put it. But for the England and Arsenal captain, for Tony Adams, the defeat was a moment of rupture. The next morning he went to his local pub in Essex and, sitting up at the bar, began to drink pint after pint of Guinness. He continued drinking through most of the next six weeks, until, early one morning, he woke to find himself in bed in a central London hotel room with a young woman whose name he didn't know and for whom he cared nothing. His next memory, as he tells it in his autobiography, 'is of daylight coming through the curtain . . . having sex with the girl but looking at my watch to read seven a.m. and wondering where I could get a drink at this time of day. That was the grip which booze had on me . . . No longer was I concerned with the feelings of another human being. There was no pleasure in anything, only need. I just wanted to have her and for her to leave, so that I could get back to my drinking . . . Cans and miniature bottles from the now-empty minibar littered the room.'

Addicted is a study in what Nietzsche called self-overcoming. It tells of how Adams overcame alcoholism, self-contempt, a poor education, class insecurities and peer pressure to become the person he is today, an autodidact who, after retirement, studied sports science and psychology at Brunel University; the founder of the Sporting Chance clinic, a charity for sportsmen and women with addictive illness; a patron of young writers at the Royal Court theatre, and now manager of Portsmouth football club. He has a grand house in the Cotswolds, which he shares with his aristocratic second wife, Oxford graduate Poppy Teacher, of the whisky dynasty. He has, in effect, become culturally middle class, in a way that old socialists romantically envisaged would happen if the working class could be freed from economic hardship and toil. 'Today I am not just Tony Adams the footballer, I am Tony Adams the human being,' he has said, lapsing forgivably into therapy speak. 'I do my best every day in every walk of life and seek to treat myself and other people with respect. In that there is also victory.'

'I still speak often to Tony,' Lee Dixon says. 'He's probably the person I'm closest to from those days. Football is a really testosterone-filled environment. Some of my close friends have been through Alcoholics Anonymous – and this made me more aware of what Tony had been through. I was never part of his drinking group at Arsenal but when he came out of the clinic we became really good friends. We'd sit at the back of the coach on match day, and you'd say to him, "All right then, how you doing?" And he'd say, "Well, I'm feeling a bit sad today." You'd see the other lads raise their eyebrows, as if to say, "Oh, here we go again." But you could speak openly to Tony, in a way you couldn't with the others.'

I met Adams at the launch of his autobiography, at an afternoon event held in a back room at Highbury, and in conversation he presents a portrait of his former self notable for its candour and disgust. He speaks of his old aggression and arrogance, his persistent bed-wetting in disturbed early adulthood, his careless drunken rampages in bars and night-clubs, his prison sentence (he was jailed for fifty-eight days for drink-driving in 1990), his failed first marriage and his complete dependence on alcohol, first as a means to help overcome shyness and later, as his drinking became more desperate, as a means through which to escape the inertia and boredom of life away from the pitch. He speaks of all this with a sense that he has known the worst of which he was capable – that he has looked as deeply into himself as he or anyone would dare – and has overcome it. As Wenger once remarked, it was a wonder, with the complications and stresses in his life, that Adams was able to play as well and for as long as he did.

Graham knew about his captain's drinking and the Tuesday-Night Club, knew that some of his players were arriving for training with hangovers; but this was the way things were then, before sports science, objective analysis of data provided by ProZone and Opta and strict dietary controls transformed the way footballers are coached at the highest level. Adams and Merson – who also later publicly admitted to alcoholism – as well as others could drink as much as they wanted during the week so long as they were fit to play at weekends, as they invariably were.

On the Tuesday before the last game at Anfield, Alan Smith and several team-mates attended the annual Football Writers' Association dinner. The choice of Player of the Year was Liverpool's Steve Nicol, who was otherwise engaged in action against West Ham. The guests at the dinner were kept informed of what was happening at Anfield, where Liverpool, after a slow start, were beating West Ham 5–1. Midway through the match Liverpool began to play with a fluency and cohesion that was perhaps without equal in Europe. Their best attacking moves were symphonies of collaboration.

'At the writers' dinner,' Smith says, 'the Liverpool score kept coming in: one, two, three . . . people were trying to do the maths as each goal went in, to work out what we'd have to win by at Anfield on Friday. I left the dinner thinking we had no chance. The next day at London Colney George said we had to win by only two goals. So only two, then!'

Graham's decision to allow the players time away had seemed to have worked. Their mood when they resumed training was less fretful and harshly self-interrogative. Goalkeeping coach Bob Wilson told the players during training that 'this is the week you'll win the title'.

'I did say that,' he says now, 'but, to be honest, I didn't really believe it. I simply wanted to boost their spirits.'

'The build-up was different that week,' Smith remembers. 'It was much more lighthearted. We had quite a few five-a-sides in training, which we didn't usually have. Everyone else had packed up. It was like preparing for a FA Cup Final, except that the Cup Final had been and gone. It was a sunny week, the weather was good. The whole atmosphere was weird.'

Graham chose to travel up to Liverpool early on the morning of the game rather than on the day before, in spite of the risk of Bank Holiday motorway congestion. 'I don't think he wanted us to arrive too early in enemy territory, and be affected by all the hype,' Smith recalls.

'I remember the journey up to Liverpool being stress-free, which seemed to settle us,' says Paul Davis. He had missed much of the season through injury and yet, like the other injured players – notably the winger Brian Marwood, whose accurate free-kicks, corners and crosses, as well as his goals from midfield, had led to an England call-up at the age of twenty-nine – he was on the coach to Anfield and, on arrival there, would go through the same routine as those who were playing: the lunch, the afternoon sleep, the pre-match meal, the team briefing.

'It was painful travelling to Liverpool knowing that I wouldn't be playing,' says Davis, who brought calm and, through his fine touch and clean passing, aesthetic surprise to the Arsenal midfield. 'It was exciting to be on the coach travelling up but sad as well. I was injured. I was missing out. I was missing out on what had the potential to be the greatest game of all our lives.'

In my own small, different way, I felt as if I too would be missing out. The game had been originally scheduled for Sunday 23 April and my father had through a business acquaintance bought two tickets for it; they would be valid for the rearranged fixture but the trouble was that we no longer had them. Even if we'd had them I wouldn't have been able to go, because I had to sit finals on both the Friday afternoon of the game and the morning after it. *A three-hour exam on the history of philosophy on an early summer Saturday morning!* I was aghast when I discovered that, between exams, there would be no way that I could get to Liverpool and back to Southampton in time; that I was, in effect, a prisoner of the exam timetable. I was confronted with the reality of missing out, of not being there. I tried to tell myself that it didn't matter, that Arsenal had no chance of winning anyway. But of course it did matter.

I would lie awake at night thinking of what might happen in the game, tantalised by unknowns and what-ifs. I'd think about the two tickets we no longer had and how we might be able to get some more. I'd dream about the game, and always my dreams would be fevered. I'd be locked outside

Anfield as the game began, or stuck on a motionless train outside Lime Street station as the game began, or stalled in traffic on the M6 as the game began. Sometimes I'd wake up, sweating, with the feeling of there being something important missing from my life beyond the match, something just out of reach, an absence that could be felt but not articulated, a void that could never be filled.

There was also something else worrying me beyond my forthcoming finals, beyond the non-negotiable reality of the exam timetable – and this was to do with my father. Even if I still had tickets or had been free to go to the game he wouldn't have been going with me. This was because my father had been characteristically true to his word: the season had finished for him on 15 April and on that day or thereabouts, thinking that I shared his sense of utter hopelessness and desolation, he'd thrown away our tickets for Anfield as if they were mere sweet-wrappers.

Four: A Moment of Pause

On the morning of Friday 26 May the Liverpool players met for a final training session at Melwood, in preparation for what would be their third game in six days: the Cup Final on the previous Saturday, West Ham at Anfield on Tuesday night and now that evening's title-decider. The city of Liverpool had been in a condition of continuous mourning throughout the late spring, most poignantly so in the first few days after Hillsborough when Stanley Park and Anfield stadium were transformed into shrines of remembrance as fans laid down wreaths, scarves, flags, banners, photographs, and many other mementos. Everyone who visited Anfield during that period remembers how perfumed the air was with the scent of cut flowers. It was impossible as a fan to think of Hillsborough without imagining yourself or some-one you knew in the tumult and torture of the Leppings Lane end. A school-friend had been at Hillsborough for an FA Cup semi-final in 1981, when fans were injured on the terraces because of a crush caused by overcrowding. No one had died, but people were injured. My friend spoke of the fear he'd felt as the crowd closed in around him and he was pow-erless to move or do anything about it. For him, then, it was powerlessness becoming not-quite-hopelessness.

The Liverpool players, some more than others, had been attending the funerals of the Hillsborough dead. 'I was learning about what was relevant in life,' said John Aldridge, who is from Liverpool. 'I didn't really see the point in football. Reading about the parents who lost sons or daughters at Hillsborough made me think of my own children. My son, Paul, was only seven at the time. I was only a little older when I went to my first football match, in the 1960s.'

The experience of the funerals never became any easier; each funeral was as gruelling as the one before it. Each player spoke of how the experience of grief seemed not to lessen but to intensify on each occasion. 'After each funeral, when another set of parents buried a beloved son or daughter, when another grieving family mourned a relative who died following Liverpool, I would come home and climb into bed with my eldest son, just to hold him, just to hear him breathing,' John Barnes said. 'Before Hillsborough I had always tried to keep things in perspective, but what happened on the Leppings Lane terraces made me question so much in my life. Football lost its obsessive significance.'

Two days after Hillsborough the Liverpool players visited the North General Hospital in Sheffield, where the injured had been taken. Some fans were in comas, without hope of recovery, and yet the players were encouraged to talk to them, to cajole, to whisper. John Aldridge was so affected by his experience of the hospital that, for a short time afterwards, he was convinced he would never play professionally again. He remembered speaking to one boy who was in a coma, Lee Nicol from Bootle. 'He reminded me of my son, Paul,' Aldridge wrote in his autobiography. 'Lee was in the middle of the crush at Leppings Lane but was still alive when he was pulled out. I went to see him in hospital. He looked a lovely kid. As he lay there in a coma, I whispered words into his ears. I asked the doctor about his chances of recovery. "He's clinically dead, John," he said. I hadn't realised how badly he was injured. That news ripped into me.'

Kenny Dalglish showed extraordinary resilience throughout this period of mourning, representing the club with patience and dignity at innumerable public events, ceremonies of remembrance and funerals. On one occasion he went in to Walton prison to address inmates at a special service. But he was profoundly affected by the experience of those weeks; I am told by friends of Dalglish that Hillsborough and its aftermath changed him profoundly and ultimately contributed to his sudden resignation as Liverpool manager on 22 February 1991. The night before, Liverpool had drawn 4–4 with Everton in the FA Cup, a game in which they led four times. Hillsborough had taken away his uncomplicated love of football, and, in something close to despair, he turned inwards. To date Liverpool have not won the championship since he left.

Dalglish joined the club from Celtic, as a replacement for Kevin Keegan, for £440,000 in August 1977 – then a British transfer record. He scored the only goal in the European Cup Final at the end of his first season. He would become one of the club's greatest players, a forward of exceptional touch and balance; he scored 172 goals in 515 appearances, and was appointed player-manager following the resignation of Joe Fagan after Heysel. 'One thing about Liverpool, even under Shankly,' says Peter Robinson, 'is that we always liked to sign star players – from Ian St John and Peter Thompson in the sixties through to Kenny to John Barnes and then Stan

Collymore, for whom, don't forget, we paid a British record of £8.5million in 1995.'

Born in March 1951, Dalglish grew up in Glasgow; he would later live in Govan in the southwest of the city, close to Ibrox, the home stadium of Rangers, the team he supported. The Dalglish family were Protestants but this did not deter Jock Stein, the great manager of Celtic who was himself a Protestant, from pursuing and eventually signing the player in May 1967 – the year Celtic won the European Cup. It used to be said that, if you wanted to discover someone's religion in Glasgow, you simply asked which football team they supported: the Protestant blue of Rangers or the Catholic green of Celtic. The East End of Glasgow, where Dalglish was born, is often described as a Catholic stronghold – this was where many thousands of Irish immigrants settled in the second half of the nineteenth century (it was from within this community that Celtic was founded in 1887). And yet, intriguingly, some of the estates close to the Celtic stadium in Parkhead are Protestant enclaves, areas from which Rangers draw their support and from where members of the Orange Order set off to march every summer, in grotesque parody of rituals taking place across the Irish Sea. When Margaret Thatcher was guest of honour at a Scottish Cup Final in the 1980s she was shocked to see Celtic fans waving Irish republican tricolours, and to hear them jeering the national anthem and singing pro-IRA songs. The prime minister had obviously never visited Celtic Park, where the Irish and Scottish flags, but not the Union one, are raised above the stadium. Nor had she listened to Rangers fans singing the 'Sash' or cruel songs about the dead IRA hunger striker Bobby Sands.

When the Protestant Dalglish signed for Celtic sectarianism was much more deeply ingrained in Glasgow and its effects more insidious than they are today, when both Celtic and Rangers freely sign players of all nationalities and of all religions and none. Jock Stein, a former miner, as Shankly had been, understood all of this of course and in his wisdom and good humour sought to transcend it. Jock, he was once asked, 'if there were two players, one Catholic and one Protestant, who would you sign?'

'The Protestant,' he replied.

'Why?'

'Because I know that Rangers would never sign the Catholic.'

'Kenny grew up in a close-knit family, and playing under Jock Stein was a great formative experience for him,' a former Liverpool director told me on condition of anonymity. 'It was hard to get to know Kenny well, to know what he was really thinking; he's a very private man and there are only a few people outside his family he really trusts, Alan Hansen being one. At the beginning of the nineties he signed a new three-year contract with us and we thought all was well. But that February day, early the next morning after the Everton draw, he came to us and said that he simply couldn't go on. He was ashen-faced; he just looked dreadful. We told him to take the rest of the season off, to go away with his wife on a long holiday. We wanted him to stay, of course. We were prepared to wait for him. [A fellow director] Tom Saunders, who was very close to Kenny, spoke to him, tried to dissuade him from resigning. He said to him: "You just need a long rest, Kenny. Get away from football, spend some time on the golf course and come back refreshed next season." But he told us he was too stressed to continue. He'd reached the end of the road. He couldn't go on – and you could see how much he was hurting, how tormented he'd become. It was a terrible day for the club when he left.'

Dalglish would return to club management, first at Blackburn in October 1991, with whom he won the Premier League (1994–95), and then at Newcastle, from where he was sacked in 1998. Unlike Hansen, who since retirement has become the BBC's best football pundit, with a nice line in understated, self-deprecating humour, Dalglish has shown little desire to become a media talking-head and pontificant.

On the afternoon of 26 May the *Liverpool Echo* led the paper with a story about Chief Superintendent David Duckenfield, whose fatal decision it had been to authorise the opening of an exit gate outside the Leppings Lane terrace on the afternoon of 15 April. This had led directly to the surge of Liverpool fans into the stadium and straight into the tunnel that passed beneath the West Stand and into the two already densely populated central pens. The people who were already in those central pens were, in effect, caged, like cattle being transported for slaughter. High fences prevented them from escaping on to the pitch or sideways across the terrace into the less-congested side pens. The fans at or near the front of the central pens – many of them children or teenagers – had nowhere to go as more people surged up from the tunnel and fought for space. The resulting crush was immediate and unendurable – and it was being watched live on television around the world as those fans who were able to scrambled for survival, trying to force their way on to the pitch by scaling the starkly unyielding security fences; some fans were pulled to safety by those above them in an upper-stand seating area.

We know that the overcrowding outside Hillsborough was exacerbated by motorway congestion caused by roadworks and by the late arrival of fans' coaches. In addition there was strict and oppressive policing outside the stadium restricting the movement and flow of fans, many of whom had turned up without tickets. Liverpool had been given the Leppings Lane end when, because of their huge support, common sense suggested that they should have had the larger Kop end, where the Forest fans were. Liverpool had, oddly, also been allocated fewer tickets than Forest – 24,000 to 28,000 – which was why so many fans had arrived in Sheffield without tickets.

In spite of the crush developing before the game around the narrow outer concourse of the Leppings Lane turnstiles, the kick-off was not delayed, a simple and sensible measure that would have reduced the anxiety of those concerned about missing the start. 'It was clear as early as half past two that both central pens at the Leppings Lane terrace were full,' the academic Phil Scraton, who has written a fine book about Hillsborough, told me in anguished reflection nearly twenty years later. 'But even before the decision was taken to open the exit gates allowing the fans to pour in, the situation was still recoverable. Yes, I think people would have died outside the stadium in the crush if the exit gates hadn't been opened, but two things should have happened before they were: the kick-off should have been delayed, and the middle tunnel through which fans passed into the two central pens should have been sealed off, so that they would have then been forced to move into the side pens. Trevor Hicks, whose two daughters died in the central pens, was in one of the side pens. Those side pens weren't full.'

It was not until the match had begun, with Liverpool's Peter Beardsley striking the bar early on, that the players on both sides realised that something was seriously wrong behind the goal at the Leppings Lane end. Goalkeeper Bruce Grobbelaar heard voices calling to him: 'People are dying in here, Bruce. Help us.'

At six minutes past three referee Ray Lewis blew his whistle to halt the game. The players were ordered back to their dressing-rooms. The game would not restart.

Chief Superintendent David Duckenfield refused to accept responsibility for his decision to authorise the opening of the exit gate and, in the confused aftermath, he told Graham Kelly, chief executive of the FA, that Liverpool supporters had forced open the gate, precipitating the catastrophe. Within minutes, Phil Scraton has written, Duckenfield's 'version of events was broadcast worldwide. Jacques Georges, President of UEFA, railed against "people's frenzy to enter the stadium come what may, whatever the risk to the lives of others". They "were beasts waiting to charge into the arena". Thus, Liverpool fans were responsible for the deaths of their own. The lens of hooliganism was firmly in place.'

Chief Superintendent Duckenfield has since been pursued into uneasy retirement by the families of the victims who continue to campaign to establish criminal liability for what happened. What is accepted is that in the days after Hillsborough someone or several people within the Sheffield Constabulary attempted to attribute blame by briefing reporters about the supposed 'drunkenness' and 'recklessness' of Liverpool supporters. The suggestion was that their violent irresponsibility rather than police panic and incompetence caused the deaths. Once again the subtext was clear: there was something uniquely wrong with Liverpool and its people.

Liverpudlians are often accused of excessive self-pity and mawkishness, and this accusation is widely repeated whenever a crisis in the city becomes a matter of national moment: Heysel, Hillsborough, the murder by two boys of toddler James Bulger, the random and fatal shooting by a member of a drugs gang of twelve-year-old Rhys Jones as he was on his way home from football training.

On 19 April 1989 the *Sun*, edited by Kelvin MacKenzie, published a front-page report – headlined 'The Truth' – in which it was said that hooliganism was to blame for the Hillsborough tragedy. Drunken fans had urinated on the dying; they had stolen money from them; a female police officer had been attacked as she assisted an injured girl; and so on. None of this was true, as Lord Justice Taylor's interim report into the disaster established four months later. But there were many people who wanted to believe that it was.

It has been suggested that, instead of 'The Truth', MacKenzie had wanted to use a more provocative one-word headline: 'Scum'. When I called to confirm the veracity of this, he said: 'No, no, no, I'm not going to talk to you about Hillsborough. I think I'll save that for my own book.'

Then he was gone.

'Much has been written about Liverpool and Liverpool people, saying that we don't show the same concern over Heysel as we do Hillsborough, and that we are a self-pitying people,' Phil Scraton says. 'The explanation is this: Heysel was caused by a group of Liverpool supporters who probably had too much to drink and wanted to give a group of Juventus supporters a hard time. But the real scandal is that the Heysel stadium was falling apart, the ticketing arrangements were appalling and the policing was terrible. So you had the combination of bad policing, bad ground, tickets being bought on the black market, and the panic caused by the Liverpool fans. Hillsborough was completely different.

Taylor got it right in his report. It was caused by overcrowding and misjudgement by the police. The fans were not to blame.'

But even if the 'real scandal' of Heysel was that the stadium was decrepit, the match would have passed without incident and English clubs would never have been banned from Europe had there not been a pre-match rampage by Liverpool fans. Everton supporters remain especially bitter about the ban, because their club won both the First Division title and the European Cup Winners' Cup in 1985. Everton were then widely considered to be the best team in Europe, and yet they never had the opportunity in the European Cup to show how good they could have been.

'My problem with Liverpool fans, including someone like Phil Scraton, is that they never take responsibility for their own actions,' says James Corbett, Liverpudlian and author of *Everton: The School of Science.* 'You can romanticise them all you like – and it's true that they're often more sporting than most fans – but human shit has been thrown at Manchester United fans at Anfield. Nowadays they are always singing songs celebrating the serial killer Harold Shipman, because he murdered Mancunians. Above all, the terrible, inescapable irony of Hillsborough wasn't that Liverpool fans were responsible on the day, but that their previous actions – and also, to an extent, what had happened in the city during the 1980s – created a climate of fear, which Taylor mentions in his report, and this governed the police response.'

The Hillsborough deaths happened at a time when the behaviour of fans and the atmosphere at most grounds was, on the whole, improving; attendances were beginning to rise after falling to a record postwar low during the season after Heysel; racism was becoming less widespread and certainly less virulent; the fanzine movement that showcased a new kind of fandom was flourishing, with its witty, irreverent magazines and flyers; the ITV Saturday-morning show *Saint & Greavsie* – featuring former players Ian St John and Jimmy Greaves – was introducing a new informality and humour to football broadcasting, later adapted and developed with greater sophistication by shows such as Baddiel and Skinner's *Fantasy Football*; the Football Supporters Association, established after Heysel, was providing guidance and leadership; and fans were turning up at games not with darts and bricks and knives, as of old, but with giant plastic inflatable toys.

The social backgrounds of the ninety-six who died at Hillsborough were diverse: people of all classes from all over the country, men and women, boys and girls. They weren't in Sheffield to fight and agitate. They weren't part of the monolithic mass, the hostile crowd. They were there to watch and enjoy an FA Cup semi-final, no more nor less. Yet we needed an event of the gravity of Hillsborough – an English disaster played out before a global television audience – for the government and those who ran the game to accept that, in its centenary season, English football had reached its psychological moment, the point of no return. The culture of the game had to change definitively if football was ever to be perceived as anything more than the preserve of the white, working-class male, a theatre of hate and of violent, often racist and misogynistic excesses, if it was to survive at all.

Perceptions at this time were all important, by which I mean the perceptions that we as a society had of the game of football and of its followers, and that we the fans had of ourselves and of those who ran the game. My own perceptions were certainly skewed. In the late seventies I went to a

Charity Shield match at Wembley with my father and so imbued was I with a sense of threat and menace that I can remember how uncomfortable I felt, as we walked along Wembley Way, for the simple reason that I was wearing an Arsenal shirt beneath my jacket. Nothing would have happened to me if I'd removed my jacket; I was just an ordinary boy out with his dad. But it was anxiety about what *might* happen at football rather than what ever *actually* happened that eventually led some of my friends to start carrying knives to games, just in case. I'm sure it's a similar anxiety that leads young lads in urban gangs today to carry knives, just in case. I was lucky: I was never beaten up, attacked, jumped or mugged at football; yet I was convinced one day I would be. At one Spurs game, in the late seventies, my friend Mike was ejected after he was found to be carrying a knife on his way in to White Hart Lane. 'I bet you'd love to shove that in my stomach,' the copper said, as he confiscated the knife and bundled Mike out of the ground; he had been carrying a plastic bag full of ticker-tape and this was why he was stopped and searched.

Once outside, Mike was at liberty to pay at a different turnstile and come back in, which is what he did. My friends and I found the whole incident hilarious. He didn't expect or want to use the knife; it was just that carrying it seemed the right thing to do, an expression of who he thought he was as a fan and what he thought he should be doing. All of us assumed that the guys who ran the firms that did the fighting carried knives. There were older boys at school who claimed to know some of the terrace leaders, and we knew that these older guys carried knives. If they carried knives, so should the rest of us – if only as theatrical props.

I've spoken to many fans who were at a match on the day of the Hillsborough tragedy, and so despairing was the national mood and so unreasonably self-hating were many supporters that, before the facts of what had happened were known, the automatic assumption was that the deaths must have been caused not by police error but irresponsibility and violence, as had happened at Heysel: *We hate Scousers/We Hate Scousers* . . .

These assumptions were just as corrosive as our (mis)perceptions. Here's the novelist Martin Amis, for instance, writing about football in the early nineties:

> 'Every British male, at some time or another, goes to his last football match. It may very well be his first football match. You stay home, thereafter, and watch it on TV. At my last football match, I noticed that the fans all had the complexion and body-scent of a cheese-and-onion crisp, and the eyes of pitbulls. But what I felt most conclusively, above and below and on every side, was ugliness – and a love of ugliness.'

When my father called on the Sunday morning after Hillsborough he reminded me of an evening the previous November when together we'd been to Highbury for a Littlewoods Cup replay against Liverpool. 'Do you remember what happened outside, before the game?' he said.

Arsenal played Liverpool an improbable six times that 1988–89 season: twice in the League, three times in the third round of the Littlewoods Cup, and once in the Football League's own celebratory Mercantile Credit Centenary Trophy. The first Littlewoods Cup match at Anfield finished 1–1; my father and I went to the replay, another draw.

Liverpool eventually won the second replay at the neutral ground of Villa Park.

We met in central London before the game, had something to eat at Ronnie Scott's jazz club in Soho, and then took the Underground out to Finsbury Park. Neither of us could get a seat on the train; we stood facing each other, in the harsh light of the carriage, keeping our balance by holding on to the plastic straps suspended from above. I noticed something different about my father as he stood being rocked by the motion of the train, a new vulnerability. He seemed physically reduced, somehow shorter than his usual six feet, and so tired. I could see the dim shine of the gathering perspiration on his forehead. I knew that there was uncertainty in his work and that he had changed jobs several times without explanation and at short notice, moving from what seemed, to me on the outside at least, to be one precariously financed operation after another, until, by this time, I sensed that he was no longer quite in control of his own destiny. He was doing less designing and more selling; the intensity of the travelling was great. I didn't like to think of him in a diminished role, as a kind of Willy Loman of the rag trade; to me, he remained a fashion designer, and a good one.

'The next stop is Finsbury,' he said.

'Right,' I said.

He seemed awkward and out of place in a carriage full of football fans, in a way he never once had on the terraces at Upton Park. There he was exhibiting the same majestic restraint as of usual, revealing nothing. His fine, flat hair was cut short, thinning slightly at the front, and greyer than even six months before. There was something stiff and formal about his manner: he was wearing a dark-brown leather jacket, baggy double-pleated black needle-point cords, thick-soled brown suede shoes, and he held a book in his right hand, a paperback of Arthur Miller's autobiography, *Timebends*. I thought of how often people would comment on his courtesy and charm – still everybody's favourite after all these years. My friends professed to like him because he was different from their fathers. He used to be younger in attitude and outlook, alert to and interested in popular-cultural trends. He used to buy style magazines such as *ID* and *Italian Vogue*, as well as the *New Statesman*, the *Listener*, *City Limits*. As new bands formed at the end of the seventies and began experimenting with synthesizers and new technologies, combining a punk ethos with new ways of making and recording music, he'd listened to early albums by Simple Minds, Kraftwerk, the Human League. My friends and I had borrowed these records and were impressed by their strange, cold, computerised sound – 'the sound of the future,' my father said.

The train pulled in at Finsbury Park. We crossed the platform to pick up the Piccadilly Line and went the one additional stop to Arsenal. Formerly known as Gillespie Road, the station had been renamed in November 1932 after some extensive lobbying by Herbert Chapman; the original name remains on the ornately tiled walls of the platform. 'Whoever heard of Gillespie Road?' Chapman said. 'It is Arsenal around here.'

There are no escalators or lifts at the station and it's a long walk up from the platform through a steep, winding network of narrow, white-painted tunnels to the street-level exit. The low-ceilinged tunnels seemed even more claustrophobic than usual: there were so many of us down there and we were all making our methodical, slightly impatient way up to the street. There wasn't much of the usual pre-match chat or singing; it was as if everyone was unsettled by the close proximity of so many other bodies, by the press and density of them, and by how closed in we were. It was obvious from the congestion in the tunnels that the crowd would be very big tonight; it turned out to be 54,000, the largest of the season at Arsenal, in any competition.

I'd watched the highlights of the first match at Anfield and had seen enough to know that Arsenal, inspired by David Rocastle, who scored an excellent goal and played with such skill and muscular influence from the flank, had the potential now not only to compete with Liverpool but also to start beating them. It felt as if we were approaching a shift in the balance of power, and in Rocastle Arsenal had a player of exceptional promise, with the ability to become the equal of John Barnes. When he made his debut at eighteen, against Newcastle in September 1985 at Highbury, manager Don Howe said: 'David passed when he should have shot, and shot when he should have passed, but he's going to be a great player.'

Howe was correct in his judgement, as he usually was about a player, and very quickly Rocastle established himself in the first team. Because of his obvious ability and character – his hard running, his willingness to tackle and to take a tackle, even as he sought opportunities to score and create – the fans responded to him. He soon became their favourite, my favourite. In the years ahead we would love other black players, notably Ian Wright and France midfielder Patrick Vieira, but in the modern era no player, black or white, has been as loved as David 'Rocky' Rocastle by Arsenal fans.

It was his name we heard being chanted as we came out on to Gillespie Road. We were late, it was very close to kick-off, yet still there were dense queues outside the narrow entrance to the North Bank on Gillespie Road. The match wasn't all-ticket; as many as 15,000 more people had turned up than was usual for a home game at that time; the police were struggling to keep order and control; and we, the fans, were restless to get inside. Police on horseback were trying to force us into orderly lines but we were mostly ignoring their bellowed instructions as we formed our own irregular lines, seeking to fast-track our way to the front. The floodlights were on, tempting us with their promise, and the noise from inside was intensifying. Then there was another surge. I felt myself being bundled along, scarcely able to stay on my feet. It was a cold November night yet I was beginning to perspire. In front people were being pushed up against the turnstiles; the guys taking the money were shouting at us to go back. We couldn't, but nor could those in front of us pass through the turnstiles. From behind there was more pushing as the crowd thickened and heaved. Police on horses were trying to calm us, shouting out instructions through loud hailers. I looked for my father, from whom I'd become separated, and saw that he was being carried away as if in a rolling maul. People were shouting, the stench of drink and cigarettes on their breath. I reached out for my father, tried to grab his hand; our fingers fleetingly touched before I lost him in another surge and could only look on, helplessly, as he went down. I struggled through the crowd, forcing my way through. I reached him just as the pressure began to lessen, with the police regaining a semblance of control as they drove those pushing from behind away from the turnstiles and out into the throbbing streets.

My father was being helped up by the time I reached him. He was smiling. He was all right. 'I think I've lost my book,' he said.

*

'Yes, I remember,' I said to him down the phone line to Hong Kong. 'Outside Highbury, you fell over. That could've been bad.'

'It could have been bad and now it really is, as bad as it gets,' he said. 'The season's over. What's left for any of us now?'

And then, soon afterwards, that statement: 'I'm finished with football.'

Five: North and South

As Arsenal were travelling north to Liverpool on the last day of the season, Margaret Thatcher set off on a much shorter journey of her own from 10 Downing Street to the Guildhall. There she would accept the freedom of the City of London at a ceremony to mark ten years of her premiership. She spoke with unrestrained triumphalism of how her policies had revitalised Britain. The virtues she valued most – enterprise, freedom, democracy – were in the process of remaking the world. We were, she said, witnessing the beginning of the end of communist hegemony, of the collapsing legitimacy of authoritarian regimes and the ultimate triumph of capitalism. She went on, addressing the Lord Mayor of London:

> These ten years have included triumph and tragedy, joy and sadness. Above all they have been years of achievement for our country. You referred to them, Mr Chamberlain, as 'a kind of revolution'. In a way they were, for what we had to do was nothing less than redress the balance of power between Government and the citizen, in favour of the citizen; to limit the power of Government and enlarge the liberty of the people . . . Our vision was, and remains, to rekindle the

spirit of enterprise in our people, to bring back hope and opportunity to those who had lost it, to spread ownership evermore widely, to restore the authority of the rule of law, to use prosperity to enhance our sense of community, and at all times to be strong in the defence of liberty.

In her mission to remake society, Mrs Thatcher and her party had been, I think, too neglectful of those who depended on the state for welfare support. Nor did she think hard enough about the broader social consequences of her economic reforms, of how they had ravaged traditional working-class communities in the industrial north as the country was transformed from a manufacturing to a service-led economy. She said that she believed in the family – such that, once we were liberated from excessive state control, it would restrain our more atavistic desires. But what if the family was already broken? What if, for some people, the wider community served as the family?

Mrs Thatcher was adored and despised in equal intensity, as Tony Blair would be. She had an irritating, hushed, remodelled voice – which the theatre director Jonathan Miller once snobbishly likened to a 'perfumed fart' – and a hectoring manner. She was especially despised in the old manufacturing heartlands of England and Scotland – in Manchester, Newcastle and Glasgow, where the Labour Party, though it had been routed elsewhere in the country, remained strong throughout the eighties, when the party was in embattled retreat, first rancorously splitting in 1981 and then, under the leadership of Neil Kinnock, seeking more pragmatically to adapt to the new Thatcherite realities. (From when the Conservative were re-elected in May 1979 to the winter of 1988, ninety-four per cent of all jobs lost in Britain were north of a metaphoric line running from the Wash to the Bristol Channel, according to the Census of Employment.)

If there was one city in which Thatcher was despised above all others, it was Liverpool. Even at the end of the eighties, because of the decline of the docks there and the closure of many hundreds of factories, including Tate and Lyle's long-established refinery at Love Lane, Merseyside had a sixteen per cent unemployment rate (it had been as high as twenty per cent). 'I believe with a passion that Margaret Thatcher contributed hugely to a decline in care, community and decency of values,' Alan Bleasdale, Liverpudlian and author of the BBC drama *Boys from the Blackstuff*, said. 'By the time she had finished with us, our society was battered.'

First broadcast in 1982, Bleasdale's drama depicted the struggles and despair of a group of unemployed men in Liverpool during the economic depression of the early Thatcher years, when it seemed as if even Liverpool's two bishops, the Anglican David Sheppard and the Catholic Derek Worlock, were united in their opposition to the government. (The Conservative Party remains even today largely unacceptable and unelectable on Merseyside, where it has no MPs or city councillors.) Wrenchingly sad but also enraged, caustic, and often bleakly funny, *Blackstuff* was one of the defining political dramas of the eighties and its popularity alerted the nation at large to how Liverpool, this once great and now decaying former industrial city, was being affected by the recession. It certainly changed the way I thought about the city, its history and its decline.

The last time I'd been in Liverpool was in May 1984. It was only my second visit to the city, but I wasn't there to watch football as I had been on my first visit: this was the period when I'd ceased going to games. I had tickets for an Echo & the Bunnymen gig, the centrepiece of an eccentric all-day event called 'Crystal Day', organised in association with the Channel 4 rock show *The Tube*. The Bunnymen's leader was, and still is, the singer-songwriter Ian McCulloch, a tall, spiky-haired, motor-mouthed agitator, and an unashamed Liverpool patriot. Crystal Day, after the title of a Bunnymen song, was less about music than it was about the band's home city: they wanted to bring their fans into Liverpool to celebrate its cultural richness and diversity, even as its factories were being pulled down and its dockside warehouses were standing derelict. Many of the Bunnymen's young fans dressed as they did, in long dark overcoats, in faded blacks and greys, in the colours of a damp, overcast northern English city morning. To see them all arriving in Liverpool from different parts of the country was like being present at the gathering of a secret society; it felt clandestine, with people speaking in code.

I caught an early train up from the south with two friends, and during the journey we darkened our eyebrows with pencil, encrusted our lashes with mascara, and attempted to disguise our razor burn and pale, blotchy late-teenage complexions with foundation and powder: all this make-up stolen from our mothers' or sisters' bags. This was the early eighties, after all, when androgyny and cross-dressing were so much part of mainstream culture.

As part of the build-up to the gig, we had the choice once we were in Liverpool of participating in various 'happenings': a bicycle rally, a ferry ride on the Mersey, a choir recital at the gothic Anglican cathedral, a haircut at a Bunnymen-favoured salon or something to eat using prepaid vouchers

87

at their favourite local café, Eric's. (The Bunnymen were then managed by Bill Drummond, who founded the K Foundation, notorious for their various situationist-style stunts or art happenings.) Jools Holland was in town that day, working for *The Tube*, and he opened the proceedings by letting off helium balloons from a platform erected outside the city's modern Catholic cathedral, which is shaped like a giant ice-cream cone turned upside-down and is at the northern end of Hope Street.

I don't know what exactly I expected from Liverpool but I certainly had an exaggerated sense of its misfortune as our train pulled into Lime Street station. I felt imaginatively as if I were entering a warzone, a defeated city, bombed-out and shattered by the mortars of Thatcherism. With its industrial unrest and strikes, its Militant-controlled Labour council and rejection of Thatcherite individualism, Liverpool seemed to me, living in the south-east, to be profoundly unstable, and yet its instability seemed exciting from the outside. It was of England and yet somehow apart from it, and I knew this sense of anti-establishment difference had become a source of stubborn pride for Liverpudlians. Scousers could be bolshy; they had their own vernacular, their own sense of humour and ways of talking.

The overwhelming sense of Liverpool on the day was not one of wider despondency but of promise. For all the self-conscious gloom and melodrama of their music, the Bunnymen were determined to showcase not only themselves but also what was best and most dynamic about Liverpool and they made a good job of it. They wanted you to discover what they as locals knew of the city, to walk its secret streets and learn of its hidden histories. A group of Chinese dancers, representing one of Liverpool's long-established but often-ignored minority racial groupings, supported the band on stage at the main gig, as if to say, *We are here and part of the city as well*.

The chosen venue for the gig was eccentric but consistent with the purpose of Crystal Day: the once-grand but now abandoned St George's Hall, the neoclassical building opened in the city centre in 1854 as both a concert hall and law courts. It was from the steps of this building that Bill Shankly had addressed 100,000 people shortly before his retirement. When it was opened St George's embodied all the confidence and wealth of the imperial port city; in 1984 it was an empty, dust-filled relic, a reminder of a lost prosperity.

In the afternoon, in the long queue outside Eric's, we met a group of local girls, sixth-formers, who had tickets for the gig and were as proud of their city as the Bunnymen were. We bantered with and teased them: outpourings of the usual regional rivalries and mockeries. One of the girls, Fiona, was quieter than her friends, more softly spoken, reserved, and rather detached. She wore an ankle-length dark-grey raincoat, and her long, blonde-streaked fringe was, like McCulloch's, tousled and spiky. I liked her, and, after eating together at Eric's – egg and chips, or sausage and chips, or fish and chips – and in a pub before the gig at St George's, we talked. She was studying for her A levels, and wanted to do history or English at university. 'Where will you go?' I asked. 'I'll stay here in the north,' she said. 'Maybe Leeds or Newcastle.'

When she asked about my life, I instinctively lied. It amused us, my friends and me, to invent fictive identities for ourselves, to deny the truth of what we were doing and where we were at in our lives – I'd dropped out of sixth-form college, having failed to complete my A levels the year before. Now I was doing nothing much beyond signing on once a fortnight and spending most afternoons sitting around at my friend Matthew's house; he, too, had dropped out of sixth-form. We idled our days away by coming up with elaborate plans for the future. We wanted to form a band, but our approach to our putative pop career was cerebral and exhibitionistic; we liked the talk, and we liked the clothes. As for the music, we were sure that would take care of itself as and when the opportunity arose, because what was the use of attempting to do great things if we could have a better time telling each other what we were going to do?

Matthew and I were career fantasists, and one of my most enduring fantasies was that I was an emerging rock journalist, already widely published; I guess, on reflection, I was always more attracted by the idea of talking and writing about music than I was by the prospect of learning an instrument or writing songs. I told Fiona that my first reviews and interviews were being published in the *NME* and *Record Mirror*. She was obviously impressed. 'Have you interviewed Mac?' she asked. 'No,' I said, 'but I will soon. I'm here today as part of my research.'

I was excited by her – by her accent, her vivacity, reticence, prettiness, knowledge of and enthusiasm for music. She sat there beside me in the pub, in her long coat, her white shirt buttoned to the neck, her grey-blue eyes ablaze, and it seemed to me then that I'd never met anyone as engaging or as desirable. 'What's your favourite Bunnymen track?' she asked. '"The Cutter",' I said. 'I like the tempo change midway through and that bit when he lowers his voice to sound like Bowie.'

'I love the video,' she said, 'the one filmed in Iceland.'

Later, at the gig in the Grand Hall of St George's, she reached out to take my hand as the Bunnymen struck up the first, jarring, sitar-like chords of 'The Cutter'. In the brief interval after the Bunnymen had finished their set and we waited for the inevitable encore, people around us began to sing 'You'll Never Walk Alone' and I thought of that first visit to Liverpool and to Anfield: the swaying on the Kop, the togetherness. Then I kissed her.

Afterwards, instead of searching for a party or nightclub to go to, I explained to the others that Fiona and I were going for a walk – 'to explore'.

'But it's dark!' one of Fiona's friends said.

'Oh, you're such a woolyback,' she replied.

We were all slightly drunk, and our friends whistled and jeered, before, obligingly, heading off towards the city centre, leaving us together, alone, sitting on the cold stone steps of St George's Hall, watched over by a statue of Disraeli, around whose neck someone had tied a Manchester United scarf. Liverpool: a once proud Tory city, but now one of its finest buildings was empty, its disuse and near-dereliction a rebuke to those who purported to run and serve the best interests of Liverpool and its people. Just across the way was Lime Street station and after a while we crossed the road and went into the station itself. We sat on a bench looking up at the high glass roof, with its intricate lattice-work of iron stanchions; the station's large ornate clock, mounted high above of a wall, showed that it was past midnight.

Fiona asked where my friends and I planned to spend the night. I told her (and for once I was telling the truth) that sometimes when we went out as a group to nightclubs in central London – to the Camden Palace, say, or the Wag or the Electric Ballroom – we'd stay right through to the end, to when the music stopped, the lights came on, and then, if we knew of no party to crash, we would hang around the streets, sometimes gathering at an all-night Wimpy, until we could catch the first train back to Essex. 'We planned to do something similar tonight . . . But of course I knew I'd meet someone.' She stood on tiptoes and kissed me softly on the cheek. 'You're funny,' she said.

We sat in the station for a long time talking in staged whispers, as if we were fearful of being overheard, and continued talking until we both began to feel cold.

'You can come back to mine, if you want, for coffee,' she said.

We took a taxi to her parents' house somewhere in north Liverpool, and, as we stopped outside, she kept apologising. 'I'm afraid it's not very grand,' she said of the house as we moved into the hallway.

'How far is Anfield from here?' I asked her.

'We're nearer to Goodison.'

'But what about Anfield?'

'Not far – about a fifteen-minute walk.'

'Shall we go and have a look?' I said.

'But I'm a blue,' she said. 'I'll take you to Goodison but I'm going nowhere near Anfield.'

The semi-detached rendered-brick house was small but neat and clean – there was a kitchen, a sitting-room, at one end of which, beneath a window, was a dining table, and three upstairs bedrooms. There was one lavatory and a bathroom, both upstairs. She made coffee and then, holding our mugs tightly, we went upstairs to her small, narrow bedroom, where she used cotton-wool to clean away the mascara smudges from around my eyes. On the walls there were posters of McCulloch and Pete DeFreitas, the

Bunnymen drummer who would be killed in a motorbike accident, of Robert Smith of the Cure, of David Bowie, and David Sylvian. The room had an odour of perfume and hair-spray. She apologised again, for the make-up scattered across a small dressing-table, on which was propped a stainless-steel-framed circular mirror on a narrow stand and scattered across it the brushes, the creams, the tubes, the cotton-wool pads, the eyebrow pencils.

We lay together on her single bed and complained of how our clothes stank of cigarette smoke; and then we began to kiss, hesitantly. The only light was from the insipid yellow wash of streetlamps outside. She was so young, and beautiful, and near. When I tried to unbutton her shirt, aware of the rapid beat of her heart against my chest, she looked at me and said: 'No, I don't want sex.'

I felt oddly relieved when she said this.

We did not speak for a while but then, becoming uncomfortable with the silence, I asked about her father – she'd not once mentioned him. Speaking softly, as if she were worried that someone else other than me was listening, she said that her father had been having a hard time and was no longer living at home but with his brother in Birmingham, where he'd gone to find work.

'It's just me, me mum and brother at home now.'

So her father had done what Norman Tebbit had asked of the longterm unemployed, I thought: he had got on his bike and looked for work.

He'd been unemployed for several years, since the closure of the Dunlop factory at Speke, she explained. She spoke of her father with distraction and sorrow: of how, before he went to Birmingham, he used to spend long days mooning around the house, often drinking too much; of how her mother became frustrated by his loss of purpose and motivation, and raged at him; of how he had lost interest in so much, even in the football.

As she told me about her father, I heard the distant reverberations of the football songs I used to sing: '*In your Liverpool slums/You find a dead cat/And think it's a treat . . .*'

Lying beside her, my throat dry from the drinking and all of that day's talking, I felt ashamed for having boasted about the thrilling things I'd be doing next when, in truth, I wouldn't be doing much more than sitting around at Matthew's house speculating on what we'd like to be doing next.

'Why did you call your friend a woolyback?' I said.

'Because she's not from Liverpool proper. She's a posho Wirral woolyback.'

'Say that again.'

'Posho Wirral woolyback.'

We both started laughing and she put her hand over my mouth to quieten me.

It was starting to get light outside.

'I think you should go,' she said, 'if you're not to miss the first train. I'll phone for a taxi.'

What she really meant was: *You must go before my mother and brother are up.*

The early-morning light was straining against the curtains. I was thirsty, the room felt airless, and my head felt thick from all the cheap drink.

Soon we were standing at the open front door, just inside the porch. 'I'll call and write to you,' I said. 'I promise.'

I never saw Fiona again. But that evening in Liverpool left me with a lingering, romantic attachment to the city. As with all great port cities, the history and identity of the people of Liverpool have been defined by continuous arrivals and departures, by welcome-home and goodbye parties, by long recessionals and farewells, by brief encounters and random couplings, by cultural slippage, immigration, and miscegenation. Life must have often felt provisional; work was seldom guaranteed, especially with the long-established policy of casual rather than permanent labour in the docks; relationships were fragile – the sailor you'd fallen in love with the night before might have been gone by tomorrow. Geographically the city is on the edge, with its back to England: it doesn't look back into the rest of the country but out to the sea, from where it once welcomed the whole world.

The 'key to knowing what a Scouser is lies in the sea,' the novelist Linda Grant, who is from Liverpool, has written.

> The sea was always there, offering an entry and an escape: if nothing else turned up, you could always walk down the dock road and sign on a ship bound for somewhere you'd never heard of but which might be the very place your neighbour had come from. And this was true even for the middle classes . . . The decline of the port was the critical turning point in the city's fortunes. Liverpool went bust because its economy depended on the docks, and it was on the wrong side of the country for trade with Europe

Yet, for all its proud exceptionalism and its various organised expressions of workers' solidarity, Liverpool the city has long been deeply segregated, riven by sectarianism and by racial and class tensions and antagonisms. There is not one, as I used to think, but many Liverpools. There is, for instance, the Liverpool of long-settled Chinese, Somali and Caribbean communities whose origins in the city extend back to the nineteenth century, but these are people who have often been outside society, on the margins, victims of informal apartheid. The racial conflagrations of the early eighties in Toxteth were a profound and genuine response to generations of anger and racist policing.

In the 1964 *Panorama* programme about the Kop there was of course something missing from the unified, swaying crowd: black faces. According to the social historian David Renton, who has lived in the city and writes a blog about, among other things, Liverpool football club,

> There's an old idea on Merseyside that Liverpool people are incapable of racism, so many of them being recent migrants themselves. The [racist] murder [in 2006] of [black student] Anthony Walker suggests a different picture, as does the recent abuse of [boxer] Amir Khan, which a number of papers helpfully reported as having taken place in 'Everton', as if Everton was a separate city. Anyone who knows the city will acknowledge that Liverpool is far whiter than people from outside tend to think. The decent-sized Somali and Caribbean communities in Granby and Liverpool 8 aren't matched by any other sizeable black populations as you travel away from the city centre. It's still depressingly easy to spend an entire Saturday afternoon in the city centre and not see a single black face.

One of my friends recalls being at Anfield for a game against Graham's Arsenal in the eighties when, in anticipation of the emergence of Rocastle and others, a section of the crowd started chanting 'Bring on the niggers'.

'That was hateful,' he says now. 'In the end it took some-one with the stature of John Barnes to make it at Liverpool. He changed attitudes.'

Before Dalglish signed Barnes from Watford, in a £900,000 deal in 1987, Liverpool had never bought a black player. Only one black player had previously represented the club – the Toxteth-born Howard Gayle, who came up through the youth ranks. In six years as a full professional at Liverpool, from 1977 to 1983, he played only five games. Throughout the eighties Everton did not have a single black player – and this was at a time when a generation of England-born black players, mostly from Caribbean families, were establishing themselves in the game.

Yet in the late-nineteenth century Liverpool had been the most cosmopolitan city in England. It was the self-styled second city of the Empire, with more foreign consulates than even London; the docks erupted into the city centre, and there was a great surging polyglot energy in and around the landing station as the ships came in and out, providing work for tens of thousands of casual labourers. Little more than a century later Liverpool was the least ethnically diverse city in England, according to the 2001 census.

During his early months on Merseyside Barnes was received with astounding hostility even by groups of his own supporters. The abuse was much worse at Everton. In one game at Goodison Park in 1988 Barnes was pelted from the crowd with bananas; there's a famous photograph of him back-heeling one into touch during the game. Whenever he had the ball sections of the crowd made grunting monkey-like noises, a cacophony of loathing. 'I was there that night,' says the writer James Corbett, 'and the abuse he suffered was repulsive. But I think we've got to be very clear about this: Barnes suffered appalling abuse from Liverpool fans first and foremost.'

The abuse directed at Barnes was part of a general pattern repeated widely throughout the country during the seventies and much of the eighties as fans were explicit about what they thought of the black players making their way in the game. 'It was particularly bad at Sunderland, Leeds, at Chelsea and West Ham,' says Paul Davis, who made his debut for Arsenal in 1978. 'Those four grounds stick out in my memory.

'It's tough; you cannot block it out. You just have to find a way round it, and concentrate on what you're doing. Concentrate on your work. Don't retaliate. Try to get a result for yourself and the team. I remember the noise, so intense. Everyone standing. It's very intimidating. I take the corners. I'm close to the fans as I take them. It's a real tough one. It resonated for me when the England guys had that trouble in Spain a couple of years ago [when players such as Shaun Wright-Philips and Ashley Cole were racially abused by the crowd during a friendly played in Madrid]. It brought it all back.'

Unlike Davis, Rocastle and Thomas, Barnes was not born in England; he did not grow up on a deprived inner-city London estate, as the three black Arsenal midfielders did. He was born in Jamaica, the son of an army officer, and moved to England as a child. He was from a comfortable middle-class family and spoke with an accent that was a curious hybrid of the Caribbean and the Home Counties: he spoke as fluently, intelligently and as quickly as he passed and moved on the pitch. In his first season at Liverpool, 1987–88, when he became the first black player to win the Football Writers' Association Player of the Year award, he was often exhilarating. According to the Sky Sports pundit Jamie Redknapp, Barnes was the best footballer he ever played with or against. 'I was with him at Liverpool towards the end of his career, but he was still a class act. If there had been the same hype around the game in the late eighties as there is now, people would have been making the same fuss about him as they do over Thierry Henry.'

To his critics, Barnes never performed as well for England as he did for Liverpool, even if his finest moment was the audaciously self-created goal he scored against Brazil, in a 2–0 win at the Maracana stadium in Rio de Janeiro in June 1984. Taking the ball on his chest and then cutting in from wide on the left, he beat one defender after another as he moved at speed into the box, the ball remaining, always, as though attached to his feet as he swerved around the humbled keeper and pushed it in nonchalantly with his right foot, with the kind of casual ease which suggests that nothing much has gone before it, that nothing has really happened at all.

Afterwards, a group of travelling England supporters affiliated to the National Front stated that the result was only 1–0; the Barnes goal did not count because 'it was scored by a black'. On the return flight to London, Barnes, at the front of the plane with the rest of the squad, could hear some of the fans at the back chanting 'There ain't no black in the Union Jack'.

Barnes said that he never felt patriotic and 'tried hard for England out of professional pride not patriotism. Nationalism causes so many problems. I hate it.'

Did he feel this way because he was born in Jamaica? Or is it more likely that he wearied of being disrespected, with his achievements ignored or erased even as he scored one of England's greatest goals, and against Brazil, in Rio; a goal against the country that, at the 1970 World Cup, played the team game as well as it has ever been played. After that goal the expectation on Barnes must have been unbearable: we wanted him – demanded of him – to repeat what he had done in Rio. That he did not, could not, led many of us unfairly to resent him. He was never resented by Liverpool fans. They knew how good he was.

Barnes remembers how in his first season at the club he was continuously being stopped while out and about in the city. 'Fans kept approaching me in the street and saying, "We love you". I appreciated the compliments but naivety had never featured in my make-up. I knew Liverpool fans would have slaughtered me if I wasn't delivering.'

But he was delivering and, through his dignity, on-field virtuosity and off-field articulacy, he helped to create the circumstances in which racism would become increasingly unacceptable on Merseyside, even at Everton, who today have several Nigerians in the first team. 'The real political point,' says historian David Renton, 'is that all anti-racist traditions have to be made and remade and *constantly* remade.'

Back at the end of the eighties I watched with interest at how Barnes was being received on Merseyside, because race was a vexed issue in our family as I was growing up. Both my grandfathers were Londoners; their fathers had worked in the Thames-side docks, one as a stevedore, the other as a more casual labourer, always scrambling for work, nothing guaranteed. They did not want their sons to follow them into the docks: my maternal grandfather, Edgar, became a carpenter and joiner, while my paternal grandfather, Frank, got a job 'on the buses', driving red double-deckers in

London's West End. In retirement, when he moved out to live near us in a modest flat in our Essex new town – as Edgar also did – Frank suffered acutely from tinnitus, which he believed had been caused by his decades working on the buses. 'Always the sound of the engine in my ears, the constant ringing,' he used to say.

The two aged Londoners, whose wives died long before them, could not have been more different in attitude and behaviour. Edgar was gregarious, a trencherman, an optimist, industrious, thrifty; he rode a motorbike until he was in his late seventies; he was treasurer of the local 'old people's club'. He was a true Cockney, born in the City of London, within the sound of the Bow Bells, and he had a gruff, unsophisticated voice and reduced vocabulary. 'Wrap it up and I'll take it home,' he used to say, if any food remained on the table after a family meal. He had known terrible deprivation. There were times as a young boy when he and his many brothers and sisters did not have any shoes. Edgar did not like sport, as Frank did; he purported to support West Ham, but you knew he didn't really know about them or care about the game. What I noticed above all else about Edgar, unusual for someone of his generation, upbringing and class, was that he was not racist. I never heard him utter a racist remark. It was said in the family that he was once well cared for by a black nurse from the Caribbean while in hospital – as if that explained it. Maybe it did.

Frank used to box in East End pubs, and he supported Millwall. (The oddity of our family was that son did not follow father in his team of choice: Millwall, West Ham, Arsenal, each time a slight geographic and social distancing.) Frank was a strange man, with a pale, open face, and, surprisingly for a former boxer, a fine straight nose. I remember how the skin of the nicotine-stained padded tips of his fingers was split and cracked and how there would be little patches of silvery hair on his face which the razor had left untouched – though they would never be the same patches, in the same place. He would sometimes purse his lips, tightly, like a trumpeter and spit-blow air through them, making little farting noises which I wondered if he could hear or not. He was introspective, quietly spoken, courteous, generous with what little money he had. And he preferred to be alone, perhaps because his tinnitus made it so difficult for him to hear and to be in company, when the buzz and chatter around him, the white noise of so many voices, reminded him of being back on the buses, always surrounded by people, the throb and throttle of the engine. 'So much noise, all the time,' he used to say. Now I wonder if it was the boxing, rather than the bus-driving, that contributed to his tinnitus: the battering around the head and ears he must have taken during his years as a fighter, the thick thud and sharp sting of gloved hands in his face.

Frank was an ascetic and a smoker; he ate very little – cheese, white bread, tinned ham, eggs, apples, dark chocolate, custard-cream biscuits – and refused to have a working fridge in his flat; he had a fridge but never switched it on and instead used it as a cupboard. Nor would he have a telephone connected. He kept his milk on the windowsill in his narrow front room, which overlooked a school, and when you visited him in summer the tea he served would be rancid with sun-warmed, curdled milk. In the end I took to asking that he serve my tea without milk. 'Funny,' he said, 'your sister has it like that as well.'

I was fond of Frank but I was disturbed by his racism, which was fierce and continuous. 'The darkies overran the buses,' he used to say. 'They're good at sport because they're used to swinging around in trees and running in and out of holes.'

In September 1975, Millwall, Frank's team, signed two black players, Trevor Lee and Phil Walker, from the same club, non-League Epsom & Ewell. Their performances quickly became noticed as Millwall won promotion to the Second Division in 1976. Frank wanted to know more about Walker, who played in midfield, and Lee, a forward: who they were, what they were doing, what they were like as people. Had the fans accepted them? It's said they work hard, is that right? He read what he could about them in the papers and was always grateful when Millwall were featured, however briefly, on ITV's Sunday-afternoon football-highlights show, *The Big Match*. Slowly, through the seventies, I noticed how his attitudes on race began to soften even as they seemed to be hardening in wider society – this was a period when Rock Against Racism and the Anti-Nazi League were founded in direct opposition to the rise of the National Front.

The contradictions continued. To Frank, Walker and Lee were still 'darkies', but they were, when in the blue of Millwall, 'our darkies' – because they played with pride and commitment, for the cause. This attitude was common among many fans at that time: they often cheered their own black players even as they traduced those of rival teams.

One Saturday afternoon in the autumn of 1980 my father took Frank and me to watch our local team in first-round FA Cup action against Charlton. The previous season Harlow, from the lowly Isthmian League, had, improbably, made it through to the fourth round of the Cup, eventually losing 4–3 away to Elton John and Graham Taylor's Watford in a game shown on *Match of the Day*. I was at the match that afternoon, as I had been for the earlier second- and third-round ties against Southend United and Leicester City, both superior professional League opposition and both beaten 1–0, after replays.

Harlow played at the Sportcentre, which was scarcely a football stadium at all; it was part of a larger sporting complex opened in 1960. The stadium had one covered stand with as few as 200 plastic orange seats, and there were steep mud banks behind each goal and opposite the stand. The pitch was enclosed by a running track. It is hard to believe now but 10,000 people were squeezed into the Sportcentre stadium for the Leicester game.

But we watched as Harlow against Charlton failed to repeat the form of the previous season, when they were so fleetingly famous. My abiding memory of the match isn't of the two goals Charlton scored, or the atmosphere on the mud banks, but of the racial abuse directed throughout at Charlton's black striker. The racism was without pause, as viciously sustained as any I've heard at football.

On one unusually warm autumn afternoon in the late seventies some friends and I slipped illicitly into Harlow's high-rise town hall, which was located in the town centre, known locally as the High because it was built on the highest part of the town. The town hall overlooked the Water Gardens, at the entrance to which was a Henry Moore sculpture named 'The Family', which, my father said, symbolised all the new families that had started in the 1960s when Harlow was known as 'pram town'. That afternoon we took the lift up to the glass observation tower that afforded superb views across the surrounding landscape through which we moved each day. There, laid out before us, was the clean, hard geometry of our once-optimistic town. We stayed up there for the whole afternoon, until it was almost dark, and watched as the lights came on in the distant houses below, shimmering amber in the encroaching blackness.

In those days Harlow was resolutely monoethnic, a largely working-class and insular town; there were no black boys in my year at school, and very few of Hong Kong Chinese or Indian and Pakistan origin. There were, however, several boys at the school who would become members of the Inter City Firm, or ICF, the feared and ruthless collective of hardcore West Ham hooligans. One of my closest boy-hood friends was convicted and imprisoned for his part in a riot by West Ham fans on a cross-Channel ferry. My father always protested that he was innocent; he could not equate such violence with the boy who used to come to our house to play Subbuteo or watch the Cup Final – the boy who stood with us on the Chicken Run at West Ham and celebrated when the home team scored with a fervour that I, as an Arsenal fan, never shared. He was the boy whose mother was a classroom technician at our school, familiar and pop-ular as she assisted the language teachers in preparing lessons. No, my father did not believe that my friend could have been guilty as charged. 'They got it wrong,' he said. 'They made a terrible mistake.' He contacted my old friend's mother to say as much.

Some of the Harlow ICF were there at the Sportcentre for the Charlton match that day in 1980; and, as the end approached, with Harlow abjectly beaten, the mood soured. Many of the guys around us on the mud banks were agitat-ing for violence. 'You're gonna get your fucking heads kicked in,' they taunted the Charlton fans, who were being protected by a tight ring of police. Coins and cans were being hurled in their direction.

'We should go,' my father said. 'It's getting dark, and we've lost anyway.'

I looked carefully at father and son as we made our way back to the car. My father was at least four inches taller than Frank but recognisably his son; they both had the same strong, narrow straight noses, though the bridge of my father's was flatter and more pronounced; they had the same soft, moist eyes and chin dimples; the same fine, flat hair and open expressions. Once we were in the car, Frank continued to wear his flat cap as usual. I watched from the back as he turned to my father and said: 'It was tough for that black fella up front this afternoon, Tone, wasn't it?'

'So it was, Frank,' my father said, 'so it was.'

Black fella. My grandfather had always used the word 'darkie'.

Six: This is Anfield

England seemed at the end of the eighties to be a more confident and more racially tolerant country than it had been at the beginning of the decade: generally more at ease. The small, bitter wars between the government and the striking miners, between the government and the print unions and other vested interests opposing its reforms, had been fought and, often painfully, won (though another war would soon break out, over the implementation of the poll tax – which had been introduced in Scotland ahead of the rest of the United Kingdom in April 1989). Tory tax cuts had been argued for and made. The deregulation of the City – the so-called Big Bang – the liberalisation of financial markets, the boon of privatising what had been in effect a socialist economy, North Sea oil revenues . . . All of this had powered economic growth. Unemployment was falling. In spite of having scant support in Scotland and in Labour's traditional northern England heartlands, the Conservatives had won the 1987 election with a majority of 102 seats.

Yet for all our new wealth it still felt as if you were living in a divided country; England was still very much two nations. London and the southeast, where property prices had risen exponentially through the decade, had become increasingly prosperous; those who were making money wanted to make more and there was a new harshness in the culture as the language of the old welfare paternalism was replaced by the rhetoric of market individualism. As an undergraduate from 1986–89 I was surprised by how many people I knew at university who were committed Conservatives and by the efficiency of the Conservative Students' Association, the dominant group at debates. Everyone seemed to be talking about wanting to make money in the City, and then of making some more: much more. Apparently the urge was no longer to change the world, even superficially in the old spirit of student idealism and adolescent rebellion, but rather to prosper in it. When I asked how my friends and acquaintances planned to do that, the answer was invariably the same: by working in the money markets or as City lawyers. The main opposition in student politics came from the well-motivated but ultimately deluded Socialist Workers Party; the student Labour Group was, like the national party, demoralised and disorganised (though it was enthusiastically led, by a likeable mature student who dressed in army fatigues, wore dark glasses and had a long dry, wispy beard, like he was auditioning for a place in ZZ Top).

Okay, I was at a university in the south of England, a bastion of middle-class privilege, popular with nearly-Sloanes and Oxbridge miss-outs – but still something didn't seem quite right. Elsewhere in the country something exciting was happening in and around the universities of the northwest, especially in Manchester. This something was the rave scene and it was spilling out of the Hacienda night-club and into wider society. Bands like Happy Mondays and the Stone Roses, with their leftover Beatles chords and floral shirts, high on the freely circulating drug ecstasy, were making a new kind of hybrid music, fusing eighties dance and indie with 1960s-style psychedelia. Here, if not in becalmed Southampton, was a stirring of cultural resistance. We were witnessing the return of psychedelia, but this time the drugs were different; the year of 1989 with its political disturbances and convulsions was turning out to be the 1968 of the post-sixties generation, but this time it was all about counter-revolution, not revolution; we were hearing not about the world-changing potential but about the end of socialism and Marxism. Yet what if anything would replace them?

Occasionally at weekends during the warm and settled late spring of 1989 I'd return home to the Herts and Essex borders and find myself driving around remote country lanes looking for a rave or pay party for which I had a ticket but no clear instructions as to where to go exactly. The whole rave scene was clandestine, diffuse and unregulated, with hastily organised and often police-disrupted pay parties being held in farmers' fields or near-derelict barns, and with tickets exchanging hands furtively. I'd been too young to take part in the punk revolution but now the rave scene was offering something similar – an exhilarating can-do attitude, something politically challenging and subversive. I was seeking sensation, a new way of being; and being at a rave was a bit like being at an especially intense football match – the idea was to lose yourself in the abandon and anonymity of the crowd.

It was during this period of being suspended between the presumed and often complacent liberties of late adolescence and the encroaching responsibilities of early adulthood that I became once more properly interested in football.

Graham's arrival at Arsenal had initially excited my interest; and even before that, in the 1985–86 season, West Ham had finished third in the First Division, their highest-ever position, an achievement that had got my father and I talking about football again just as I was preparing to leave home for university. For the first part of the 1985–86 season (the season after Heysel, when people were as disgusted with and as despairing of the game as they had ever been) a rights dispute resulted in no football being shown on television, not even highlights. Good riddance to it, many thought, we're better off without it. But my father and I felt this absence acutely – we weren't able to take a look, for instance, at West Ham's new goalscoring sensation, Frank McAvennie – and so we started going to games again, and continued going even when the dispute was settled and football was back on TV.

When I arrived at university I started to play again. I found that playing as well as watching, reading and talking about the game gave shape and definition to my often idle, drifting days – and I discovered that there were many other students who loved football just as much as I did but who had none of my tortured class anxieties about it. They read books and they played and watched football – what was the problem?

I understand now that my father's reasons for attempting to re-engage with football were different from mine. This was because his preoccupations were increasingly with the past, with his *own* past. He once told me that something disappeared from football about the time Bobby Moore retired in the mid-1970s. What exactly? I asked him. He couldn't really explain. All he said was that this loss had something to do with what he described as our once having had a 'common culture' – by which he meant, I presume, a greater sense of national purpose and togetherness. But where did Bobby Moore, former captain of West Ham and England, our World Cup-winning captain, fit into all this? Maybe my father meant something more than that. Whatever he had meant, it sounded like old-style, romantic socialism to me – all those guys with cloth caps standing together on the terraces – and I said as much to him, with my usual haughty young man's indifference.

For me the present and near future were all that mattered. I wasn't interested in the past, least of all in my father's past. I didn't want to know about ten years ago or even last year. I wanted to know only about what would happen next . . . Next week, next month, next year. Forward, forward, forward.

On the day of 26 May, the day of the match, the Arsenal team arrived at around lunchtime in Liverpool after an uneventful journey and checked into the Atlantic Tower Hotel on Chapel Street. The hotel is a short walk from the stately Liver Building, completed on the river at Pier Head in 1911; the building is famous for its two signature cormorants, which stand tall atop the two clock towers with wings wide open as if startled into flight. The front of the hotel is shaped like the prow of a ship; it's not hard to imagine the hotel itself pushing off from dry land and out into the Mersey.

It was on this waterfront earlier in the decade that the former Conservative cabinet minister Michael Heseltine had based himself as he sought ways to regenerate the blighted city. For a period Heseltine became known as the 'Minister for Merseyside' or 'Mr Merseyside'. He was never a Thatcherite, never a true believer: he positioned himself against Thatcher, as her overt rival, a dissident in the ranks. He was, unlike her, a Europhile, not a radical but a true conservative. Thatcher was appalled by Liverpool, especially by the recklessness of its local Labour politicians, whom she blamed for bankrupting the city council; Heseltine, by contrast, cared for the city and, as he grandly saw it, wanted to save it.

At night he stood with a drink at the window of his hotel, looking out, as he would later recall,

> at the magnificent view over the river, and [asking] myself what had gone wrong for this great English city. The Mersey, its lifeblood, flowed as majestically as ever down from the hills. Its monumental Georgian and Victorian buildings, created with such pride, still dominated the skyline. The Liver Building itself, the epicentre of a trading system that had reached out to the four corners of the earth, stood defiant and from my perspective very alone . . . everything had gone wrong.

That was one view, the government view. But how could anyone, even at this time of high unemployment, suggest that *everything* had gone wrong when the city still had its two great football clubs? Steve McMahon played for both Everton and Liverpool in the eighties. Born in 1961, in Halewood, Merseyside, best known for its Ford car-manu-facturing plant, McMahon was first a ball-boy at Everton, then an apprentice, and then, finally, club captain in his early twenties. Today he lives in Singapore, where he works as a football pundit for ESPN Asia. As a player, the fine-haired, thick-thighed McMahon was a resolute destroyer. In 1983, after three years in the first team at Everton, he was approaching the end of his contract; he wanted to sign an extension but was offered a rise of only £10 per week. 'I was insulted by that,' he says. 'I thought I was worth more.' He was approached by Liverpool, and he and his father met manager Bob Paisley. 'He was very persuasive,' McMahon says, 'he wanted me to join. I'd also been approached by Aston Villa, but Mr Paisley offered me twice what Villa did. But the circumstances weren't right. I didn't think I could join Liverpool, because of my Everton connections, and I'd already agreed in principle to join Villa.'

McMahon moved south to Birmingham, and there he watched enviously as, in 1985, the club of his schoolboy ambitions, the club he'd left over a wage dispute, won their first title since 1970 under manager Howard Kendall. He eventually returned to Merseyside in September 1985, but as a Liverpool player, becoming player-manager Kenny Dalglish's first signing; Liverpool would win the Double that season. 'I was delighted to be back playing football in my home city,' he says. 'I know I'm biased but I think Liverpool is special, the most special football city in Britain, if not also the world. The people work, live and save up to go to watch Everton or Liverpool. Their devotion is total. The game is in their heart. It gives meaning to their lives. You learn this from an early age, and you never forget it.'

Once settled at the Atlantic Tower, the Arsenal players had lunch before being instructed to return to their rooms to rest. On the night before games some of them would take sleeping pills, but never on match day. 'I was sharing a room with David O'Leary,' Alan Smith told me. 'We drew the curtains and had a good few hours' sleep. I didn't always sleep well on match day, but we both woke up that afternoon and said we'd slept well. It was the same when we went down to meet the others. Everyone said they'd slept well.'

Graham received his players at the five o'clock team meeting dressed in club blazer, white shirt, and a red and white tie. The players were served tea with toast and honey, and then Graham asked the waiters to clear the tables and close the door. 'There we were,' he has said, 'the enemy, right in the heart of Liverpool.'

Graham confirmed what the team would be and that they would play with five at the back, with O'Leary as sweeper. This was his great gamble – to bolster the defence in a game he needed to win by two goals! Using a flipchart as an aid, he discussed tactics and explained who would be marking whom at set-plays. He then told the players exactly what he expected of them: that they should 'keep it tight', frustrate Liverpool so as to subdue the crowd; and that, above all, they shouldn't concede a goal. They shouldn't worry or panic if the score was still 0–0 at halftime, he said. In the second half they should 'open up a bit', and seek to score an early goal. The greater pressure would then be on Liverpool: they had the title to lose; they would 'fall apart under the pressure'.

Nobody expected Arsenal to win. 'All the pressure is going to be on Liverpool. They will not be able to breathe out there for the weight of expectancy. Their fans, the media and probably even some of their players think the title is in the bag. The television cameras will be bringing the game live to the nation, and all the viewers at home will be sitting there expecting to see a Liverpool victory.'

Graham reminded his players that he himself had won the championship as an Arsenal player. 'I promise you there's nothing quite like it, and you can experience that feeling tonight.'

It was nearly five-thirty p.m.; very soon Arsenal would be making the short journey by coach to Anfield.

There was just under an hour and a half to go before kick-off when the coach arrived at the stadium. The players disembarked, went to their dressing-room in the Main Stand and then, before changing into their kit, out to inspect the pitch – 'firm and in excellent condition considering this was the final match of the season,' was Graham's verdict. On their way out they would have passed beneath the sign every player must notice before he leaves the narrow tunnel for the last time: 'This is Anfield', the sign introduced under Shankly.

There were thousands of people already waiting for the London team on the terraces; the noise they made pressed in on the Arsenal players, enclosing and entrapping them, making them halt or step back, as if they'd bumped up against a sheet of glass. *This is Anfield*. 'It's at that moment when you go out on the pitch,' Kevin Richardson says, 'and are hit by the noise around you that you think: "I'm involved in one hell of a game here."'

After the pitch inspection the players returned to the dressing-room to begin their methodical pre-match preparations: the ritualised stretches and rub-downs, the tactical rehearsals and team talks. Players were kicking balls around in the tiled space of the communal shower and bathing area while others undressed and began to put on their kit. The most superstitious among them was David O'Leary, who always undressed in the same way, putting each piece of kit on in the same order. Last of all he would take his crucifix from a pocket and repeatedly kiss it. Some of the players were silent but others nervously chatted. Adams was the loudest, as usual: *This is our fucking chance. We can win it, we've come this far, we've got nothing to fucking fear.*

Back in the hotel lobby Arsenal's assistant manager Theo Foley had received a visit from his daughter, who had a ticket for the game. She was holding her baby, his grandson, and she wanted her father to know that no matter what happened in the game she believed in him. He shouldn't 'get too worked up because it's been a great season, Dad, hasn't it? It's great to be second, Dad, isn't it? That's why you shouldn't be too despondent.'

Foley had also been Graham's confidant and assistant at Millwall. His role was that of in-house optimist and man-motivator; he was a fast talker and a joke-teller, with a rich, peaty Irish accent. The players liked and trusted Foley, felt as if they could talk openly to him, confide in him, in a way they never could with the elegantly austere Graham. Now, in the changing-room at Anfield, Foley found himself reflecting on the conversation he'd had with his daughter. He'd told her that the season could only be described as great if Arsenal ended it as champions. That was what he'd told her in the lobby and now here he was telling the players exactly the same thing, only this time his phrases were punctuated with expletives, with the casual, routine obscenities of the dressing-room.

By this time, match referee Dave Hutchinson, from Oxfordshire, had been at the ground for nearly two hours. 'Because the match was originally to be played in April, I knew as early as March that it would be mine,' he says. 'The fixture then obviously wasn't as critical as it subsequently turned out to be. When I finally knew its importance, I didn't get nervous so much as I just thought, "This is one game in which I've got to get everything right." I travelled up in the early afternoon. I suppose I got there about three hours before. I just went though my normal routine; there was nothing extra to do. I was very conscious that I needed to be as calm as I possibly could be. Also it was essential that I got to know and feel comfortable with my two linesmen.'

The ITV broadcasting team, led by Jim Rosenthal and Elton Welsby, had also settled in at Anfield and were preparing to go live. 'It was phenomenal,' Rosenthal says. 'I don't think there's ever been a climax to a season like it. I think Sky have been begging for an ending like that ever since – a one-off game to decide the title – and of course they have never had it.

'Liverpool had gone something like twenty-four games unbeaten, while Arsenal had wobbled a bit. It was a real long shot. Before the game I thought back to the previous summer, when I'd had a bet with Tony Adams. I'd been the England reporter at the European Championship in Germany that summer and those were the days when we mixed quite freely with players. Over a drink we'd had a £100 bet: I'd said they wouldn't win the championship next season and he'd said they would. So the bet was still on.'

Just before the start it was announced that the kick-off would be delayed by ten minutes: at least twenty coaches of fans were caught up in slow-moving traffic on the M6; in the event, some of those fans would not arrive until halftime.

The pitch-side security fences at Anfield had been removed in the days after Hillsborough and, before kick-off, a police officer came on to the pitch to address the crowd. 'There are millions watching us tonight,' he said, speaking through a microphone. 'Please do not come on to the pitch at any time. If we can achieve that, you will see the presentation [of the championship trophy].'

Most neutrals would no doubt have expected and indeed wanted Liverpool to win, because of Hillsborough but also because of Dalglish's commitment to the passing game, which contrasted markedly with the much more direct style of Graham's Arsenal. 'Boring, Boring Arsenal,' was the immemorial chant that had greeted the players when they came out to inspect the pitch.

To compare Graham's young Arsenal side with the extravagantly accomplished multinational side of the Wenger years is to accept that there's no comparison: the present team, in technique and ability, are superior. Yet the group of '89 had special qualities of resolution and endurance during an era of intense on-field physicality, when few teams played a passing game and an ultra-physical side such as Wimbledon bullied their way to winning the FA Cup. Many of our leading coaches, notably Watford's Graham Taylor, who would become England manager, were unapologetic exponents of the long-ball game. English domestic football through much of the eighties was, when contrasted with how the game was played in France, the Netherlands or Spain, characterised by a pragmatic brutalism; it was dismaying but indicative of the era that a player of such creative gifts as Glenn Hoddle ended up being so marginalised by the national team.

Graham's Arsenal may not have had the homogeneity of the Celtic team that won the 1967 European Cup in Portugal, the Lisbon Lions of whom, it is said, the entire team were born and brought up within a thirty-mile radius of Celtic Park in Glasgow, but they had a distinct local identity all the same. All thirteen players who took part at Anfield, including the two substitutes, were born in England, though

David O'Leary, from an Irish family, would represent Ireland as an international. Six of them had signed for the club as schoolboys: O'Leary, Adams, Rocastle, Thomas, Merson and Hayes (one of the two substitutes). 'Coming through the ranks is really great,' Rocastle said. 'We've got the club in our heart, the passion is there. We've come through; we don't want the club to lose. We are all winners and we have a lot to prove and we'll fight to prove it.'

Another youth-team graduate who was not fit to play at Anfield was Paul Davis, though he and the other injured or non-selected squad members were still present in the dressing-room before the start. 'I went down to the changing room, but no one seemed to have any tickets for us,' Davis recalls. 'I thought we'd be sitting on the bench – great, I thought, right in with the action. But then just before the start George came over and gave us some tickets. They weren't for up in the main stand in the seats, but were for out on the terraces, with the Arsenal fans. We had to go out of the stadium and then come back in again to take our place down at the front behind the goal.'

Davis remembers leaving the stadium and, once outside, being caught up in the pre-match hustle. He felt a fan's keen excitement as he queued to get back in the stadium from inside which, paradoxically, he'd just come. He was a privileged insider and yet here he was as an outsider, queuing for a place on the terraces. 'I've been an Arsenal fan ever since I was a young boy, so it was an amazing surprise to find myself in with the fans. Some of them recognised me. They were saying, "Good on you, Paul", that kind of thing.'

Before sending his players out, Graham repeated more succinctly much of what he'd already said at the Atlantic

Tower: keep it tight, the pressure is on them, and above all be patient.

'What if they score?' Adams asked.

'We'll score three,' Graham quipped back. 'But don't let them score.'

Graham shook the hand of each player as he left the dressing-room for the last time before giving a brief interview to ITV's Jim Rosenthal. 'He was so calm,' Rosenthal recalls. 'I remember thinking that if you were an Arsenal fan looking at that you would think, "We've got a chance here." I always think you can tell a heck of a lot by mannerisms and how people are before big sporting events and he was super-controlled.'

Graham preferred to watch the first half of games from up on high, in the directors' box. On his way up to his seat in the Main Stand he encountered Dalglish in the narrow tunnel outside the dressing-rooms. They wished each other well at a reserved distance and Graham observed how 'he looked much more strained than I felt'. Graham continued to the box, where he took his seat alongside chairman Peter Hill-Wood and the club's most influential director, David Dein. Dein was the entrepreneur and trader who had done so much to modernise Arsenal since paying £300,000 to buy a fifteen per cent stake in the club in 1983. Investing in football was, Peter Hill-Wood commented at the time after selling shares to Dein, 'dead money', just as the Bergkamp signing was 'complete madness'.

It was Dein who brought Wenger to Arsenal from the Japanese club Grampus Eight in October 1996; it was also Dein, as vice-chairman of the FA, who encouraged Sven-Goran Eriksson, then of Lazio, to become England manager. In August 2007, in dispute with the board over the future ownership of the club, he resigned and soon afterwards – to the widespread outrage of fans – sold his shareholding for £70million to an Uzbek billionaire, Alisher Usmanov. Usmanov has since increased his stake in the club to twenty-five per cent. The Arsenal board have in response agreed to sign a 'lockdown' agreement, which prevents any of them from selling their shares to outside investors until 2012.

Was it a mistake to sell his shares to Dein? 'No,' Hill-Wood says. 'You can't look back. What do you want me to do? Cry every night about it? No, there's no point jobbing [sic] back. Arsenal has never been about making money for me or my family. In fact, none of the board is in it for the money – otherwise they'd have sold out by now and not signed the lockdown agreement. We see ourselves as custodians of the club. It's our duty to protect its best interests.'

Book publisher Ernest Hecht, owner of Souvenir Press, who has followed Arsenal since arriving in England from Czechoslovakia as a child on the *Kindertransport*, has known Dein for many decades. 'One of his best friends was working for me as an audit clerk,' Hecht says, recalling his first encounter with Dein. 'I was off to Barbados to watch the cricket – Australia versus West Indies – and my clerk mentioned that a friend of his, a fellow Arsenal fan called David Dein, would be on the same flight out to the Caribbean. He was going out to do some business. We met at the airport lounge, and it was obvious who Dein was: he was very dark and was like a caged panther in the lounge. We got talking and it was clear that he was a complete Arsenal nut. He was going out there to buy exotic tropical foods for the family trading business in Shepherd's Bush. He was about twenty-one at the time, and very well mannered. I wasn't sure what he would go on to do, but it was clear he would do something significant. He's a hustler. A deal-maker. Above all, he's a genuine fan.'

It was Dein, together with Hill-Wood and the then chief executive Ken Friar, who first interviewed Graham for the manager's job – 'a businesslike first meeting,' Graham recalled nearly twenty years later. 'I was the manager of Millwall. That was a giant leap from a little club to the big boys – perhaps one that will never be made again – but they knew about me, my way of doing things. I was a different [as a] manager than I was as a player. George Graham the player would not have got the Arsenal job, no way.'

Hill-Wood was impressed by Graham's authority and confidence at that first interview. 'We knew him as a player, knew he'd done well at Millwall,' he told me. 'His teams never played attractive football, but we weren't looking for that. It's always a gamble when you appoint a manager. You never know what you're going to get. George inherited some good young players, but then we always produce good players from within the club. He was strong and disciplined. We liked that. We made a lot of progress under him.'

As he took his seat in the directors' box in the Main Stand, Graham looked out over the green turf, with its scarred and dark, mud-worn patches around the centre-circle and each penalty box. He observed the rival sets of fans positioned territorially at either end of the ground, restless with anticipation, their loyalties marked out by team colours and scarves and flags. He looked out over all this and then down at his players, who were just then emerging from the tunnel into the early evening sunshine. Seeing them led out by Adams, Graham felt a strange sense of serenity. He turned to his chairman and said: 'We're going to be all right. We've got the game plan to cause a major upset.'

Part Two: The Last Game

Seven: The First Half

Arsenal emerge up the steps from the narrow tunnel wearing their away kit of yellow shirts with navy-blue short sleeves, and tight blue shorts; it's a wonder that they're not blown back or frozen by the force of the high-decibel roar into which they run, by the tremendous, reverberating power of it. Each player wears a white memorial armband; white, rather than the more conventional black as worn by the Liverpool players, because black would not have shown up against their dark shirt sleeves. Liverpool wear their traditional all-red kit; and on this warm evening, so late in the season, so early in the summer, they too are in short-sleeves. The Arsenal players are holding bouquets of flowers. After lining up briefly inside the centre circle to wave to and applaud the crowd, they spin off in different directions, as if in choreographed formation, carrying the flowers to all parts of the ground, where they are then passed into the crowd. The home fans respond to this gesture with harmonious applause. The mood is one of tolerance and mutual respect; Hillsborough has cooled the fans' hatreds without diminishing their ardour.

Liverpool and Arsenal, north and south: just for now, just before the game, there's a sense of unity and reconciliation.

'The flowers were a good idea,' says Theo Foley. 'We walked out and were respectful – that was important.'

Liverpool are to kick-off, attacking the Anfield Road End. Arsenal line up in a 5-4-1 formation: John Lukic; Lee Dixon, Tony Adams, David O'Leary, Steve Bould, Nigel Winterburn; David Rocastle, Kevin Richardson, Michael Thomas, Paul Merson; Alan Smith. Liverpool are as 4-4-2: Bruce Grobbelaar; Steve Nicol, Alan Hansen, Gary Ablett, Steve Staunton; Ray Houghton, Ronnie Whelan, Steve McMahon, John Barnes; Ian Rush, John Aldridge.

In this last minute before the match begins the players are in formation, with Barnes and Rocastle facing each other, separated only by the chalky thickness of the halfway line. They embrace and shake hands, these two black athletes who through their excellence and example have done so much to alter terrace attitudes to racial difference. The whistle blows; the match begins. Arsenal immediately retreat, inviting Liverpool to come to them, like a boxer confident of his defence and ability to counter-attack. It's as if right from the start they want to demonstrate that they shall not be reckless, that their game plan is to be patient, as Graham has asked of them. Caution and patience: the grand theme. So back it goes, from Merson to Richardson to Bould, and then all the way to goalkeeper Lukic. He gathers the ball and prepares to kick long and high up-field, as he has been doing all season.

In these opening minutes there is little fluency of play to excite the crowd, as Arsenal hustle and run hard in their usual manner, each player taking no more than two touches, never pausing on the ball. They are determined not to allow Liverpool the opportunity to establish a pattern or dictate the tempo. What Arsenal fear most is Liverpool's passing game, the force of its momentum, of the way the ball can be moved so swiftly and accurately between Barnes, Beardsley, McMahon, Houghton and others. Except that tonight there's no Beardsley in the starting line-up. The little man is a substitute, with Dalglish opting to play two central strikers, in Aldridge and Rush, supported from wide positions by Barnes and Houghton. Rush and Aldridge are, perhaps, too similar in style and method, finishers both rather than one of them being a subordinate or shadow striker in the model of the astute and nimble Beardsley. Can Liverpool succeed without Beardsley, the player who goes deep to receive the ball from midfield, who links play and beguiles with his trickery and control?

Dalglish believes in and trusts the Italy-returned Rush – his old partner in attack – who came off the bench in the Cup Final the previous Saturday to score twice. Since rejoining Liverpool at the start of the season, after just a single season at Juventus, Rush has scored only seven League goals in twenty-four appearances. For much of the season there's been something distracted, even melancholy about him; he plays now sometimes with the burden of one who's forgotten how to play, how to relax into his natural game. Once, before the move to Juventus, it must have all seemed so simple for him: he knew instinctively when to move and when to run into space and why. First in his season-long absence and now in his presence it's Aldridge, signed from Oxford United as Rush's replacement, who has become the supreme marksman at Liverpool, despite his technical inferiority to Rush.

Rush was ridiculed while at Juventus for his introversion and failure to adapt to life in Turin. During Serie A's winter break he returned to England and spent a week training with his old team-mates at Liverpool. Upon being re-signed by the club he reportedly said: 'I couldn't settle in Italy. It was like living in a foreign country.'

This remark has been used ever since as representative of the average British footballer's insularity and monoglot limitations. But did Rush say it? When I was editing the *Observer Sport Monthly* magazine, we contacted him to ask. 'I was set up,' he said. 'It was someone's idea of fun – probably one of my Liverpool team-mates joked that I'd said it and things went from there. I had just re-joined the club [in August 1988] and wanted to get back to playing football, not worry what was being written about me. I was homesick at times [in Italy], but it is one of the best things I've done in my life. I flew into Turin airport on what was supposed to be a secret flight but, when I arrived, there were 5,000 fans waiting for me. I started off living in a hotel but had my own place before long. On the downside, I never realised that Turin was such an industrial area. There wasn't much to do and I wasn't allowed an interpreter. The only other English-speaking player at the club was the Dane Michael Laudrup. He helped me out as much as he could but he had his own life to lead and couldn't hold my hand the whole time. Looking back, Juventus were the right club at the wrong time. They had just signed seven players and were happy to get 0–0 draws away from home. That negative approach didn't play to my strengths. I would have been better joining Mark Hughes and Gary Lineker playing under Terry Venables at Barcelona . . . Still, I can look back on my career and not wonder about what might have been.'

In this early phase of the game Arsenal's tackling has a premeditated ferocity. It's easy now to forget how subtle changes in the laws, such as the banning of the tackle from behind or the preventing of goalkeepers from picking up back-passes, have since refined the game, quickened it, made it more fluid. Graham's Arsenal were adept at using the tackle from behind not only to thwart but also to intimidate. Bould, who is lean with dark-brown receding hair swept back from a high forehead, is the master cruncher, eager to let both Rush and Aldridge know from the beginning that he's insistently there, right behind them, always behind them. So the game is being interrupted by ankle-wounding tackles and free kicks; neither side is able to build momentum or establish a coherent pattern of play.

'When I was part of the old back four we used to go on to the pitch not expecting to concede a goal,' says Lee Dixon. 'We knew exactly how to defend and what we wanted to achieve. We took it for granted that the others would be there; if the ball went over my head I knew Tony or Bouldy would be covering, that they'd help me out. So whenever we lost a goal, or indeed lost a game, we couldn't believe it. "Hold on, what's happened here?" we used to think. It really messed us up.

'If we conceded, Adams would say: "Look, this is going off here, we've got to get our heads down and fight." He led by example. You'd get a tingle down the back of your spine when he was trying to inspire you, especially when we needed to get a goal back.'

Arsenal continue to hit the ball long, by-passing midfield as they seek out Smith, who is operating largely on his own up front, with Rocastle and Merson supporting from wide positions when they can. Wherever Smith goes he is shadowed by Ablett; they move as if engaged in an elaborate dance, nervous partners rather than antagonists.

The first chance of the match falls to Arsenal when, improbably, Bould arrives from deep to head a cross towards goal; the ball beats Grobbelaar, only to be headed up and over the bar by a retreating defender. Arsenal may be playing Graham's version of the sweeper system, with three central defenders, but their game tonight has fluidity and no little surprise: the full-backs as well as Bould keep pushing up whenever they can, but never carelessly. *Above all, you must be patient*, Graham had said.

In response and frustration, Liverpool begin to mimic Arsenal's direct style rather than seeking to outplay them. Working as the co-commentator for ITV alongside Brian Moore, David Pleat, a former Spurs manager, remarks on how Arsenal are 'looking the more relaxed side'. They have settled the better, it's true; the long ten-day break between this and their final home game has calmed them, perhaps even liberated them.

Playing for Liverpool after an injury-interrupted season is Alan Hansen. Tall, slim and long-legged, he moves gracefully, never seeming to overexert himself even at moments of stress and danger. Both he and his partner in central defence, Ablett, seek to bring the ball out, to pass short and simply, playing through midfield. Liverpool's sustained success has been founded on the solidity of their defence and of how accomplished their defenders are in possession, never hurrying, always seeking to use the ball constructively. 'If we needed to, we could keep the ball all night,' Hansen once said, remarking on how Liverpool controlled so many European Cup games away from Anfield. 'We could pass teams to death.' They could also bore them to death by continuously playing the ball back to the goalkeeper as a tactic to retain possession and lower the tempo of a game.

This evening Hansen is not as comfortable in possession as usual, because he has missed so much of the season through injury (this is only his sixth League game) but also because so much of the match is being played above him, in the air, as Arsenal scramble, and indeed gamble, for position. Yet how carelessly Arsenal surrender the ball, as if they feel they can control the game without it, through pressure, presence, power. So much of their play is speculative as they go in pursuit of knock-downs and ricochets, foraging for scraps, taking what they can as and when they can. This is Graham's preferred way, perhaps the true Arsenal way: an anti-style, extending back to the 1930s when Chapman schooled his teams to play on the break, to become masters of the counter-attack.

'Before Arsène came, Arsenal was never remembered for the sophisticated football they now play,' Graham has said. 'Go back to the 1930s; it was always "lucky Arsenal", "boring Arsenal", "Bank of England Arsenal". Even Chapman said sometimes you can have too much possession. So he didn't mind the opposition having lots of possession, which happened regularly away, but Arsenal would still win 3–0!'

The home crowd is muted, and it's the away fans at the Anfield Road End who are beginning to find more confident voice as the match enters its twenty-first minute. Now McMahon has the ball and, evading a challenge, he finds Houghton, wide on the right. The Ireland midfielder plays a pass with the outside of his boot to Rush, moving just inside the box; Rush returns the ball to Houghton, who crosses for

Barnes coming in fast from the far left. But a straining Dixon is there, just, to intercept with a header that gives Liverpool their first corner. Soon afterwards, in open play, Barnes passes to Rush, who moves the ball on to Aldridge only to receive it again in return. He shoots spontaneously from just outside the box, a hard, abrupt shot that travels fast and straight into the arms of Lukic, who gathers the ball to his chest as if he never wants to let it go.

The game is opening up, with Merson now on a wounded rhino's run down the left; there's something gloriously uninhibited in the way he runs, in his uncomplicated method, the way he charges head-down, broad shoulders lowered, with a surging, loping stride, his long-layered, bleached, unkempt hair flowing raggedly behind. There's something uncoached in all this, a supreme naturalness. It's easy to imagine Merson, 'the Merse', as a young boy in the playground or on a scrap of wasteland during an impromptu game after school: the keeper rolls the ball to the Merse, because he's so much better than the rest, and off he goes on one of his solo runs, beating players at will, and then beating them again because he can, because it all seems so much fun, so *natural*. Merson is predominantly right-footed, but has over time adapted to this limitation and now exercises his right to do whatever he wants with it.

Merson is still running and, with Thomas arriving late from midfield, he sends over a cross but it's headed out. Thomas's long run from deep has been in vain but he will keep on trying to make these late runs, keep on going, as if each failure is motivation enough to try again, to try better, even if it means failing again, failing better.

A former captain of England schoolboys, Michael Thomas

first came into the side as a teenager under Graham at right-back; but, because of his stamina and physique, his excellent technique and desire to attack, it was soon apparent that he would be best positioned in central midfield. When I first saw him play I called him 'the Brazilian': he looked like a new kind of English footballer to me, a full-back with the muscularity and power of a defender but with the skill and speed of a forward. For Graham, Thomas can be too inconsistent, too much of the would-be Brazilian: one game imposing, the next wasteful and inefficient. His team-mates speak of how 'laid-back' he is, of how easy the game can seem to him. *Does he care enough?* Graham has asked. *Does he want it enough?*

Thomas is the one player who is perhaps less willing to fit unquestioningly into the system. He doesn't want to be a mere cog in Graham's rigid, grinding machine. In person he's quiet and thoughtful but also stubborn and wilful. He has all the attributes that Graham most admires: pace, power, stamina, hardness. He never stops running. But as he himself says he loves to watch Brazil; and, like the best Brazilians, he wants to be free to express himself, to able to *play*, to pause a while on the ball, not to have to release it so quickly. 'When I was coming through at Highbury the player I most admired was Graham Rix,' Thomas said. 'He was skilful, so good in possession. I wanted to be like that.'

Thomas wants sometimes to have a licence to stroll, as Rix did, and indeed as Graham once did. But Graham as we know does not like strollers. He wants his players to run, run fast, run harder; to tackle, to keep forcing the game, not to try to reinvent it, to call the play, in the style of an American quarterback.

Liverpool are beginning to settle, to command with some short passing, quick and simple, and always to the nearest player – 'the style Shankly began,' says David Pleat.

Just after the half hour, Rush, pained, leaves the field to be replaced by Beardsley. He pulled a thigh muscle when striking the shot at Lukic, his one significant contribution. There's that air of melancholy again as he lowers his head as he leaves the field, limping, applauded on his way by the fans, his season at an end. Once again you wonder about that year in Italy, its disappointments and lingering frustrations.

Earlier in the week, on Tuesday, Beardsley came on as a second-half substitute against West Ham and immediately helped to dictate play with his superior passing and control. The goals followed. But on Tuesday the imperative was for Liverpool only to win, and win well; tonight they can lose and still be champions. Is this why, then, there is absent now the urgency of recent weeks, when they had to win every game as they chased down long-time leaders Arsenal? Are they becalmed in the knowledge that even a one-goal defeat would be good enough? Or is it just that they're feeling the effects of playing their third game in a week, as would anyone? Maybe Arsenal are just too well organised, playing too well. Whatever the reasons, in terms of expectation there are, as Brian Moore says, 'not quite the flashpoints, not quite the atmosphere, and indeed not the excitement in the opening thirty-five minutes.'

What were we expecting? For Arsenal to come at Liverpool, attacking with the exuberance of their opening-day thrashing of Wimbledon or with the immense power of their 4–1 November victory at Nottingham Forest's City Ground, perhaps their most complete performance of the season? Were we expecting Liverpool to play with the abandon of the closing twenty minutes of Tuesday night's West Ham game?

Be patient, Graham had said before the game, *the pressure will get to them and you will be rewarded.*

Boring, boring Arsenal, taunt the Kop.

'Perhaps Liverpool are happy to settle for a draw, knowing that it will be enough for them,' says Brian Moore.

No, replies his co-commentator, David Pleat, they will still want to win, 'to show that the standards set here are the standards we must all set ourselves'.

'Our manager Kenny Dalglish told us to go out and win the game and play in the positive manner that had served us so well that season,' Alan Hansen has said. 'He certainly did not tell us to remember that a 1–0 defeat would still do us; in fact, he told us the opposite.'

'Yes, of course we wanted to win, desperately,' Steve McMahon says. 'We always wanted to win. The club was built on winning.'

Now Rocastle has the ball, having switched to the left, perhaps frustrated at how little he has been able to influence the game so far. In his first prominent attack he runs directly at the Liverpool defence, slipping past Whelan. Then, with Hansen advancing, he plays a short pass to Richardson, whose shot is of no consequence.

Rocastle hustles back to take up a defensive position in front of the right-back, just as Graham would have demanded. From his first training sessions at Arsenal as a fifteen-year-old, Rocastle had impressed all at the club with his resolution and purpose. His father died when he was only five; he was raised by his mother, a nurse, on a southeast London council estate. The family were poor. As the eldest of four children, Rocastle felt a special responsibility to provide leadership and moral example for the rest of the family. 'It made my mum more secure when she knew I was going to have a job,' he told Kate Hoey. (A few weeks after the Anfield match, Rocastle and Thomas were out campaigning for Hoey during the Vauxhall by-election, which she won for Labour.)

'I often used to give David a lift home after training,' Hoey says now. 'I particularly remember the day he signed his first professional contract. He was so excited and desperate to tell his mum. He lived with her and his sisters and I think he always felt he had to look after them all. I think that feeling always meant he was very responsible, and worked hard to succeed.'

Ian Wright remembers how Rocastle, as a young Arsenal apprentice, would encourage him when he was playing non-League football. 'He was seventeen and coming home from Arsenal every day,' Wright said. 'I was twenty and working on building sites and in chemical plants. Rocky always told me not to waste my talent, to keep going, to get myself into the professional game.'

Which of course he eventually did – even for a short time playing alongside Rocastle at Arsenal.

With the half nearing its end, Liverpool once more advance down the right, working the ball between Nicol and Whelan. Their progress draws Adams away from his usual central position, in the safety zone. He harries Whelan into a mistake but then panics in possession, hacking the ball into the crowd. The response is at once gleeful and familiar: the sound of a braying donkey reverberates mightily around the old stadium. Adams – this giant man-boy, simultaneously vulnerable and yet fanatically resolute, the team's leader – retreats, hurt, until he is once more flanked on each side by O'Leary and Bould. The Arsenal fans respond to the mockery of their captain with a chant of their own: *There's only one Tony Adams/One Tony Adams*. Adams has heard this and, bolstered, he takes a deep breath and puffs out his chest, inspired once more.

The referee blows for half-time.

The club directors make their way to have drinks in the boardroom, which overlooks not the pitch but the main car park at Anfield; across the corridor is the trophy room, where dinner is being served for those with corporate-hospitality tickets. Peter Hill-Wood is in the boardroom, as is the Liverpool chairman John Smith, as is the England manager Bobby Robson, who has flown down from Glasgow, where England are preparing for an end-of-season international against Scotland to be played the next afternoon. Peter Robinson never goes to the boardroom at half-time and instead follows his usual routine and is back in his office. Much of the chatter is about the match but there's some sad news, too – the former Leeds and England manager Don Revie has died this very day in an Edinburgh hospital. He was suffering from motor neurone disease and at the end his weight had dropped to below eight stone. It is said that he communicated by blinking his eyelids: twice for yes and once for no.

All around the country those watching on TV begin to stir as the commercial breaks come on. ITV will report that there was a national television audience of eight million at the start of the match but many hundreds of thousands more will switch on in the second half. Regular live League football is a recent introduction to British television – the first live League game for more than twenty years was broadcast in October 1983; before that the Football League refused to allow games to be shown live because it was believed this would adversely affect attendances. Throughout the seventies and eighties only highlights were permitted to be shown on ITV and the BBC.

Earlier in the day it has been reported that the launch of BSkyB, the Rupert Murdoch satellite channel that will soon change forever the way football is sold, marketed and watched in the country, has been delayed by technical problems. Within a few years, however, Sky will have won an auction for exclusive rights to the new Premier League in a deal worth £304million to the clubs, and fans who want to watch live football on television will be paying subscription fees for what was in the eighties free to view. It would be this match at Anfield that would convince many in and around the game of the huge untapped revenue-generating potential of live football on television.

Meanwhile, in the same stand but down in the dressing-rooms, Graham and Dalglish are addressing their players for the last time before sending them out. Graham is telling his players that before the game he kept reading that Arsenal's trip to Anfield would be a wasted journey. 'Does this feel like a wasted journey?' he asks. He is extraordinarily calm. He does not raise his voice; there's no shouting. He simply wants to reassure the players that everything is going to plan. *Everything's going to plan*, he keeps saying. *We've kept a clean sheet. Just start to get forward more now*, he says, *be more positive on the ball. The pressure is on them*, he says. *The pressure is on them*. 'He wasn't swearing or shouting, nothing like that,' says Alan Smith. 'He just wanted to get his message across very calmly, to make some small adjustments to the game plan and to make sure we didn't start to panic because we hadn't scored. He sent us back out on to the pitch feeling enormously confident.'

Eight: The Second Half

Liverpool start the half by seeking to establish sustained passing movements and to dictate play. During the break Dalglish has urged them to do so, has implored them to assert their own game. But, no matter what they try in these early phases of the half, their attacks continue to break up against the hard, high wall of Arsenal's three-man central defence. The Kop are chanting: *Champions, Champions*. A 'chant they know well', says Brian Moore. In contrast to Liverpool's passing game, Arsenal continue to hit the ball long while beginning to show more attacking intent, with Winterburn a continuous threat down the left. 'The more Arsenal press, the more spaces they'll leave behind at the back,' warns David Pleat.

Six minutes into the half the referee blows for a foul on Rocastle – high feet against Whelan. Rocastle senses an opportunity; his eyes are ablaze, he punches his right fist into an open left palm, his teeth are gritted. It's an indirect free-kick, to be taken from the right-hand side of the penalty box, about thirty yards out. Winterburn and Richardson stand over the ball while Arsenal's tallest – Bould, Smith, Adams, Merson – jostle for position just around the edge of the box, twisting, pivoting, sprinting and then retreating as

they seek to slip their markers. So much movement, the ren-
actment of all those training-ground drills: *pressure, pressure,
pressure*, said Graham. 'We paid so much attention to set-
pieces,' Smith says. 'We'd be in a line: me, Tony, Bouldy. One
of us would peel away, one would dart to the near post as a
decoy.'

There is a long pause before Winterburn with his left foot
curls the ball in precisely towards the far side of the box.
Adams breaks between Nicol and Staunton, but stumbles
and goes down in front of the keeper, around about the
penalty spot. Just behind him, Smith has found space and
he's there, alone, with his marker distracted by Adams,
about six yards out; with the lightest of touches he glances
the ball into the far right-hand corner of the net, with
Grobbelaar beaten before he has had the chance even to dive.
The Arsenal fans, clustered at the Anfield Road End, just to
the right-hand side of the goal, are celebrating; a few of them
spill from the terraces on to the cinder track that separates
the pitch from the crowd. Just a few, but there's a moment of
mayhem as a lone copper, wearing a traditional British
bobby's helmet, scrambles to round them up. So animated
are his movements that it's as if he too is celebrating the
goal.

The Liverpool players have reacted to the goal with indig-
nance and incredulity; they descend upon the referee,
enclosing him in a ring of fire. The most vehement protestor
is the captain, Whelan, who conceded the free kick. Close
behind him are Nicol, Ablett, Houghton, McMahon,
Aldridge, Barnes: a terrifying army of disgusts. Was Smith
offside? Did the indirect free kick go straight in without his
getting a touch? The referee hurries over to his linesman and
rests a reassuring hand on his left shoulder, addressing him

143

as a policeman might an errant youth: *Now, tell me calmly exactly what happened*. The linesman has wiry, thinning hair, and a neat moustache; his faced is harrowed by anxiety.

'The only way to deal with it was not to threaten to book them but to say, "Right I'll go and talk with my linesman,"' Hutchinson says now. 'I always found it easy to communicate with players. I don't know if it was because I'd been a copper. I'd always been a fairly gregarious sort of ref; I didn't mind talking with players. If someone wanted a chat with me that was fine. I didn't take their frustrations to heart. When the ball first went in the net I looked at my linesman; he'd done what I asked him to do if a goal was scored, which was just to turn back and go to the centre. The players' reaction throws a doubt in your mind. I remember thinking, *I hope television proves us right*. It wasn't that I thought the players would be more inclined to cheat because it was such a big game. Now, yes, I would think that – there's so much more money in the game and so many other influences. Whereas my gut feeling is that back in those days it was a different atmosphere. I think we knew the players a bit better. We all spoke the same language.'

The referee and linesman stand facing each other, so close together that they must be able to smell each other's breath, so close because they are trying to hear each other above the harsh, wrenching dissonances of the crowd, because at that moment they want to be sure, in agreement. A vein in Hutchinson's left temple throbs. The linesman scratches his nose. Ablett is close by, straining to hear what is being said; he is soon replaced by Whelan, keeping watch, waiting.

Hutchinson continues: 'I went over to my linesman and said, "A couple of quickies. Did I have my hand up for the indirect free kick?" He said yes. "Was there a touch by Smithy in the middle?" He said, "In my view, yes." I said, "Was there any possibility of offside?" He said no. I said, "Foul?" He said no. So I said, "Then it's a goal."'

Then it's a goal. Whelan has heard this before his players, certainly before the crowd know what's been decided, and his face carries the pallid look of disappointment as he turns away.

1–0 to Arsenal.

'I remember Nigel curled in the free kick and I glanced it in,' Smith says. 'I was told at the time that the linesman's flag had gone up and then gone down. The ref went over to the linesman, with 40,000 Scousers breathing down his neck. You're thinking, *We don't have much chance here.* Anfield's a fortress. All their big players are over there. O'Leary went over to see what was going on. He expected the ref to indicate that the goal had been disallowed but, amazingly, he gave it.'

Liverpool are becoming distracted; in the dug-out just below pitch-level Dalglish, sitting with fellow coaches Roy Evans and Ronnie Moran, looks on, troubled, as Grobbelaar rages at Ablett, at his own man, after confusion between them results in the goalkeeper dropping the ball. With his receding hair cropped razor-short, his thick, dark moustache and tufts of chest hair, Grobbelaar has the look of an angry Soho leather-boy.

Liverpool must reassert their control, keep the ball, to start passing out of the defence – but Arsenal will not allow them to settle. They push up, compress, hustle, press. The balls they hit into the box in open play are often random and improvised, but they are also persistent. That's the key: persistence. For the first time you begin to feel that with so much of the game being played in Liverpool's half it will be difficult for the home team to withstand the persistence of this aerial bombardment; at some point the ball will fall fortuitously for an Arsenal player in the box and he will have a clear chance to score.

Merson is on another buccaneering run, setting off from deep inside his own half; his run emboldens the Arsenal fans, who take a familiar chant and turn it against their tormentors at the opposite end of the ground: *Boring, boring Scousers*.

Then Arsenal have their chance. Winterburn, on the halfway line, collects a glancing header from Richardson and plays it long to Smith; it's an accurate pass rather than a speculative hit-and-hope. Smith, with Ablett diligently following as usual, keeping time, doing the two-step shuffle, holds up the ball, turns and lays it off to Merson, who plays it quickly with his left-foot to Richardson, up on the edge of the box now. Richardson slips the ball through to Thomas, who has run from deep in midfield and beyond his own central striker and the Liverpool centre-backs. Thomas is clear and in space, alone, just around the penalty spot, but he shoots too quickly, straight at Grobbelaar.

'I just said to Mickey,' Richardson recalls, 'not in a criticism way, just as a bit of banter, I said, "Mickey, I've put it on a plate for you, you've got to put it in the back of the net. We're not going to have many more chances. They've got to count."'

It did not count, but it served as warning of what could be achieved if Arsenal stilled themselves to play with guile and patience as well as with power and athleticism; if they tried to pass short as well as long.

Now Graham makes the first of two tactical substitutions

as Merson is replaced by Hayes, who shuffles on, with that distinctive, hunched running style, like a postman carrying a heavy sack; soon afterwards Groves comes on for Bould, as the formation is switched to a more conventional 4-4-2, with Groves operating as a fleet-footed flier up front. With Bould gone, Liverpool are finding more space to push on, winning consecutive free kicks in and around the Arsenal box. The first free kick is awarded as a result of a wayward lunge by Richardson on Houghton – for which he receives the first yellow card of the match – and then soon afterwards McMahon is brought down in a similar position, prompting a chant of *You dirty Cockney bastards* from the Kop. As McMahon receives lengthy treatment, the Kop moves from attack to the more mournful as thousands on that great standing terrace sing 'You'll Never Walk Alone'. Scarves are raised and stretched tightly to show the colours of the crest.

Barnes is standing over the ball; he has the ease and fluency of a natural virtuoso. This free kick could be his moment, this is it . . . Up he comes, only to curl his shot wide. Wasted. Now Rocastle is being booked for dissent; now Nicol is running hard with the ball straight at the Arsenal defence – but he goes down under a clumsy challenge, just outside the box. Another free-kick and another chance for Liverpool and for Barnes. This time the free-kick is played short into the box; Barnes collects the return pass but is bundled off the ball before he can shoot. Wasted. Still Liverpool are coming forward, exploiting the spaces that in Bould's absence are opening up behind the Arsenal full-backs. From the left-hand side of the penalty area Aldridge plays a pass through to Houghton but his shot is sliced into the Kop. Wasted. Then Aldridge is played in by Barnes, but he knows he's offside even as he steadies himself to shoot low past Lukic. The 'goal' is received with an ironic cheer from the Kop.

We are entering the eighty-seventh minute. Pat Rice and Theo Foley are standing up in the Arsenal dug-out, urging their team forward – and forward they go, with Adams supplementing the attack whenever he can. Police are beginning to bunch at the Anfield Road End, some of them clasping long, narrow black batons in tensed hands, watching not the action but the Arsenal fans, prepared for trouble. But it's not trouble these fans want; they're too absorbed by the game, chanting *Come on, you yellows/Come on, you yellows*, singing the same refrain over and again, as if it's possible to will a team to score.

Barnes and Aldridge are on the counter-attack now, exchanging neat passes, making up ground, with Richardson in pursuit. It's then that Richardson goes down, exhausted, cramp-stricken. The game is stopped as he receives treatment. We're so close to the end. The crowd knows this – the Liverpool supporters have been whistling incessantly for many minutes now, imploring the referee to blow for time. McMahon knows this – he raises his right index finger, but as a warning rather than in complacent celebration. He looks on as team-mates Aldridge and Barnes pass each other and, fleetingly, touch hands, a reassuring gesture of unity. 'Come on,' says Barnes, clapping his hands together. 'Come on.' McMahon is perspiring as he stands before the Kop, before the steeped banked terraces of his own people, at the end of an exhausting game and of what has been an unimaginably protracted and traumatic season. He paces the pitch, his finger still raised, the muscular thickness of his pale thighs exaggerated by his tight red shorts. He spits repeatedly, thin jet streams of anxiety. His blue eyes burn. It's obvious what he's telling his team-mates: that there's one minute to go. You can see him saying this, again and again: *One minute, only one minute*. The camera continues to follow McMahon, as Brian Moore says of him: 'There's a real competitor, there's a man who's really earned a championship medal.'

'I was just trying to get the team to concentrate, to concentrate hard, and then we'd have another Double,' McMahon says. 'Even today people come up to me and mention that one-minute-to-go moment. I try to laugh it off, but it still hurts. The whole evening had such a weird atmosphere – because of Hillsborough, because we'd already played the Cup Final, because we didn't have to win the game to be champions.'

The great American sports of basketball, baseball and football, with their ritualised stoppages and time-outs, can be reduced to countable, repeated moments. The interruptions in American sports are there to enhance dramatic tension and to allow for the last-minute reversal or turn-around, for what's been called the Hollywood ending. Time-outs allow participants and spectators alike to catch their breath and space enough in which to assess the logic of the situation as the end nears – and for a whole game to be decided in one final sequence of play. You are not rushed to the end; the end is delayed, the drama is stretched out. The time-out is as important as the action itself.

Here at Anfield, with Richardson down, we are not being rushed to the end: we are being made to wait for it. It feels as if the whole season is being distilled into these final few moments, into one final passage of play, in imitation of the American model. Dalglish, pale and rather wan, stands on the touchline. He is alone, speaking to no one, just there pensively looking out over the pitch.

Hurry up, gentlemen, it's time.

The clock is running down – beyond ninety minutes now. The floodlights are bright in their hardness. 'I guess I was so dehydrated when I went down,' Richardson says. 'I'd put so much into it, just like the other lads: being in midfield, in the engine-room, all that running . . . I just went down with cramp. It definitely wasn't a tactic. [Physio] Gary Lewin came on and just said, "Can you carry on? We need fresh legs as it's near the end." I said, "I'm staying on. I'm not going off." You just want to be part of it to the end.'

Lewin massages and then stretches Richardson's right leg; the player is still in pain. Lewin continues to massage the leg and then tries again. This time Richardson responds well; he rises to stand.

Game on: Adams has the ball and, against his natural style, seeks to carry it with him out of defence and into midfield. He is swiftly dispossessed by Barnes who, with Adams scampering back after him, dribbles towards the Arsenal box, rather than heading towards the corner flag, where he would have had the chance to hold up play, to run down the clock. There's something aimless about Barnes's run, an absence of conviction, like much of his play tonight, and the ball is taken away from him by a recovered Richardson, who slips it neatly to his goalkeeper. From the touchline Theo Foley is screaming at Lukic, urging him to release it. He wants the goalkeeper to kick it long, to punt it up high into the night sky and deep into the Liverpool half. He's cursing Lukic. *Why now the delay, when there's so little fucking time. For fuck's sake hit it, fucking hit it.*

'I was calling him every name under the son,' Foley says. 'I couldn't believe he wanted to throw it out to Dixon.'

Just hit it, man. Even if he can hear Foley raging at him

from the touchline, Lukic knows what he must not do – and that's punt it speculatively up-field. Instead, he throws the ball out to his right-back, Dixon. 'It was the sensible thing to do, when you look back,' says Richardson. 'Barnes had just dribbled the ball into the corner of the box so we'd have had most of our players back near the box. So for Lukic to kick it up-field ... Maybe only Alan Smith would have been up there. If he'd flicked it on or not controlled it then it would have been a waste of time. We would have lost control of the ball.'

Dixon plays the ball long and accurately and it's collected by Smith. 'I didn't really want the ball,' Dixon says. 'I was running up the pitch, and the next minute the ball comes whizzing out to me. I'm thinking: "Why has he done that?" My first instinct was just to whack it as far as I could up the pitch. But when I looked up Alan Smith had pulled into the hole, and I thought, 'Well we can't score from there but there's nobody else up front, so I had to hit the ball into him.'

Smith receives the pass and, with his usual economy of movement, turns to play the ball through to Thomas, rushing forward from midfield, as he has, tirelessly and without reward, throughout the match. 'At Anfield there was no clock,' says Smith. 'You had no idea of the time, except the whistles of the crowd and George waving us forward. We knew it was getting close. I gathered the ball well from Dixon – it was one of those nights when all my touches came off. I didn't want to hold it up, so turned at the same time and helped it on to Michael, who was coming through. I jogged after him, and watched what happened next.'

Unmarked and sprinting deep into Liverpool territory,

Thomas miscontrols Smith's pass; the ball spins away, bounces against Nicol before, improbably, falling for Thomas. 'How do you explain that?' says Nicol. 'The ball is played up, Thomas is running through on it, he miscontrols it, it bounces straight off me and back to him. You try to coach *that*. When the ball bounced off me it could have gone anywhere, but it just fell perfectly for him. How do you explain *that*? You can't, except to say that things happen. You can prepare all you want in training for a match, and then something happens you can't account for. Now I'm a coach I try to explain to players that sometimes things just happen in life and there's nothing you can do about it. You can't put your finger on why they happen. They just do.'

Sensing danger, Grobbelaar moves towards Thomas just as he reaches the edge of the penalty box. Red-shirted Liverpool defenders are pursuing Thomas. As many as 42,000 spectators are watching inside the ground suspended at a point of heightened crisis. It's all happening so fast, yet there's also something curiously hallucinatory about what's unfolding, as if time itself is being slowed.

Here he comes, Thomas, free, lost to the moment, as he would later describe it. He must know that the defenders are closing on him, must feel the hot rush and strain of their exertion. He has the ball and is moving towards the penalty spot. The goalkeeper is coming towards him. Thomas has the ball. He is waiting for the goalkeeper to commit, just waiting; his momentum carries him forward as he lifts the ball up and over Grobbelaar and – look, watch it now, follow it as it goes up and over the goalkeeper and continues on its way into the net.

2–0.

Thomas continues running – how can he stop? – and does a somersault in wild celebration, and begins to writhe and thrash around on the ground, like a huge marlin hooked on a fly.

'When Mickey was running through I could see the defenders getting near him, but the composure he showed, the ability, the confidence – it was all spot-on,' says Richardson. 'I couldn't see where the ball had gone at first; I just saw Mickey doing his celebration and our fans jumping up and down. It was all just a dream, considering what we'd had to do and then to score so late.'

His team-mates are embracing Thomas, reeling him in. Smith is there, Hayes is there. One Arsenal player is on his own, still running – it's Winterburn, both arms raised straight up in triumph, fixed in position, as if he's just clean and jerked a big weight to win Olympic gold; he runs, arms up, straight towards the Arsenal fans massed in their corner at the Anfield Road End, and it's as if he'll never stop, as if he'll go straight on into the crowd, into the thick of the celebrations. Dixon is standing on the halfway line, and he is weeping uncontrollably; the elation and shock are too great. Meanwhile, some of the Liverpool players are dropping to their knees. Barnes is down, Aldridge is down. Nicol is on his knees. McMahon is on his knees. 'Dalglish,' reports Brian Moore, 'just stands there.' And so he does, as if immobilised.

He is like a general looking out in shocked and silent contemplation over a battlefield of defeat, his exhausted men collapsed before him. 'It was just devastating,' says McMahon. 'If we'd had to win the game, we would have. It happened because we didn't have to win to be champions. We didn't have to win. There I was a minute earlier just trying to get my team-mates to concentrate and then you end up with egg on your face. That's just devastating.'

Looking down from the directors' box, Peter Robinson is in the process of making a phone call. 'Barclays, the League sponsors, had provided champagne for the winners,' he says. 'The champagne was being chilled in the kitchen of the Main Stand, two floors up from the dressing-room. Barclays had stipulated that they wanted the champagne to be in the winners' dressing-room at the final whistle. When Arsenal scored I rang the kitchen to find out what was happening to the champagne. I panicked when I was told it was already on its way to our dressing-room. "For God's sake get it back," I said, "Arsenal have just scored again." We managed to intercept the champagne and redirect it to the Arsenal dressing-room.'

There's still time enough for the referee to restart the game, however; still time enough for Liverpool to mount one last attack. But no, that's it, there's no more time. The game and the season are, at last, over. The longest season, the last of the eighties – yes, that's it, all over. Arsenal and Liverpool have finished with the same number of points (76) and the same goal difference (+37), but Arsenal are champions because they have scored more goals (73 to Liverpool's 65). From the touchline Graham is trying to remain in control; he holds his arms out in front of him, palms open, as if staying a small rebellion, trying and failing to hold back the celebrations that are erupting around him. *Be calm*, he seems to be saying, *just be calm*. But how can they be calm? Out on the pitch Aldridge is still lying slumped; O'Leary, his Ireland team-mate, goes over to console him but is pushed away. Aldridge is inconsolable. Barnes remains down, as if felled by a sniper's bullet.

Up in the directors' box Peter Hill-Wood turns to David Dein and Ken Friar. He pauses to draw on a thick cigar, then says, in his characteristic patrician drawl, 'It was never in any doubt.'

The Arsenal fans have transmuted into a crowd of night-club ravers: look at their manic movement, their twisted dance patterns! Scarves and flags and yellow plastic inflatable bananas are being tossed up in the air. In their midst is a large black man in a jester's hat, dancing wildly. Massed pitch-side in front of them are the police, still holding on to their long batons, still expecting trouble.

No one is attempting to invade the pitch; nor are the Liverpool fans leaving the ground. They are staying on in their tens of thousands to applaud the new champions. There is no booing. *There is only resounding applause.*

'I looked out and saw the whole crowd clapping,' says Peter Robinson. 'I think the Arsenal players and their fans were stunned by that.'

Referee Dave Hutchinson is on his way to the tunnel. 'As we were coming off Jim Rosenthal was there for ITV and I looked at him and said, "Was it okay, Jim?" He said, "Don't you worry, perfectly okay."'

Rosenthal remembers the moment. 'In those days there weren't all the monitors that are now so easily available, but Dave's relief when he found out that Smith had definitely touched it . . . The colour immediately came back into his face. It wasn't a decision you'd want to be remembered by if you'd got it wrong.'

Now Dalglish is there before the referee, blocking his way. 'Kenny put his face in front of me – not in an aggressive way, but there he was,' says Hutchinson. 'He said, "Are you sure about that goal?" I said, "Kenny, you may have had a chance to look at it and I haven't but I'm sure." Give him his due, about half an hour later there was a knock on the door and he's stood there with a bottle of champagne. He said, "Okay, no problems at all, you'd better have this."'

The Arsenal players are celebrating on the pitch, embracing one another, dancing in that slightly self-conscious way of those who know they're being watched. Graham is out there among them now, and he holds on to Rocastle and Richardson with special affection. Later he will express surprise at how 'subdued' Liverpool had been on the night. 'They didn't want to play their usual game. That suited us.'

'The goal which won the League championship for Arsenal last season,' wrote David Lacey in the *Guardian* at the start of the following season,

with the final shot of the First Division programme, did more than provide a unique moment in a sport which was beginning to think it had seen everything.

The speed and audacity of a movement that took the Kop's breath away and left Kenny Dalglish standing open-mouthed in disbelief by the Liverpool bench epitomized the healthier qualities of English football as the game approaches the Nineties. That goal will be seen over and over again as the videos are played and replayed. Those who consistently criticize the English game for its lack of imagination would be hard put to win their argument given such well-documented evidence. Here you had intelligent distribution by a goalkeeper, good attacking instincts by a full-back, an outstanding example of a centre-forward coming deep followed by the perfect demonstration of how to strike from midfield.

It was August, only a few months after the end of the season, and Arsenal's title-clinching winner was already being referred to as *that goal*.

It was already legendary.

Nine: Outside the Cage

When Thomas scored to win the championship for Arsenal I was sitting among friends in the cramped, humid TV room of a student hall of residence in Southampton. Even though I wasn't on the terraces at Anfield in person, nothing before or since compares to what I felt then: self-abandonment, a complete surrendering to the frenzy of the moment. I was free, outside what Buddhists call the 'limited cage', unbounded.

A feeling of euphoria stayed with me for days and weeks afterwards. I felt it throughout my final exams – during which I was unusually self-possessed, at ease, and success-ful – and this lightness, this sense of heady self-contentment, stayed with me through the long, drifting summer months that followed. For Arsenal fans, this period was, as Nick Hornby wrote in *Fever Pitch*, his memoir of a life of obsessive fandom, 'the greatest moment ever'. For Liverpool fans, as my friend the Liverpudlian writer Andrew Hussey says now, the defeat that night at Anfield remains a source 'nearly two decades later of acute physical pain. That night coming after what we'd been through already – well, it was a kind of metaphysical insult.'

I wasn't as bitter as I thought I would be about missing

out on Anfield. The joy and wonder of the surprise of the final result were so complete as to compensate for any regret. At the time, I'd no idea where exactly my father was or whether he was watching as Thomas scored. I knew he was in India, away at short notice on another trip. He didn't call that night and I didn't call home to ask my mother if there had been any word from him. After the game was over, I didn't join my friends in the bar to celebrate. Instead I went back to my room, sat at my desk, and continued working until about two in the morning in preparation for that day's exam in the history of philosophy. I briefly attempted to write about how I felt but my words – amazing, unbeliev-able, astonishing – were as predictable as they were banal. I did not have the vocabulary to express how I felt or the verbal facility to describe what had happened. In the end, I settled for one word: happiness.

'You can't ever describe the feeling,' Nigel Winterburn said of how he felt when Thomas scored. 'The disbelief of the Anfield faithful, the silence, and then this explosion of sound from one corner of the ground.'

It's often dismissed as cliché when sportsmen speak of their disbelief, of their inability to describe how they feel at moments of intense triumph or despair. Winterburn is cor-rect: sometimes you simply cannot describe how you feel; words are not enough. At such moments true meaning seems to reside outside language, beyond rational articula-tion. You're in the realm of pure, inarticulate feeling, beyond which there is only silence. When Kelly Holmes won a gold medal in the 1,500m at the 2004 Athens Olympics, she was asked by a track-side interviewer how she felt. 'I'm gobs-macked,' she said. She was mocked by some for choosing such a lazy word. She shouldn't have been; nor was there any need to have asked her how she felt in the first place. Why ask the question when you could see from the wonderment on her face how she felt as she crossed the line to win? Why seek always for the word that is beyond speech?

As I sat working in my room that night I wondered about the scenes in the two different dressing-rooms at Anfield, the contrasting moods of desolation and delight. Jim Rosenthal of ITV remembers being in among the Arsenal celebrations. 'One of our broadcasting team, a guy called Mel Batty, who was once the ten-mile World Record holder, was a fervent Arsenal fan and somehow got in the changing-room. I remember going in after him and you can't help but get caught up in the moment. I got the whole treatment with the champagne being sprayed. I think nights like that you should have cameras in there, because fans watching would want to see what's going on. The fans want to be part of the celebration.

'I feel sorry for the guys who are doing now what I did then: nowadays things are so much more controlled. The spontaneity of that night I think was something that you don't get now. It probably was the end of a more innocent era. The players were very much still in touch with their public. I think the sad thing is that because they have so much money there's now the attitude that's sort of blackened windows and red rope across everything.'

Rosenthal remembers, too, Adams coming up to claim the £100 bet on which they'd shaken hands the previous summer. 'After the game the first thing he did was come up to me and say, "Where's my money?" I was very happy to pay up. Whenever I see him now he always reminds me of it.'

From the changing-room the Arsenal players dressed

formally in their club suits and ties and went straight on to the team bus to begin the journey south. On this long, celebratory return, the coach was followed or flanked on the motorway by fans in their cars, horns sounding, scarves streaming from or being waved out of windows.

The coach eventually arrived at London Colney, where many of the players and officials had left their cars the previous morning. 'We had a few drinks on the bus,' says Kevin Richardson. 'Most of the lads were telling the bus driver to slow down, to go back to London as slowly as possible. We wanted to savour everything, even the journey home. But lots were being careful because they were driving. I was picked up by the missus. We got back late, but it was wonderful to see so many fans still out on the streets.'

Back at London Colney a group of players – the Tuesday-Night Club, plus assorted extras and groupies – went off to find a nightclub in which to continue the party. 'Nothing was open,' says Paul Davis, 'nothing was planned. We ended up, I think, in this pub called the South Herts, and then went to a club next to it. It was a crazy, crazy night.'

Perry Groves remembers it differently. 'Someone had radioed ahead that a nightclub out Cockfosters way was being kept open for us. We said to the Gaffer, "Any chance?" And he said, "We're all going – let's take the coach." Even at that hour there were people on the streets cheering us and inside the club there were birds everywhere – it was mayhem. We all went in and George came in for a drink and then left us to it. Me, I stayed until six a.m.'

This is Steve Bould's recollection. 'We got a police escort to a nightclub in Muswell Hill. It was called Champions, I think – a great name.'

'I think the club was in Southgate and it was called

Winners,' says Alan Smith. 'I'm not sure how we got there. Perhaps the coach took us. We'd all drunk a lot of champagne on the way back from Liverpool.'

These memories of the aftermath of the title win may be unreliable (there is some distance between Muswell Hill and Southgate, for example), but this much we know: they were champions; they celebrated.

My father hadn't watched the game on television in India; he said he saw the result in an Indian newspaper. Phil Scraton, author of *Hillsborough: The Truth*, the best account I've read of the Hillsborough disaster, hadn't watched it either; for him, the match at Anfield was, and remains, an occasion of profound grief, unforgettable for the wrong reasons. 'It should never have been played,' he says. 'The season should have been abandoned. There were people still in hospital, for goodness' sake.'

Would he have felt the same if Liverpool had won?

'Absolutely. People kept saying before the game that Liverpool would win the title for the dead of Hillsborough, then they wouldn't have died in vain. I thought that was ridiculous then and I still think it's ridiculous now. And don't forget, what happened broke Dalglish. He never recovered from Hillsborough. He was one of the victims. No, I stand by what I said. It's a disgrace that the game was ever played.'

He is particularly critical of the film adaptation of *Fever Pitch* (1997), directed by David Evans. It stars Colin Firth as Paul, a truculent and cynical London teacher in his thirties for whom supporting Arsenal provides the one fixed point of meaning in an otherwise careless life: football offers him public occasion for the private expression of emotions that would otherwise be repressed. For Paul, fandom has less to do with sport than with the larger evasion of the responsibilities of mature adulthood, notably his failure as a boyfriend (his girlfriend is pregnant) and as a teacher (he's about to lose his job). Paul is an archetype of willed indecision: he knows he must stop equivocating if his life is ever to have any purpose or direction, and yet he cannot. The Liverpool–Arsenal game at Anfield provides the film's dramatic climax, and is the moment at which Paul, in exultation and relief, accepts that he must finally act purposefully if he is to save both his career and the relationship with the mother of his unborn child. The exhilaration of Thomas's goal lifts him from despondency and helps to create the circumstances in which he can rebuild his life. In his book, Nick Hornby's own life-changing epiphany occurs not at Anfield, as in the film, but two years earlier at White Hart Lane, when a late goal by, improbably, substitute Ian Allinson wins Arsenal an epic League Cup semi-final and helps to liberate Hornby from a 'decade-long downer'.

'The way *Fever Pitch* the film builds to the magic moment at the end, I watched it with mounting fury,' says Phil Scraton. 'By then, I knew many of the families who suffered at Hillsborough. I'd lived through it with them. Like them, I was still so angry. Hillsborough was only the second Liverpool semi-final I'd missed in fifteen years. If I'd been there, I'd have been on the Leppings Lane terrace. At the time of the Arsenal game I couldn't believe all the fuss in the papers about this one game. Football supporters had died only a few weeks earlier and now we were all meant to be celebrating this supposedly wonderful match. I remember on the night itself I went into a pub with some of my students and it was on. I just walked out.'

But there is an alternative view and it's this: that having the will to go on when the instinct is to stop can itself be a form of memorial. For me there was something cathartic about the whole evening. After all the grief, rage, anger, and suffering that had preceded it, here was a game that brought palpable release *for nearly all football fans* who watched it, with the obvious exception of those who supported Liverpool – and perhaps even for some of them there was release too – at the very fact of the match having taken place, of the season having been completed rather than abandoned. If the home fans had reacted differently to defeat, if they had rioted or raged, or even skulked off in fury at the end of the game instead of staying on to applaud, no one would now remember that night at Anfield as the point at which the fortunes of English football seemed to turn. The fans did not riot. They stayed on to witness Arsenal being presented with the championship trophy, to witness a conquering army sinking the flag of victory into the Anfield turf at the worst possible moment for the home team. *The Liverpool fans applauded*. It was as if they understood that we were at the start of something new; that there would be no returning to the ways of old. Six weeks after Hillsborough those fans demonstrated that they understood the real meaning of sporting glory.

I went alone to Islington on the Sunday morning after the game to follow Arsenal's champions' parade through the North London streets in an open-top, red double-decker bus, a soft wind on a sunny day rustling the roadside avenues of trees around Highbury stadium. As many as 250,000 turned out for what was a spontaneous street carnival, an expression of ecstatic sociality. There was manager Graham in his well-cut suit, his shrewd, dark eyes staring megalomaniacally into the far distance; Adams, the captain, leering and clowning from the top of the bus with the trophy in his hands, a good night's drinking ahead; Thomas and Rocastle were huddled together, both wearing dark sunglasses, brothers-in-arms, inseparable; the Merse, like a boy raver, with his goofy grin; Smith and Marwood (who missed the game), exhibiting their usual restraint and good manners, like two young graduate accountants on a work's outing; Groves, the hyperactive ginger genius, bouncing as amazed and joyful as if a giant hand had reached out from the top of the bus and plucked him straight from the crowd below; Winterburn quietly taking it all in; Lukic waving shyly, as unknowable and unheralded as he would ever remain; Dixon and Bould, former Stoke City team-mates and now saying a few words to each other – *How did that happen, then?*; Richardson, with his clipped moustache and soul-boy's coiffure, the man from the northeast but now finding acclaim in the capital; Hayes on the periphery, as usual, but playing his part. They were all there with the exception of O'Leary, the low-voiced statesman, the best-paid player, a title winner at last in his sixteenth season at the club. He was away on international duty with Ireland but was represented by his wife, who spoke of how Friday 26 May had been the day of their son John's sixth birthday and as a present his father had promised the boy a championship-winning medal.

And so the bus moved on in stately procession through those red and white streets, moved on to a civic reception at Islington Town Hall, and on and on into the indeterminate future.

Part Three: After the Game

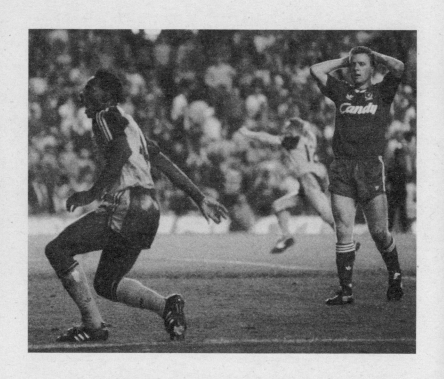

Ten: World in Motion

Occasionally now, if I need reminding of how I felt about the long summer days of the year of 1989 and about the world in general at the end of the eighties and into the nineties, I key the words 'New Order' and 'World in Motion' into the YouTube search engine and watch the video of the official England World Cup song for the 1990 World Cup in Italy. If it can be said that Arsenal's title win at Anfield signified the start of a new era for English football, Italia '90 was confirmation of it.

The year of 1989 was politically the most turbulent of an often turbulent decade. There was a profound sense, for the first time, that the Cold War was coming to an end; that communist totalitarianism was collapsing. Also obvious was the imminent demise of entire political eras, with Europe's aged dictators being toppled from within: Jaruzelski, Honecker, Zhivkov, Ceaușescu. Worldwide, it was the year of the restless crowd. There were the rebellious crowds massing in the great cities of central and eastern Europe, their collective and heroic agitation for change precipitating the eventual breach, in November, of the Berlin Wall. There were the crowds of courageous students, workers groups and democracy campaigners in Tiananmen Square, Beijing, their aspirations so murderously suppressed by state dictatorship. (Here, the Chinese Communist Party responded with extreme violence; on 4 June tanks smashed into the square and many thousands of people died.) There were the crowds of frenzied mourners at the Ayatollah Khomeini's funeral in Tehran. There were the smaller crowds of marchers and book-burners in Bradford, inflamed by Salman Rushdie's novel *The Satanic Verses*. And there was of course the crowd at Hillsborough.

In August 1989 Chief Justice Taylor published his interim report into the Hillsborough disaster; the final report was published in January 1990. In the eighties, whenever Margaret Thatcher and her advisors had been forced by unhappy circumstance – a riot by Millwall fans at Luton in 1984, or Heysel – to address the crisis in English football, it was as if they could only look and then look away; it was as if the prime minister could not bear to think imaginatively or conceptually about the game, its problems or the culture of chauvinism and violence that was perceived to have surrounded it. The morning after the deaths at Heysel, the deaths of those thirty-nine Juventus fans, Mrs Thatcher's official response was: 'There are no words, there are no justifications; the blame is entirely for England.'

It was as if little that was sensible occurred to the government when confronted by the game of football and what could be done to reform it. There was no guidance. The blame was, simply, for England. Instead, the Conservatives came up with the Football Supporters' Bill. Had the bill become law fans would have been required to carry identity cards – in effect they would have been criminalised. It had been assumed that in his report Lord Chief Justice Taylor would endorse the government's plan to introduce ID cards, but in the event he rejected it. 'Taylor was interested in much more than security issues,' says John Williams of Leicester University's football unit. 'His was a liberal, wide-ranging review that looked at the culture of the game, at why this thing called football was so important to us. None of the inquiries into the game had done this before. He also gave supporters an opportunity to contribute through the Football Supporters Association. The symbolic importance of this was huge. Hillsborough was not about hooliganism, but it was framed by our obsession with it. What he gave us was a blueprint for change.'

The Taylor Report, with its recommendation for all-seater stadiums and its enlightened liberalism, changed English football forever – to the extent that at a distance of twenty years one can now speak of the game of football in England as it was before and after Hillsborough, in the same way as one speaks of cinema before and after the advent of sound; as the transition between two epochs, as a moment of profound and irreversible cultural shift.

Also in the year of 1989, on 5 February, Rupert Murdoch's Sky Television (renamed BSkyB in 1990 after its takeover of the rival satellite broadcaster BSB Alliance) launched its British service via Astra satellite. Buying exclusive broadcasting rights to sport, notably to the new Premier League when it was established in 1992, would be the means by which Sky would grow its subscription base in the United Kingdom. It was obvious that we were ready for a new contract to be signed between football and society and in the years ahead it would be Sky's role to dictate many of the terms and clauses of that new contract as football began its move from the margins to the very centre of the culture.

The last season of the eighties began in August 1988, towards the end of the 'Second Summer of Love', and extended right through into the following summer, a period which coincided with the rise of new-style dance and drug subcultures. A more benign, less drunken and more druggy and laid-back form of fandom flowed out of the pay parties and nightclubs of the rave scene and on to the terraces – and this found fuller expression at the 1990 World Cup finals in Italy. Italia '90 is not remembered for the quality of its football but is remembered as a great tournament all the same because, against so many expectations, England excelled. Having reached the semifinals, which they lost following a penalty shoot-out to the eventual winners, Germany, they returned home not as world champions but still with honour. And they did this to an optimistic summer soundtrack of New Order's 'World in Motion' and the arias of Pavarotti, as well as to the memory of Gazza's tears – when he cried after being booked towards the end of England's semifinal defeat against Germany it was as if the whole of England cried with him. Because the England fans had, on the whole, behaved well in Italy, the ban on English clubs playing in Europe was soon afterwards lifted. This was a new start for the national game – it could even be called a renaissance – and it began at Anfield on the evening of 26 May 1989.

The 1989–90 season, which reached its climax with the World Cup in Italy, was one of anxious transition for the game in England as clubs awaited the final publication of the Taylor Report. Domestically it was a season of disappointment for Arsenal and Liverpool, for different reasons. For Arsenal it was a disappointment because their defence of the title withered mid-season and, after many weeks of indifferent form, their best players – Adams, Smith, Rocastle, Thomas, Merson, Dixon – all missed out on selection for the final

England World Cup squad. 'We had won the title and the only way we could have maintained momentum was to win it again,' Graham once told me. 'I think the players relaxed; they didn't lift their game. We were basically suffering a hangover from the dramatic success of the previous season.'

'Italia '90 pointed the way for a new kind of fan culture,' Alan Smith says. 'I was in Bobby Robson's provisional squad of twenty-six for the tournament, as were Adams, Rocastle and Thomas. We were called back from a tour in Singapore to the England camp at Burnham Beeches and told we had just failed to make the final twenty-two. I just felt sick. I went on holiday during the tournament to get away. To Florida, with Lee Dixon and his family. We were close at the time. We watched the England–Germany semifinal in a hotel over there. It felt terrible to miss out. There was just something so positive about the tournament and England's involvement in it, and from there everything began to change.'

For Liverpool the season was a disappointment because, although they won the title for what would turn out to be the last time to date, the players knew that something was missing and that as a group they were approaching the end of an extraordinary period of dominance. The defeat at Anfield on the last day of the previous season had made them feel mortal, time-haunted. They knew that the fortress that was Anfield had been definitively breached. 'Something was missing in that following season, principally because of Hillsborough,' Steve Nicol says. 'It didn't feel the same. It was only the professionalism of the players that kept us going through to the end and helped us win the title in 1990. But none of us had recovered from what happened the previous season, especially Kenny. The mood, the atmosphere, the desire – something wasn't there, something wasn't right. You could say it never returned. What we'd had was gone. Maybe it took us a year to realise it.'

Midway through the following season Dalglish had gone too, and with him the long period of Liverpool supremacy.

'It was traumatic when Kenny resigned,' says Steve McMahon. 'Souness came in [as manager] and tried to revolutionise things at the club. There was unrest among the players. Souness thought too many of us were too old. I believe most of us had at least another couple of good years in us but he didn't agree. He tried to change things too quickly. He'd been in Italy and had his own way, all these new ideas about diet, training methods. He tried to implement these new ways too soon. But you don't need to teach old dogs new tricks. You don't fix something if it ain't broke. And I don't think the club was broken.'

One of the players signed by Souness during his rapid reshaping of the club was none other than Michael Thomas, in December 1991. Thomas scored a good goal for Liverpool in the 1992 FA Cup Final but his time at the club would be undistinguished. Nor did he ever establish himself as an England international, which he once told me was his defining ambition. He played just twice for England during the 1988–89 season but never afterwards. He followed Souness to Portugal in the late nineties, playing under him at Benfica, and he lingered on disconsolately in Lisbon, in dispute with the club, long after Souness had been sacked and returned to England. Thomas eventually retired in 2001, with his final season being at Wimbledon. The 'Brazilian' never quite fulfilled the promise he'd showed in those luminous early seasons at Arsenal.

Arsenal under Graham won the title for the second and

final time in 1990–91, losing just once and conceding only eighteen goals while scoring seventy-four in thirty-eight games. That was the best it would be for Graham at the club. In February 1995 he was sacked in disgrace, his authority in the dressing-room already diminished, after he was found guilty of illegally profiting from transfers. In the vernacular: he took bungs, but then so did many other managers during a period when transfers were so inadequately regulated.

Moving into the nineties Arsenal remained competitive in the League but, under the fanatically determined management of Alex Ferguson, it was Manchester United who replaced Liverpool as England's outstanding club side. Arsenal won both the FA Cup and League Cup in 1993, and, improbably, against a much-superior Parma side, the European Cup-Winners' Cup in 1994. But their style was becoming dour and defensive, ever more reliant on the destructive arts: the squeezing and compression of space, the expert manipulation of the offside trap, the long ball, the brutal and swingeing tackle. There was little investment in players of attacking excellence, with the exception of Ian Wright, who was signed from Crystal Palace in 1991 and became a prolific goalscorer for the club. The once steady flow of players progressing from the youth to the first team became little more than a trickle; it eventually dried up altogether. The defence of Adams, Bould, Dixon and Winterburn remained resolute season after season and they played on together into the early Wenger years; but in the period between the championship win of 1991 and the arrival of Wenger in 1996 aesthetic surprise and attacking dynamism disappeared from Arsenal's game, notably with the sale of Thomas and, in the summer of 1992, of Rocastle. The following season, the first of the new Premier League, Arsenal finished tenth, scoring just forty goals, the fewest of any team in the League.

The departure of a favourite player is often experienced as a form of bereavement by fans. You don't quite know why he went or what precipitated his going. You feel helpless and lost. Sometimes you even feel betrayed, as if a great wrong has been committed. You're nostalgic. You find your-self longing for the player's return. Sometimes you dream he's back, once more playing in an Arsenal shirt, yet wake to feel the fall of dark not day: it was just a dream; he's not there; he's never going to be there.

I felt all of this and more in the months after Rocastle was sold by Arsenal. It happened like this. One afternoon after training, shortly before the start of the new Premier League in 1992, Graham had an impromptu meeting with Rocastle in the car park at London Colney. The meeting took place in Rocastle's car and lasted for at least an hour; by the end, Rocastle was weeping. Graham had told the player that the club were prepared to sell him to Leeds United, the then League champions, for £2million. Graham had ceased to believe in the once-indomitable Rocastle, who had been in and out of the team and hindered by a persistent knee injury. 'Rocky told us that the club wanted to sell him after his meeting with George,' Paul Davis says now. 'He was crying. He said, "The club want to let me go. But I don't want to go." He was devastated.'

As a very young man it had seemed as if Rocastle had everything he could possibly have wanted. The future must have seemed infinitely inviting for him. It was felt that he could achieve whatever he wanted in the game. But it didn't work out for him as he – and we – hoped and expected. It didn't work out for him at Leeds. Nor at Manchester City after that. Nor did it work out at Chelsea, Norwich or Hull City. For whatever reason – injuries, loss of confidence – too much began to go wrong too quickly for him. He lost his clear, pure talent for winning and much of his luck; the game was no longer such an innocent joy for him. His injury-haunted last years as he became a kind of ghost, a spectral presence moving from club to club in search of first-team football, were especially poignant. He died, from cancer, at the age of thirty-three, having spent his final days playing club football in Malaysia.

'He never really recovered from being forced to leave Arsenal,' Davis says. 'He didn't enjoy Leeds. Then he went to City, to Chelsea and then abroad . . . He struggled all the way through. Psychologically he never recovered from going. He couldn't understand why the club would let him go. George said his knee wasn't right – that was the story, anyway. He went to Malaysia and stayed out there for a while. I kept in touch with him and his family but didn't see him. Then I found out he was ill, but he didn't want anyone to see him during that last year. I still keep in touch with his wife; the club, to be fair, have looked after the family. He has two girls and a boy, and they are invited to the games. The wife has been remarkably strong. I see her at games or functions sometimes.'

Rocastle made 260 appearances in all competitions for Arsenal, and fourteen for England, and he will never be forgotten. To this day, his name is sung by the fans, just as it was at the first home game after his death, when we stood for a minute's silence, with not even a murmur of dissent from the Spurs fans, our opponents that day. This plangent chorus of loss was sung again a few months later at the FA Cup Final, played on a hot May day in 2001 at Cardiff's

Millennium Stadium, when Arsenal lost 2–1 to Liverpool. It was sung as the referee blew his whistle to begin Arsenal's Champions League quarter-final at the Emirates in 2008, and it will continue to be sung in the years ahead, as we who were fortunate enough to have seen him play tell those who came after us of the kind of man and player he was. Our memories of him – strong, muscular, athletic, alert, proud, wide-eyed, committed, loyal, modest – shall remain forever inviolate.

Rocastle was not quite a conventional winger; he was, says the journalist Brian Glanville, 'very much in the tradition of Arsenal outside-rights, from Joe Hulme and Alf Kirchen onwards'. That *onwards* is important: it bespeaks of continuity, of an essence that underscores all change, of something imperishable and lasting – the very substance and mystery of a football club.

'Rocky was one of my best friends, not just in football,' Alan Smith says. 'He had a knee operation that wasn't carried out too well. He kept getting fluid on the knee, became less mobile, put on some weight. The operation would have been routine now. He was an amazing player; he was able to ally skill with a tough streak. He was ferocious in the tackle. He could take a tackle brilliantly. The fans loved him, absolutely worshipped him. He had such a good attitude and everyone felt for him when he couldn't get to his old level again. He was in his car in the car park for a good hour that day with George. Everyone wondered what was going on. The two of them in the car, George explaining why the club was letting him go.'

Smith remained close to Rocastle during the last year of his life. 'He went to Malaysia, and it was there that he contracted it [non-Hodgkin's lymphoma],' Smith says. 'He went to Jamaica the following summer, when all these lumps came up on his body. It was diagnosed on his return. When I heard I couldn't believe it. At the same time, I was told this strand of cancer was curable. You never thought it would end the way it did. He lost a lot of weight. His feet became so sensitive, even if you just brushed past him. I remember his wife Janet calling us at three in the morning when he passed away. It was terrible, just terrible. I'd never lost a close friend like that before. He was such an engaging personality; he never took himself too seriously. He took the mickey out of the whole brother thing – you know the phrases, the accents . . .'

His voice faded into silence.

As I write, thinking about Rocastle and how he just missed out on playing at the 1990 World Cup, the 'World in Motion' tune plays in my head. Music can reconnect you with memory, with the moods and feelings of a particular time and place. It was remarkable and unexpected, this coming together of the England squad and New Order, of the foot-balling mainstream and one of Britain's best and most subversive indie bands. Before this, England World Cup songs were an embarrassment. It's probably fair to say that, with the exception of Pat Nevin and Stuart Pearce, few foot-ballers showed much interest in hard-edged indie music or punk. Few read the *NME* or *Melody Maker* or were politically committed; Graeme Le Saux has spoken of how he was widely ridiculed by fellow players because he read the *Guardian* in the changing-room. Throughout the eighties most top-flight footballers were, on the whole, renowned for their social, sartorial and cultural conservatism. If they were members of any social tribe, they were soul-boys or casuals, habitués of the suburban disco and the wine bar, devotees of the mullet and the perm. Consider two famous England football captains representing the old and new, then and now: Kevin Keegan, with his tight bubble perm and Brut aftershave ads, and David Beckham, a fashion and style icon who even as he approaches the end of his career remains one of the most photographed men in the world. To watch recordings of the 1982 England World Cup squad, managed by Ron Greenwood (or Green Ronwood, as my father preferred to call him with stubborn whimsicality) miming their rallying song 'We're on Our Way' (who can forget that imperishable second line: 'We're Ron's twenty-two'?) on *Top of the Pops* is to encounter a group of men, dressed in V-neck Pringle sweaters and Farah golf club-style trousers, bashful in the company of so many pop stars. Today's England players would not feel similarly out of place – and it's fair to say that they'd be more extravagantly dressed, or overdressed, than the musicians. In most cases, they would be considerably wealthier, too.

Yet something happened in 1990 when New Order teamed up with Barnes, Gascoigne, Waddle, Pearce and the rest: a kind of alchemy. 'World in Motion' defines a distinct time and place while having a glorious timelessness. You can't listen to 'We're on Our Way' without being reminded of anything but football. But you can listen to 'World in Motion' and be reminded of football, yes, but also of the summer of love, ecstasy, raves, the wider sociopolitical upheavals of the end of the eighties and the slow, welcome emergence of a more socially liberal and multicultural Britain. The chorus – 'Love's got the world in motion' – is a sly and subtle reference to ecstasy, the love drug, the drug of those times; the original title of the song, cowritten by Keith Allen, father of the more famous singer, Lily, was 'E for England'. It's been said that many of the England squad felt uncomfortable about singing of love in a football song – but they had a go all the same.

The song begins with a sample from Kenneth Wolstenholme's celebrated commentary at the end of the 1966 World Cup Final: 'Well, some of the crowd are on the pitch. They think it's all over. It is now . . .' This was long before the phrase 'They think it's all over' became so much part of the culture, a catchline and quiz-show staple used and abused, to the ultimate irritation of Wolstenholme himself. The location for the video is an ordinary recreational football field, with the highrise towers of a housing estate in the background – football was still then the people's game, drawing its followers from the housing estates and urban centres. New Order's Bernard Sumner, wearing sunglasses and a short-sleeved Umbro England shirt, sings in the foreground while just behind him an unshaven, crop-haired John Barnes, in a red sweatshirt and tight black shorts, juggles a ball, with his usual nonchalance. It's a sunny day, and the pitch is clean and hard, burnt dry. The video has a simple brilliance – it's witty, urban, and cool. Football was changing, and here was an example of by just how much: an official World Cup song written and performed by a great indie band and with a black player chosen as the main attraction. It went all the way to Number One.

To watch the video is to be reminded once again of how change was the defining characteristic of those quite extraordinary times. And it wasn't just football that was changing. In her Guildhall speech Margaret Thatcher had asked whether anyone could 'now doubt that the tide is turning in the struggle for the hearts and minds of people the world over?'

It was at about this time that the American policy-thinker and teleologist Francis Fukuyama published an essay, in a journal called the *National Interest*, in which he declared that we in the West had reached the end of history and were entering a period of rest in which liberal democracies adhering to the rule of law would find it impossible to go to war with one another and would thus begin to work together towards the universal goal of progress and world peace. For Fukuyama, history (by which he meant history as a battle between rival world-transforming ideologies, not the innumerable small details and events of the everyday) had ended because the universal movement towards the realisation of human potential had found its ultimate expression in liberal democracy as the only legitimate system of government. The essay was an exercise in utopianism but it was also characteristic of the more general mood of Western triumphalism.

And yet nothing was certain; this feeling of being in suspension, of not knowing what would happen next, of living at the end of one world-historic era while waiting for another to begin. This sense, more personally, of having graduated and to now be on the cusp of adulthood at just this moment of quickening change. The feeling was heady. It was as if the world was indeed in motion, not quite spinning out of control but veering in new and strange ways: my world, our world. Sometimes I couldn't sleep for the excitement I felt. I wanted to get out of bed and get out there – to plunge straight into the world.

The summer of 1989, especially in the south of England, was extraordinarily warm: long serene days of continuous sunshine. The settled weather contributed to what seemed to me to be a more general euphoria at large in the country. I saw the multiracial Arsenal side as a product of a new, attractive cosmopolitanism; as were the black British pop act Soul II Soul, from Finsbury Park, whose dance anthem 'Back to Life (However Do You Want Me)' was Number One throughout most of June and was the soundtrack to which many Arsenal fans partied in the accelerated and vertiginous atmosphere of that summer.

I finished my finals at the end of June 1989 and soon afterwards set off with two friends from university on an InterRail around Europe. We had no set route, or any idea of which countries we wanted to visit. We often ended up sleeping on night trains as we moved through different countries, through different time zones, thinking nothing much of travelling overnight from London to Munich and, after a few days, moving on again to Salzburg and then Vienna, then, a few days later, trying to take a train to Prague. We were detained at the Czechoslovak border for not having a visa for entry, so gave up and looped all the way back to Nice. There we did nothing but lie on the shingle beach for a few days while staying at a cheap hotel close to the seafront. Through all these long train journeys, I had no idea of what I'd be doing next. I had no job to return to, nothing was fixed, set up or planned. Everything seemed boundlessly open; anything seemed possible. I wanted those summer days never to end, because their ending would force me to make life decisions, to choose. I didn't want to choose, to commit to anything. It was far better to live with the possibility of what might happen, of what you might go on to do. And I didn't want the responsibility of adulthood. I wanted to defer the future, to let it wait for me. In truth, I wanted to continue living at home, like a teenager, without responsibilities, sheltering behind the protective shield of my parents. I could have stayed on those trains for many more months, stayed on them and simply kept on moving, to the next city in a new country, moving through the new Europe, a world turning, breaking apart and reforming, a world in flux, until the money ran out.

Yet, once I'd returned from my travels in Europe and was living back at home, still without a job or any interviews to prepare for, I felt my life beginning to slow down, even to close down, just as it should have been opening up. My closest friends from university were all preparing to start new jobs or were going to live permanently overseas, in France, Portugal, the US or Canada. But I was back at home with my parents doing nothing – and so inevitably I began to spend more time with my father, and to observe him more closely.

He had changed, that much I knew. He was a different man than the one I'd lived with at home just three years before. His sense of humour remained as good as ever – he still watched his videos of Marx Brothers, W.C. Fields and Will Hay movies, chuckling along to them – but he seemed more subdued in and around the house. I took notice of the books he read, the movies he watched, the music he listened to. He had a collection of old black-and-white Hollywood films that he'd recorded from the TV and kept in a deep-bottomed drawer in a unit next to the television (the drawer was so full of VHS cassettes that he could scarcely open it). Where once he'd enjoyed talking and finding out about a range of contemporary music, he now listened really only to jazz – Chet Baker, Bill Evans, Miles Davis – and, obsessively, to the romantic crooner Al Bowlly, a Greek-South African who had been perhaps the most popular singer in Britain during the 1930s and early 1940s; his voice, my father said, was the most expressive of melancholy and yearning he'd ever heard.

My father had stopped reading contemporary fiction and no longer bought the political and current-affairs magazines he'd once read. All his books now seemed to be about the early 1940s: about the Blitz, the home front, Black Saturday. Black Saturday: 7 September 1940, the day of my father's sixth birthday, the first day of the Blitz, when as many as 1,000 German planes set off from northern France on a bombing raid on East London, on what the American writer Ben Schwarz has called 'the most concentrated force arrayed against Britain since the Spanish Armada'. The planes formed a block twenty miles wide and they were headed for the East End docks. They returned on seventy-six of the next seventy-seven nights: killing and maiming, destroying buildings, and leaving hundreds of thousands homeless.

On Christmas Day 1989 we watched news reports from Bucharest of the violent overthrow of the Ceauşescu regime. It was beyond parody when Ceauşescu, humiliated and soon to face a firing squad in a squalid room – a room as squalid and monotone as the country he'd created – defiantly announced that he answered to no one in the country except the 'working class'. So to the end, like all the fallen communist dictators of that year, he remained in his own self-image an authentic working-class hero, deluded until death.

In the Christmas card he gave me my father had written 'It's been a great year for freedom'. I felt at the time, as I do now, that he'd written that only for my benefit, because it was not in his character to make political statements of this kind and in any event he'd seemed rather detached from what had been happening, even though we were witnessing the end of the long Second World War in which he was so interested.

In fact, he was increasingly preoccupied by the books he read about London during the war, the old movies, the jazz and Al Bowlly tapes he played in his car, with their general ambience of loss.

'If someone told me that one day I'd have my own copy of *Double Indemnity* or *Sunset Boulevard*, I'd never have believed them,' he said one evening.

'Whenever he puts on Al Bowlly in the car, he seems to crumple,' my mother said.

'Oh, no, not another book about the Blitz,' we'd say, as he settled down to read.

I used to believe that my father was omnipotent, as many sons must do. When I asked he seemed to know everything I ever needed to know and he was better than me whenever we competed with each other at games, especially at table-tennis, the game he loved to play more than any other. Except that of late when talking about, say, what I was reading, I'd noticed how he did not know as much as I'd once thought he did, before I went to university. 'It's a little beyond me, son,' he said one evening when I asked what he'd read by Wittgenstein. We were sitting opposite each other at a local Chinese restaurant – my mother was with us – and I was struggling to master the chopsticks while observing how deftly he manipulated his. For some reason, my incompetence with the chopsticks coupled with his remark about Wittgenstein angered me. 'What do you mean by that?' I said. 'Come on, Dad, everyone's read Wittgenstein, don't you think?'

One evening not long after this my father and I visited an old family friend, a former neighbour who was now living with his wife in a village near Stansted Airport; he had converted his double garage there into a games and utility room and my father occasionally went over to play table-tennis with him. That evening he asked if I wanted to come along to play with them – he knew I'd been playing at university. We started by rotating games before we decided that the winner should stay at the table. As I waited for my turn I studied perhaps for the first time my father's technique. I noticed how, rather than using his backhand, he'd shift awkwardly to find space so that he could return the ball with his forehand, always and only with his forehand. In fact, he had no backhand – why had I never noticed this before? He moved in quick jerks around the table but this eccentricity of technique left him with a weakness that any good player would expose. When it came to my turn to play him, I repeatedly drilled the ball at his backhand. He was surprised at my improvement and he struggled, sending contorted forehand returns erratically beyond the table or haplessly straight up into the ceiling. As the game went on his faded grey-black T-shirt, the one he wore whenever he worked in the garden, became soaked through with perspiration. I won our game, and then beat him again when it was his next turn at the table. By this time his T-shirt was saturated, and yet I was cool.

He insisted that we played a third game. 'Come on, I've given you a start, son,' he said. 'Now for the real challenge.' There was a forced jauntiness in his voice but I could see that he was tired. 'Okay, one more game,' I said.

We played on, I worked him around the table as before, manipulating him at will, and he was becoming once more frustrated, straining to hit the ball harder but with even less control: his smashes were flying wildly beyond the table. Sweat was dripping from his hands and the bat handle, leaving damp patches on the flat green table. Every time he hit the ball long he groaned and threw his arms up in exasperation. Watching this I thought of how over the years it was through sport, and usually only sport, that I'd come to know him better, to discover more of the passionate and emotional man he was behind the face he presented to the world: behind the amiability, the courtesy, the good manners. Afterwards, slumped against a wall, he complained of numbness in his hands: 'This tingling sensation of pins and needles, I get it sometimes when I'm working in the garden.'

'Have you spoken to the doctor about it?' I said.

'The doctor!' He threw his hands up in feigned exasperation, and then laughed. 'Let's have another game?'

'You should take it easy,' our friend said to my father. 'You'll be sixty soon, old boy.'

'Sixty!' my father said. 'I'm not even fifty yet.'

'I thought you were well past fifty,' the friend said, with obvious surprise.

'No, no,' said my father, and then: 'Who wants another game?'

I knew that my father was in fact fifty-four but I presumed he was joking, as he often did about his age. He once told me of how on first meeting a colleague in the rag trade named John Tyler, who became a close friend, there was a seven-year age difference between them; over the years he'd blurred this difference to only a few years, and it was his intention 'one day to find myself younger than John'.

As we drove home that evening I thought about my

father at the table – of how he'd raged as he found himself unable to do what he'd once done so effortlessly, namely control the ping pong ball and beat me. It was almost as if the whole evening had been for him an exercise in self-measurement and he'd failed whatever test it was he had set himself. I'd always wanted to beat him at table-tennis, and yet now that I had so easily I felt no pleasure. It seemed somehow wrong, a violation of the natural order between us, one rite of passage I didn't want to undertake, and yet it was unavoidable and inevitable, because the balance of our relationship was changing from one of dependency to equality. That's what this period was all about; it was about readjustment, about reconnecting with each other but in new and complex ways.

I thought back to my early teens, when my father had started to come along again to watch me play football for my Sunday-morning team (I'd briefly been an altar boy at a local church, and organised recreational football provided an acceptable way out of that). At the age of twelve, having tried out as a striker, I'd reinvented myself as a central-midfield player. I was getting a regular game, though by the time I was sixteen I was playing centre-back: from the front to the back in six years, so much for my early boyhood dreams of goals.

My team-mates' fathers were mostly postmen, lorry-drivers or factory-workers. Some of them turned up to watch their sons wearing donkey jackets, with PVC elbow patches, and steel-capped boots, as dressed for or coming from the factory or building site. I wished that my father would dress as these other fathers did, wished that he would fit in more, be less of the dandy, more conventional. At this time he was wearing his hair quite long, and he was driving his red Alfa-Romeo

Alfetta. 'Posh,' my team-mates called him. But then, in the part of Essex where I grew up, a prawn cocktail was considered posh. (At my sister Alison's wedding party, held at a good local Indian restaurant, my grandfather Frank turned to me when he was offered a starter of prawn cocktail as an alternative to Indian food, and said: 'Isn't this what those pop-star blokes eat?' He ended up asking for egg and chips.)

The coach of my boys' team was a local butcher named John. He was tall and straight-backed, with tightly sprung curls of red-brown hair, the worried, inflamed eyes of a drinker, and a huge wart on his thumb, which often seemed to be bleeding or wrapped in a plaster. He chain-smoked, and there was something about him – the mournful eyes, the hair, the stiff, straight back – that reminded me of an Airedale terrier, but one with the eyes of a bloodhound. 'Your father's an accountant, isn't he?' he said to me once. I had no idea where he'd got that from but I nodded in agreement. It seemed more acceptable than to be working in fashion. The tag stuck. After that, he was the accountant to my team-mates as well.

The accountant was an enthusiastic supporter of my boys' team. And, occasionally, an enraged one, as I discovered one Sunday morning when, midway through the second half of what must have been a close game, we were caught offside yet again; league rules were that the referee was neutral, paid for by the home side, but that the home side were obligated to provide a couple of dads to run the line. We accepted the offside, as you do at that age, but from the touchline there came a violent interruption: 'Why don't you keep your flag down, linesman – you're ruining the game.' Then, the same voice, but this time even angrier: 'Why don't you sort this clown out, ref, he's not fit to run the line.'

It was my father's voice. The referee blew his whistle to halt the game. The linesman, who was stocky and short and wearing dark glasses, even though it was a dull day, began to shout back at my father: 'Who are you fucking calling a clown, sideburns? Keep your mouth shut, and keep it fucking shut.'

My father – 'sideburns' – went over to him. They pushed and jostled each other, the linesman threw a punch at my father, which he swerved to evade, and then they were separated. I was shocked and embarrassed – by what had happened, but also by my failure to have recognised my father's voice when he first shouted out. After the game, which we lost, we all gathered around our manager John, fathers and sons in a tight huddle, as if John were the leader of a political faction and was about to deliver a rallying speech of great public moment. In the event, he simply told us that we'd been cheated out of the game. 'You were right,' John said, addressing my father. 'That line-o was bent.' The rest of the adults looked at my father as if in renewed respect. What about that, eh? The accountant! Who'd have thought he'd had it in him.

When a few months later something similar happened, and there was more abusive shouting from the touchline at a flag-waving linesman and another confrontation, I knew right away who was to blame: it was fucking sideburns again. What I couldn't understand was why he did it, why he cared enough about a trivial boys' game to become so angered and agitated, especially when he seldom if ever raised his voice at home, never at us, never in rage. It was as if he were inhabiting a role, acting out a part. Or maybe only football provided him with the opportunity to feel an uncomplicated passion for something. It helped unlock something deep within him: the fury of the crowd.

I was thinking about all this as my father and I made our way home after the table-tennis, thinking about this and of the dampness of his sweat-darkened T-shirt, thinking about this and half-listening to the sweet melodies of the Al Bowlly songs that were playing in the car.

One night during this period of stasis, I was drinking in an Epping Forest pub, somewhere I often went, when there entered two young women in their early twenties whom I'd never seen in there before. I was still if not actually outside the cage then not fully back contained within it. The pub was small, with a ceiling of low wooden beams that trapped the cigarette smoke and created a misty haze. The pub attracted a committed band of regulars, who included several retired London footballers, such as Frank Lampard Snr, and the pop star Rod Stewart, who had a house nearby (with a football pitch in the garden) and would drop in whenever he was over from California, often with his then girlfriend, Kelly Emberg. I was with a couple of friends up at the bar, bantering about this and that but not really concentrating, because I kept glancing over, intrigued, at the two young women. One of them had red bobbed hair and pale skin; the other was slim, with blonde hair pulled into a ponytail. She was attractive, had blue eyes and a look of anxious vulnerability. They both had the stylish bohemianism of art students. My friends and I were moving on to a party but just before we left I wrote on a scrap of paper my home phone number and some pompously stilted words – *Forgive my presumption, but it would be lovely to have the opportunity to speak, perhaps even to meet . . .*

I walked over to the young women and said, 'I apologise for interrupting, but can I leave this with you?' I placed the note on the table and, without looking back, hurried out into the car park, where I unlocked my car and, eager to be off and away, promptly reversed straight into the vehicle behind.

A couple of days later I returned home to be told by my father that a young woman named Charlotte had called. I didn't know anyone by that name but wondered, just wondered. 'Oh, really,' I said, 'how did she sound?' He said that she'd had a 'slight northern accent'. 'Right,' I said. 'Did she leave a number?' 'No, but she said she'd call back.'

She did call back. Charlotte turned out to be the young woman with the red-bobbed hair from the pub. She told me she was from Wigan, in Lancashire, but was living in north Chingford, in Essex. Apparently her friend with the blonde hair, who lived with her in Chingford, was an old school-friend named Sarah; she was from the Lancashire town of Bury.

Sarah is my wife.

Eleven: Things Happen

On the evening of Saturday 26 May 2007 I attended an end-of-season dinner organised by the Arsenal Independent Supporters Association specifically to celebrate the eighteenth anniversary of the title win at Anfield – eighteen seemed an odd anniversary to choose for a special event, but there you go. The dinner was held at the new Emirates Stadium, and the guest of honour was – who else could it have been? – Michael Thomas.

Arsenal had played their final League game at Highbury in May 2006; their first Premier League game at the 60,000-capacity all-seat Emirates was in the August of the same year. The Emirates is a short walk from the old stadium at Ashburton Grove (naming rights were sold, on a fixed-term contract, for at least £100million to the Dubai-based airline).

Thomas now lives on the Wirral, where he runs his own security firm. He joined Liverpool from Arsenal after the cracks in his relationship with Graham opened up into gaping fissures. He was late arriving for the dinner at the Emirates, having driven down to London from Merseyside – it was a wet night; the roads were slow, he said. When he entered the room, with the diners sat at round tables, it was as if a favourite player was coming off the bench late in a

game, with the home side losing: the eruption was spontaneous and sustained. Meanwhile, on TV screens mounted
high on the walls the Anfield game was being replayed, as it
would be throughout the night on a continuous loop.
Thomas was shaven-headed, wore a diamond stud in his
left ear and was dressed in a pale-green double-pleated suit
and open-necked blue cotton shirt. As he made his way to
the front he glanced up at one of the screens, and there
before him was his younger self on what had turned out to
be the greatest night of his career.

Actor and journalist Tom Watt, compere for the evening,
said: 'Here comes Mickey Thomas, late tonight but bang on
time at Anfield.'

There was a huge cheer from the floor.

Thomas took his place at the top table, alongside former
players Alan Smith, Paul Davis, Perry Groves, Kenny
Sansom and Bob Wilson. He sipped anxiously from a glass
of water, and seemed unsettled as one diner after another
approached to ask for an autograph. Soon Thomas was surrounded by middle-aged men as well as some younger boys
who would never have seen him play, all requesting autographs, shaking his hand, stopping to have their photograph
taken with him.

Each former player was interviewed by Watt at intervals
throughout the evening. As each rose to speak the diners
chanted his name and sang his old signature terrace song, as
they would have done when he was playing; it was wonderful to hear again that great psychedelic anthem 'We all
live in a Perry Groves world', sung to the tune of 'Yellow
Submarine'. Groves was unchanged in character but heavier
in frame: a plump Tintin, moving towards middle age. He
was asked what he had felt as Thomas broke through on

goal at the end of the Anfield match. 'What did I think? Thank fuck it ain't me.'

Another cheer from the floor.

Groves was conforming to expectation, fulfilling his usual role as jack-the-lad, the court jester, the ginger genius, always on hand with a sharp one-liner and a cocky retort. 'It all seemed to happen in slow motion,' he went on. 'To have that composure, to wait, and wait . . . And then something exploded in your head when the goal went in. Thank God it wasn't me. But Mickey was always so laid-back, so laid-back.'

Yet tonight Mickey seemed less than laid-back; his bald head shone under the lights, he was perspiring, and from the floor came a continuous call for him to speak before his time, a chant of his name. Up on the TV screens mounted high on the walls the first half at Anfield was approaching its end, with the scores level. 'George's team talk at half-time,' recalled Smith, 'that was the finest fifteen minutes of his career.'

I was at the dinner with my friend Oliver Price and at our table were two brothers who had been at Anfield on the night of the game. One of them was carrying a ticket for the match that was initially scheduled for Sunday 23 April 1989 but that was rearranged after Hillsborough: the match for which my father had originally had tickets. The time of the kick-off was printed on the ticket as 3.05; the price was £7.

One of the brothers had brought his son along for the night. His name was Michael; there was a second son who wasn't present. His name was Thomas. One did not need to ask after whom they were named. The brothers had absolute recall of the night of their Anfield adventure: of the slow journey to Liverpool, of the kick-off being delayed because of the late-arriving fans, of how after the game they had stayed at a friend's house in the northwest, where they had eaten chili con carne and spent most of the rest of the night sleeplessly watching a recording of the game, over and again. 'His obsession with Arsenal cost him his marriage,' one brother said of the other. 'And it cost him one and a half million quid in a divorce settlement.'

Now Paul Davis was on his feet. Dressed in a dark suit, grey shirt and black tie, he was athletically lean; there was grey in his tightly cut hair but apart from that he could have easily passed for someone in his mid-thirties and who was still playing in the lower divisions. He reflected on how 'I fell out with George, just as Kenny did.' The portly Sansom, sitting by his side, looked up and nodded sadly. Davis recalled how Graham had given him and the other injured or non-selected players tickets just before kick-off. 'Did he let you 'ave 'em at face value, Davo?' quipped Watt.

There was a cheer from the floor.

'I was watching the game again recently,' Davis said, 'and I was looking for myself in the crowd. You can just about see me at the front after Mickey's goal goes in.'

Sansom, who played 314 games for Arsenal, left the club in December 1988 to join Newcastle. He missed out on being a title winner but, he told the audience, he'd still played his part. His first game back at Highbury was the match of Saturday 15 April – the day of Hillsborough. Sansom recalled scoring a disallowed goal in that match when the scores were level. 'If that goal had counted, Arsenal wouldn't have won the title. I'm glad it didn't count.'

He paused to receive applause, then spoke of his trepidation in the week preceding his return to Highbury. 'I didn't know how the fans would react to me coming back. My mum didn't dare go. She said to me, "They're gonna boo you, son." Then when I came on to the pitch and heard thirty-eight thousand people chanting my name, heard them cheering for me, I felt at least six feet tall.' Sansom is in fact about five feet six. He broke off, and broke down, weeping at the memory, and we all began to chant his name, just as we had on that distant Saturday afternoon when our former captain returned for the first time to play at Highbury in the black and white stripes of a rival team.

After three courses, we were more than ready to hear from Thomas. He rose unsteadily, swaying a little as if over-whelmed by the rousing chorus of 'There's only one Mickey Thomas'. He was asked immediately about that goal. He tried to speak, but at first could not be heard above the fizz and hiss of feedback. He started again, even more hesitantly, but there was more fizzing and popping from the speakers, discouraging him. Then at last he had some space and silence in which to speak. 'I was focussing only on Bruce Grobbelaar – just waiting for him. It was surreal, just waiting for him, just waiting for him to come. I can't watch it now. If it ever comes on TV, I can't watch it.'

It was apparent that Thomas was nervous; he stuttered slightly and shuffled awkwardly. Where the other players had been expansive, practised raconteurs, he was laconic and brief. 'When you leave here,' he said, opening his arms wide, 'you just miss being part of Arsenal. It was about the squad, back then: we all grew up together; we were all in it together. We knew each other so well. You just missed it.'

Up on the screen, the game was entering its eighty-eighth minute. I continued watching . . .

Adams is charging forward deep into the Liverpool box,

but Grobbelaar, unperturbed, gathers the ball, deflecting any threat. Adams rubs the balding goalkeeper on the head, and jogs away smiling – a nice gesture so late in the game when the mood could have been fractious.

Thomas had sat down, and many more of us were watching the TV screens now, a silence settling on the room. The camera is following McMahon; he raises his right index finger. *One minute to go*, Steve, people are calling out. *One minute.*

Now it was as if everyone in the room was watching the screens, except for Thomas, who was looking down rather bashfully at the table even as, on the screen, Lukic threw the ball out to Dixon.

We watched as Dixon played the ball long and accurately to Smith. He turns and plays a pass through to Thomas, who is rushing forward from midfield.

I was focussing only on Bruce Grobbelaar – just waiting for him. Just waiting for him.

Thomas has the ball. The goalkeeper is coming towards him. Thomas has the ball.

There was silence in the room, and I suddenly realised that I was holding my breath. I glanced over at Thomas and even he was now looking up at one of the screens, as fascinated as the rest of us, because he knew exactly what will happen next.

Here he comes, his momentum carrying him forward as he lifts the ball up and over Grobbelaar and, look, watch it now, follow it as it goes up and over the goalkeeper and continues on its way into the net.

2–0.

Many of us were on our feet, cheering now. The brothers at my table were holding on to each other, as they must have done on this same night eighteen years before, and the son, Michael, who was not even born then, was as delighted as they are, celebrating the goal as if for the first time.

It was surreal, just waiting for him – just waiting.

The atmosphere soured shortly afterwards, however, when a man collapsed at a nearby table. I hurried over and saw that he was breathing; that he was being helped by friends. An ambulance had been called, I was told. It seemed as if he'd had a fit rather than a heart attack, but he looked blanched and sickly, taking in air through his mouth, his collar open, the tie slack and loose around his neck.

I caught up with Thomas just before he left the Emirates. He was holding the very boots he'd worn at Anfield, borrowed for the night from the Arsenal Museum. They were battered and crumpled – the toe of one of them was damaged – with the three parallel stripes of the Adidas logo, in green, peeling slightly away from the leather, like a poorly sealed stamp on an envelope. This evening, he said, had been 'surreal'. That word again. He seldom returned to London, he said, and was settled on Merseyside. His business was there, his wife, his family.

'You'll never escape the memory of that goal, Michael,' I said, 'down here or up there, in the north or south, wherever you go, whatever you do.'

'I know that,' he said. 'I think I've always known it.'

He showed me the boot with which he'd struck the shot that won the title for Arsenal and I didn't know what to say or whether I should take it from him, like a gift. 'Wow,' I said. 'So that's the boot.' He nodded gravely, took my number, and then left.

As he headed for the underground car park, he looked relieved to be out of there.

As I drove home along the Seven Sisters Road, passing from Arsenal into Tottenham territory, a light, warm rain falling, I found myself thinking of the man who had collapsed earlier in the evening, of the cold, grey vacancy I'd seen in his eyes. The incident had disturbed me and I found myself thinking of my friend Salvatore – Sav – and of how much he would have enjoyed the reunion dinner at the Emirates. Sav was one of the two brothers who were with me on that first visit to Anfield and he was with me again at Highbury on the Sunday in May 1998 when Arsenal won their first title under Wenger. But within a couple of months of that game he had died, from hypertrophic cardiomyopathy, a congenital heart condition of which everyone, including Sav, was completely ignorant. He was thirty-one when he died in his sleep and he did not live to see the start of the next season.

I pictured him hanging out of my car – so young, vigorous and optimistic – and chanting 'We've got Dennis Bergkamp' as we pulled away from Blackhorse Road tube station after the Everton match. We had bonded as boys partly because of our mutual support for Arsenal; he was a strong, powerful boy, and he lived on our cul-de-sac. We were united in our opposition to all the Spurs and West Ham, not forgetting the Liverpool, fans around us. But we weren't tribally opposed to these other fans; first and foremost we were friends and when Arsenal were out of town, groups of us from our road would still occasionally go along to different London grounds, including White Hart Lane. There was one game at the Lane I especially remember. I stood with Mike, another of our friends, at the Paxton Road End. Alan Hansen was playing for Liverpool and whenever he defended a corner, or came over to pick up the ball close to where we were, men as well as boys around us kept spitting at him, until the back of his shirt was dark-sodden with saliva, with gobs of yellowy-green phlegm hanging from it. When they were not spitting at him, they were telling him to fuck off back to his northern slum. All this was a typical London welcome for Scousers.

I continued driving along the Seven Sisters Road, out of Tottenham Hotspur territory, on past Blackhorse Road station and out towards the M11 motorway, and thinking of Sav I began inevitably also to think of my father.

In the early nineties my father's company had a corporate-hospitality box at White Hart Lane, and on 12 January 1991 he finally agreed to go to his first football match since Hillsborough. He was very reluctant to go, but it was a business obligation – and, as I reminded him, it *was* the North London derby. Although I didn't have a ticket I travelled up in the car with him in the expectation of being able to buy one outside the ground from a tout or of bribing my way in at the gate. I was still then living at home with my parents in what was becoming an extended post-university torpor, getting by as best I could. Contrary to my confident expectations, I'd not been accepted for the BBC's graduate news trainee scheme (the one job I applied for in my final year at university). I knew I was beginning to flounder. Not long before, I'd applied to work as a postman for the Christmas period but was not even called for an interview. After that, I applied to be a van driver for a local bakery group named Dorringtons, which had numerous shops in and around Essex and Hertfordshire. I was interviewed, but one of the

Dorrington family was suspicious of me and refused to take my application seriously. It was serious: I liked the idea of the early mornings alone in the van, of the simplicity and discipline of the routine, of the free cakes, bread and buns to eat, of the rest of the day to do as you wished once your deliveries were completed.

On the way to the match we listened to Al Bowlly in the car; through familiarity I was beginning to like some of Bowlly's songs, notably 'Riptide' and 'The Very Thought of You'. I asked my father more about Bowlly and he provided a brief biographical sketch, explaining how Bowlly had died in a Luftwaffe raid in the early hours of 17 April 1941. A bomb had exploded in the street outside his flat in Dukes Court, Piccadilly. 'He will have been dead for fifty years in April,' my father said, crumpling into his seat.

Shortly before his death, Bowlly had received a letter from a female fan. Written on blue paper, it warned him that his life was in danger. 'Al darling,' she wrote. 'Do be careful. I dreamt last night that you were standing with a black man and you were both blown away.'

On the same morning as he received the letter, Bowlly discovered that one of his closest friends, Ken 'Snakehips' Johnson, the black bandleader with whom he often worked and made several jazz recordings of Shakespeare sonnets, had been killed in a raid while performing at the Café de Paris in Coventry Street. The letter had been posted the day before the raid. 'When I'm free,' Bowlly told a friend, 'I sing at the Café. If I'd been in London on Saturday, I'd have been standing with Ken.'

My father couldn't understand why, on the night Bowlly died, he had taken the last train from High Wycombe to London. 'I don't know why he made the journey,' he said aloud, as if in conversation with himself. 'It's possible that a self-styled superstitious Greek like Al' – he always called him Al, or Al Bowlly, never simply Bowlly – 'might have thought himself immune from death, especially after what happened to Johnson.' Then he sighed. 'I suppose that letter can be read in retrospect as the chronicle of a death foretold.'

He looked across at me as if seeking confirmation, but I simply shrugged.

My father said that he had recently visited Westminster City Cemetery, where Bowlly was buried in a communal grave without a tombstone or any special memorial of his own. It was then, saddened, that he had decided he would mark the fiftieth anniversary of the singer's death by visiting the Dukes Court apartment block in Piccadilly. There he would light a candle outside the building in which Bowlly had died: a private vigil, a strike against the forces of forgetting.

'Will you really do that?' I said.

'I'd like to.'

He and my mother also had tickets for a Bowlly celebration evening, he said, to be held at South Africa House in Trafalgar Square in April.

We went on to reminisce about the first games we'd seen together, before he'd quite understood and accepted that, unlike him, I was not a Hammer and that no matter how many times he took me to Upton Park I never would be one.

'Can you remember our first game?'

'West Ham–Derby,' I said. 'Upton Park. Nil–nil. I couldn't tell you who was playing for either side but I remember you telling me to look out for the Derby winger who wore white boots.'

'Alan Hinton.'

'Yes, that's right. Alan Hinton. I stood on that wooden stool you used to bring for me. On the Chicken Run, where we always used to stand. Everyone smoking. Loads of swearing. Everyone stinking of beer. You bringing sandwiches for me, and a flask of coffee for yourself. I can still smell it, the coffee, as you opened the flask for the first time. I couldn't understand why you kept shouting out "Come on you Irons".'

'That was our original name – Thames Ironworks. Fans have a long memory, as you know. Our second game?'

'FA Cup sixth round. Highbury. Nineteen-seventy five. West Ham. Unbelievable. Absolutely packed. Pouring with rain. Heavy pitch. Fighting everywhere in the crowd, the ICF taking the North Bank.'

'Two goals from Alan Taylor,' he said. 'A great win for us. A great day. We went on to win the Cup that year. Two–nil in the final, against Fulham. Bobby Moore playing for Fulham. Incredible to think of Bobby playing against West Ham. And two more for Taylor in the Final. I wonder what happened to him?'

'Didn't Taylor get two in the semi as well?'

'Against Ipswich. Two–one, in a replay. I went to the first game. Nil–nil at Villa Park. Green Ronwood – or was it Lyall? – bought Taylor in from Rochdale that season. Skinny little guy. Long, lankish, gingery hair. Had a tash. Cost us nothing at all. And he won us the Cup.'

We parked in a side street somewhere behind Seven Sisters station and made our way to the stadium. There were police positioned all along the tatty high street and, not far from the ground, we were stopped at an impromptu barrier and asked for our tickets.

'Tickets?' I said. 'I want to pay at the gate.'

'It's an all-ticket match.'

I feared it might be but said, 'I know. I'm meeting a friend at the Paxton Road End. He's got my ticket.'

'You wanted to pay at the gate a minute ago. You've either got a ticket or you haven't.'

'Officer, can I help?' my father said.

He turned towards my father. 'Have you got a ticket?'

'He's in one of the boxes,' I said.

'Lucky for him,' said the copper. 'But you, young man, aren't going any further without a ticket.'

This was the post-Hillsborough reality: stricter and more efficient policing in and around football grounds. I told my father that I'd head back towards Seven Sisters station to see if I could pick up a ticket from a tout. As we shook hands, he surprised me by saying, 'Son, don't go.' 'But I haven't got a ticket, Dad.' He looked at me, smiled, and placed his hand on my left shoulder; then, without saying anything else, he turned and set off, never once looking back as I stood there watching him for as long as I could until he became indistinguishable, merging into the restless accumulations of the pre-match crowd.

Unable to get a ticket at a reasonable price, and not even that keen to see the game anyway, I gave up on the idea of going and took the Underground into the West End. I didn't miss much, as it turned out: the game ended 0–0, with Arsenal reliant on several good saves from goalkeeper David Seaman for a point. The next afternoon I went for a walk in Hatfield Forest, which was a short drive away from the family home in Hertfordshire, relishing the quiet and anonymity as I moved through the thickening trees, the ground slightly wet and uneven, fallen branches kicked aside as I went. The air was heavy with winter dampness by the time I arrived back at the car. Looking behind me I could no longer see the shapes of the trees out of which I'd just come. I sat for a while in the car, looking out into the darkness. Nothing seemed to be falling into place for me. Nothing was happening. I was teaching one day a week at a school just outside Bishop's Stortford as well as doing some scraps of freelance journalism for a local paper in the town, but I wanted more: real purpose, propulsion, the start of a proper career.

There was a solitary light on in our house when I returned, burning dimly in the dining-room, where I encountered my father sitting up at the table with the faded pages of old newspapers and magazines spread out before him. One Sunday evening many years before, when we still lived in Harlow, I remember coming across him in a similar setting: alone in the dining-room of a mostly darkened house, sitting then as he was now at a table. But then he'd been reading book reviews from the *Observer*, or perhaps it was the *Sunday Times* (he bought both newspapers); and he'd tried to interest me in one of them, a review of a book about the poet Wilfred Owen.

'Have you ever read Owen?' he asked.

I said that I hadn't.

'Oh, do, when you get the chance,' he said, and began to speak from memory the opening sentences of the poem I know now as 'Dulce Et Decorum Est':

> Bent double, like old beggars under sacks,
> Knock-kneed, coughing like hags, we cursed
>   through sludge,
> Till on the haunting flares we turned our backs
> And towards our distant rest began to trudge.

Then his voice began to break, as if something solid was caught at the back of his throat, and he coughed self-consciously, turned away and made as if to continue reading the paper.

He wasn't reading a review now in this ill-lit room: he was looking at photographs, mostly black-and-white ones of wartime East End scenes; he was particularly fascinated by one double-page magazine spread, which when I'd come into the room he had been looking at intently through the box-shaped brass magnifying glass he used to scrutinise cloth constructions and shirt patterns. So intense was his concentration that he'd not heard me come in and seemed startled when I spoke. He turned to look up, the soft skin around his right eye creased and puckered from where the glass had been pressed hard against it.

'What are you doing?' I said.

'I'm looking at these old pictures.'

'Of the war years?'

He smiled.

'What is it you look for when you look at those pictures, Dad?'

'I'm not quite sure,' he said. 'Sometimes I wonder if I'll see someone I knew. Sometimes I wonder even if I might see myself –'

'By the way,' he said, digressing, 'can I borrow your trainers? I'm playing table-tennis with some of the guys from work on Wednesday. At the club down the road.'

He meant the local working-men's club on Station Road. He'd not played table-tennis or done any exercise for a while, which is why he didn't have any trainers of his own. Of late, as the effects of the recession tightened, it had all been work: early morning alarm calls, weekly flights to

Ireland and beyond, long car and train journeys, a repeating cycle of meetings. Most evenings, once he was back at home, if he was at home and not away in a hotel, he never seemed to relax; he'd be continuously on the move, making cups of tea for everyone or flicking through the paper, before, at about ten o'clock or so, he'd say that he was 'going up to read'. This became something of a family joke – because if ever you looked in on him, not long afterwards, he'd be sitting up in bed but he wouldn't be reading: he'd be asleep with the light on, a book lying open on his bare chest or by his side, where it had fallen from his hands. He was a deeply private man and never wanted any of us to see him in bed, especially like this – exposed, vulnerable, so tired. He'd recently started wearing wire-framed reading spectacles – which he used self-consciously – and he would sometimes still be wearing them when you looked in to see him there in bed.

A few days later, on Wednesday evening, shortly after six o'clock, I arrived home from the local paper where I'd spent the day working. My father's car was on the drive, which meant he was back from work much earlier than usual – yet he wasn't to be found when I went in. 'Where's Dad?' I asked my mother as I went through to the kitchen.

'He's playing table-tennis. You've just missed him.'

Of course – I'd forgotten. 'He wanted to borrow my trainers,' I said, preparing to go after him. 'I'll take them down to him.'

'No need,' she said. 'He bought some this afternoon.'

My younger sister Victoria was out at work. So my mother and I sat down to eat together, a simple, quickly prepared meal I've never forgotten of salmon-en-croute, broccoli, and some new potatoes. I drank water and she had a glass of red wine. My father would be having the same meal when he came in; my mother had served his up on a plate that she left covered on a work surface in the kitchen, presumably to reheat once he returned. The next morning I was due to take an informal A level English seminar at the local independent school where I was teaching. I told my mother about this failing school, which occupied the site of what had once been a grand stately home but which had fewer than ten pupils in its sixth-form. I was teaching a class of two tomorrow: two girls, one of whom was from the Ryan family, owners of the airline Ryan Air. I wasn't sure what I was doing at the school, since I had no previous experience of teaching, had taken no postgraduate teaching qualification, and did not even want to teach. It was something I'd stumbled into after meeting the headmaster at a party, which was comment enough on both the mediocrity of the school and my lack of direction. I hadn't even read the book we were supposed to discuss the next morning, Graham Swift's *Waterland*. I had a long night's reading ahead.

After the meal I went upstairs to my room, stretched out on the bed, put on some music and began the long, rather solemn task of working my way through *Waterland*. Soon I must have fallen asleep because I was awoken by a loud, panicky knocking from downstairs. My mother answered the door. I heard her say, 'Oh, hello, Joe.'

The only Joe I knew was our Irish window-cleaner. He was a stout-chested, short-legged man; he wore black plastic-framed glasses that magnified his eyes like marbles and his thick hair was greased into an Elvis-style quiff. I saw him sometimes late at night returning home, his face the colour of a bruised peach, from the working-men's club where he was a regular and where my father was for the first time now playing table tennis. I liked Joe; he was reliable, garrulously amiable. But now something wasn't quite right. I heard my mother say, her voice high and panicked, 'What do you mean, stroke?'

I threw the paperback of *Waterland* across the room; it folded and bent as it impacted with the white-painted wall and dropped into the wire wastepaper bin, never to be retrieved. 'Dad's had an accident,' my mother said, as I made my way downstairs. She was gathering her coat.

'He's had an accident,' Joe repeated. 'Down at the club.' I sought reassurance in Joe's eyes – so large and watery behind the thick lenses of his glasses – and saw in return only sad incomprehension.

I pulled on my trainers – the ones my father should perhaps have been wearing – and set off for the club, which was no more than a brisk five minutes' walk away. I knew my mother would be following, and I began to sprint so that I would be there ahead of her. As I reached the club – a dishevelled two-storey redbrick building with a flat-roofed, white-painted one-storey annex extension – I saw that an ambulance was parked outside in the small car park, its blue light rotating soundlessly. I wondered what could have happened: my father slipping and falling as he pivoted to play another of those contorted forehand returns. A broken ankle? A dislocated elbow? But then I remembered the alarm in my mother's voice: a *stroke*!

I pushed open the main door and went in. I paused to take in my surroundings: the ceiling was low, the air was heavy with cigarette smoke, and there were three or four men sitting right up at the bar on stools. They said nothing and received me with flat expressions, ominous in their matter-of-fact blankness. I'd walked past the club so often in the years since we'd moved out to this small riverside town in the Essex–Hertfordshire borderlands, but I'd never before been inside, never had any reason to, and I'm not sure my father had been inside before tonight either. I moved towards the bar and turned right into the annex – perhaps directed by someone who knew why I was there, why I had come. I can't remember. The door to the games room was open, and there was a dull wash of light coming from it, leading me. The lights were terribly bright in there. I turned into the room; the table-tennis table was in the middle, two wooden-handled bats were discarded on the floor, as if scattered by distracted children. At the far end of the room a huddle of men I didn't recognise stood with their backs to the window which looked out on to the street. They were staring down, evidently shocked, at the man who was lying on his back on the floor being tended to by two paramedics. The man's shirt was open and the paramedics were massaging his chest: pump, push, pump. The man was wearing stone-coloured chinos, and a pair of thick-soled white trainers, ostentatious in their newness; a price sticker was attached to one of the soles. I did not recognise the trainers but in that blurry, disorientating moment between perception and comprehension I realised that I knew the man and I went over to him. His eyes were open when I got there but they could see nothing; the stare was fixed in its vacancy, infinitely empty. I recognised the blue glint of my father's St Christopher caught up in the matted reddish-grey hairs of his chest, the cherished watch strapped to his left wrist, the dull shine of his gold wedding band. One side of his face seemed swollen or misshapen, and his eyes were open. I knew immediately from those eyes, the stare I did not recognise, the blankness I'd never seen before, that he was dead. Yes, quite dead. I began to shout, to rage. The para-medics ignored me, as they had to, and continued doing their work: pump, push, pump.

Now, when I think back to that night, I imagine a rock being dropped into a pool of stagnant water. It disappears, the surface broken by the disturbance of concentric ripples, and then I see another being dropped, and another, the surface each time resettling into the same oily smoothness, as if it had never been disturbed. But at that moment I could think only of my mother following behind. So I left my father there on the floor, left him behind, and returned the way I'd come, the men still sitting up at the bar, still saying nothing. It was as if the film of what had happened was being respooled, as if by leaving the scene I'd have the chance to return to it soon afterwards, when I'd discover that I had been wrong, that it hadn't turned out like that, that there had been a terrible mistake and it wasn't him lying on the floor after all. As I came out of the main doors my mother was breathlessly coming in, her eyes bright with confusion. I held on to her, blocking her way. I said, 'Don't, Mum, please. Don't. Dad's in there.'

I have no recollection of what followed or what I might have said next, until we saw my father being brought out into the cold night on a stretcher and hurried straight past us into the ambulance. My mother reached out as he passed and, tentatively, touched her husband's arm. 'Hold on, Tony,' she said. 'Please, hold on.'

I left her in the car park outside the club – she would follow behind in someone's car – and climbed into the back of the ambulance, which was bound for the Princess Alexandra Hospital, Harlow. It was our last journey together, my father and me, and we were on our way back to our old hometown.

It was clinically bright inside the ambulance, my father lying there with his shirt open, the paramedics using crash equipment in an attempt to restart his heart. They used a defibrillator to send electric shocks into his used-up heart; his body lunged and jerked, but nothing about him changed, repeatedly. His face was preternaturally pale, a faint blue glow around his lips. I felt his hands, which were as cold as stone. I squeezed them, and began to shake both his arms and thin legs. I shook him as hard as I could. I wanted so much to shake him back into life. 'The extremities always go first,' one of the paramedics said to me as I held my father's hand.

I knew that he knew that it was hopeless, but with intense concentration he continued, silently, doing his work, out of pure duty and professionalism, all the way to the hospital in Harlow, where my father was taken straight from the ambulance to intensive care. Shortly afterwards, he was declared dead on arrival.

Once back at home from the hospital, I turned on the television to discover that American planes had started bombing Baghdad; in the days that followed Iraq would respond by firing Scud missiles into Israel and Saudi Arabia. The first Gulf War had begun. It was as if the widespread optimism, the euphoria, even, of the year of 1989 had never been. So this was the reality of our new world order: war in the Middle East, with Baathist militarism and radical Islam presented as the enemies of the western democratic model. Here on the screen before me was an outer projection of what I was feeling: an annihilating sense of rage and futility.

So this was how it felt to be living at the end of history. I sat there watching as the night sky above Baghdad was illuminated by precision-guided missiles and searchlights. Smart and cluster bombs were being dropped. This was a desert storm of an unprecedented kind – and it had all the gaudy artificiality of a computer game.

In the time-slowed days that followed, we as a family discovered more about my father's life, about how he'd been living, about his various withholdings and secrets. It was distressing, because of what had happened, to have the opportunity to discover many of the things I'd often wondered but never directly asked about – such as how much he earned. It was distressing to have the freedom to rummage with impunity in his desk drawers, among his private papers, in his briefcase. It turned out that he'd misled his colleagues about his age at work. He was fifty-six when he died, on that Wednesday of 16 January 1991, but they believed him to be a much younger man. For whatever reason – the competitiveness and youth-fixations of the fashion business, the difficulty of getting and holding on to a job in an industry in thrall to novelty and the next trend, the hardships caused by a second recession in less than a decade – he'd sought to pass as a younger man, and yet so much of his conversation had been about wartime Britain: the Blitz, the songs of the period, the evacuations to the countryside. It seemed that nobody outside the family knew how old he was. Not one of his obituaries in the trade magazines was accurate about his age. He was obituarised as a younger man, which I guess, strangely, would have pleased him. 'I knew it didn't all add up,' one of his colleagues told me one evening on a visit to the house.

In the weeks after his death we were visited continuously by people from my father's past and present. It was consoling for my mother to discover that so many people respected her husband and spoke well of his courtesies, kindness and charm. Someone sent my mother a note in which she wrote, quoting something Raymond Chandler had once said of F. Scott Fitzgerald, that that there was only 'one word to describe TC' and that word was charming – charm as a kind of subdued magic, controlled and exquisite.

My friend Matthew, who was living in Australia, wrote to my mother to say that, to him, Tony had been 'an ideal man,' tough, aesthetic and brave, and not ashamed or embarrassed by any aspect of himself.

To me, though, those words offered little consolation and it was hard to get through those first few days after his death when I'd wake to hear my mother crying from somewhere inside the house; at night I used to tour the many pubs in the village with my sister Victoria, my girlfriend, Sarah, and my oldest friend, Mike, and we would play darts to occupy the hours, to push the night towards its end. The monotony and repetition were soothing; the soft suck of a dart as it landed and stayed fixed in the board.

The consequences of what had happened were severe for my mother, though she never complained nor spoke ill of her husband even as she struggled to cope with her double shock: first his death from a heart attack and then the discovery that he didn't have life assurance or even a pension. He'd refused to join both the company pension and health-insurance schemes; he'd taken out a second mortgage and was not properly insured to cover the debt on that. Why he'd been reluctant to take out effective insurance no one knew. My mother was convinced that it was because he suspected there was something wrong with his health and this, he must have assumed, would have prevented him from being properly insured. 'He didn't want us to know that something was wrong, he covered it up,' she said.

The numbness, I get it sometimes after I've worked in the garden.

My mother said that, when they first met, my father had told her that he had been rejected for national service because 'of my hammer toes', but that many years later he changed the story. The real reason for the rejection, he said, was that 'he had a problem with his chest, something to do with his lungs'. She didn't know exactly what the problem was. 'But if there was anything ever seriously wrong with me, Lilian,' he had told her, 'I wouldn't say.'

'Did you ask him why he wouldn't tell you?' I said. 'Didn't you think it was odd that he should say that?'

'I did ask him,' she said, 'but all he said was that he wouldn't want to worry me with anything. "But I do worry, Tony," I told him, "I do worry,"' and then she added that while on holiday in southern Italy, the previous September, he'd become breathless as they walked up a steep hill to the hotel. 'Let's stop here, Lilian,' he'd said. 'I don't want to die abroad.'

'He knew,' she said again, 'he knew.'

Yet would insurance and the various regular health checks and medicals to which he would have been entitled as a member of the various company schemes he refused to join have helped him live beyond fifty-six? Would regular medicals have revealed that he was not as healthy as he wanted us to believe? But then had he joined those schemes he would have been legally obliged to reveal both his exact age and the extent of any underlying illness. So he was trapped by a cruel paradox: he wanted to be younger, presented himself as being so, but in so doing he couldn't possibly have had the detailed recollection of the experiences that, in his last year, preoccupied him more than any other, notably an East London boyhood in the long lead up to and during the Second World War.

Among the books I found in my father's room as we sorted through his possessions was a recently purchased copy of Paul Auster's book about the sudden death of his father, *The Invention of Solitude*; among its pages I found a clipping of an obituary of the American boxer Henry Armstrong, a.k.a. Hurricane Henry or the Punching Preacher. My father had never mentioned him to me and I wondered what about the Punching Preacher it was that had interested him enough to have cut out and kept an obituary; the photograph of Johnson showed him dressed in a tight white T-shirt and working at a speed bag. The caption was intriguing: 'Glory days: Henry Armstrong training at Clacton-on-Sea in 1939'.

I wondered if my father had seen Armstrong box or just in training, perhaps while away with his mother, Jane, on one of their holidays on the Essex coast, without the ostracised Frank. It was possible. Also tucked into the book were a McDonald's lottery scratch-card and his business card – Boftex Ltd, with 'offices in Hong Kong and Mauritius'. Had he been to Mauritius? I didn't know.

I began to read the Auster book and, on page fifteen, came across a vertical pencil stroke against this paragraph:

My father's capacity for evasion was almost limitless. Because the domain of the other was unreal to him, his incursions into that domain were made with a part of himself he considered to be equally unreal, another self he had trained as an actor to represent him in the empty comedy of the world-at-large.

One day it began to snow, starting early in the morning and continuing all through the afternoon and into the evening so that by nightfall the snow had thickly settled and no cars passed on the Cambridge Road outside our house. It was overly warm in the house; I wanted to get out into the cold, away from the family and visitors, and so I walked for about a mile down to the River Stort, wading out deeply into the snow-covered, low-lying surrounding meadowlands, the branches of the trees white-bowed and heavy, the very air I breathed making my teeth ache. I scooped up snow in my bare hands and felt the hard crunchiness of ice as water oozed through my numbed fingers. For some reason, and quite suddenly, I began to run out into the field, stumbling before I finally fell backwards, toppling over with a muffled thud in the compacted snow. There was no one around to hear or see me. I lay there looking up at the darkness; flakes the size of small buttons were falling again and, for a moment, in the silence, I wondered how long I could lie there, with the snow covering me until I could not be seen, until I would be quite invisible, merely nothing and no one in that white world. I lay there and closed my eyes, feeling the wet flakes landing and dissolving on my face. Then I felt nothing more.

I thought back to that night at the hospital, when I'd discovered my father lying on a table behind a drawn curtain in a small, windowless room. Two doctors in white coats had just drawn the curtain on him and they seemed to be chuckling as they wrote down some notes.

'Why are you laughing?' I asked them, perhaps too aggressively. 'What is there to laugh about?'

'Who are you?' I was asked.

'It doesn't matter. I just want to know why you were laughing? Laughing at a dead man.'

'Why don't you calm down,' I was told.

'I am calm.'

'You don't seem it.'

'I just can't understand why you were you laughing. Why were you? Why were you laughing?'

'We weren't laughing,' one of them said. He was holding a plastic folder, into which he was pushing some sheets of paper, and I noticed how his hand seemed to be trembling. I looked on, with fury, as he motioned his colleague away, and together they walked down a long, overlit corridor. I imagined I heard the ghostly sound of more laughter filling the spaces they left behind.

I pulled back the curtain and there was my father, flat on his back on a table, a white sheet covering his body but leaving his neck and face exposed – oh, how he would have hated to have had me see him like this. I touched his face gently, which was rough from that day's stubble. I ran the middle finger of my right hand along his narrow straight nose and rested my palm on his forehead, as if I were trying to soothe him, and then touched his cold, thin lips. I reached beneath the sheet and removed from his left wrist the watch he'd worn since he was twenty-one, its face faded, old-yellow. As I stood looking down at him it was as though his face began to change, as past and present seemed to merge as in a hallucination, and I began to see him simultaneously as he was there and then, dead, but also as he'd been at different stages in his life, as a younger man, my father or always destined to be so. There he was with my mother, alongside, leaning jauntily against his

Jowett, his hair cropped GI-short. There he was leading us in a chorus of *What does Harold Wilson eat?* And here he was before me, his eyes closed, his face puffy and blue-grey. He did not seem to be at rest.

Shut your fucking mouth, sideburns.

I wondered if, momentarily, I'd fallen asleep because I became aware of the movement of the river nearby and it was as if I'd heard the very turning of the earth. I spoke some words aloud: *There's nothing either good or bad but thinking makes it so.* I was feeling cold and damp and I was shivering. I rose, knocked snow from my coat and jeans, and continued walking out into the darkness across the heavy fields.

The next morning, soon after waking, I sent a fax to Arsenal, addressed to Alan Smith. It was a speculative interview request; I didn't have a commission from a magazine or newspaper but I was desperate. I'd been reading the magazines *Ninety Minutes* and *Football Today*, to which several friends of mine had started to contribute as freelancers. The former was very much influenced by the new fanzine culture that emerged from the rubble of the broken-down stadiums of the mid-eighties; the best of them being the wonderfully titled *When Saturday Comes*. *Ninety Minutes* was breezy, smart, humorous, laddish. It seemed to understand the direction in which the game was moving. *Football Today* was more traditional, in the style of the august *Charles Buchan's Football Monthly*. It was authoritative, respectful, earnest. It looked back nostalgically to how the game had been. Neither magazine paid well for an article, I was told, but at least they paid something, and the editors were prepared to take a chance on commissioning unknown writers.

And if, as I saw it, difficult circumstance and an absence of social mobility had prevented my father from having the opportunity to pursue his careers of choice, journalism and/or acting, I was now determined not to allow my own indolence and indirection to stop me from doing what I wanted to do, which at that point was to try my hand at journalism.

To my surprise and delight I received a call the next day from Alan Smith. He'd received the fax, he wanted to talk, whenever would be convenient for me. 'Let's talk now,' I said, anxious not to lose him. 'Who are you writing for again?' he asked. *'Ninety Minutes,'* I said. 'It's a good magazine,' he said. 'Well, we're pleased with how it's all going,' I said.

That afternoon I called one of the editors at *Ninety Minutes*. He was encouraging: yes, he would be interested in an interview with Smith. I had my first commission and my first sale. This was in February 1991, when Arsenal were playing some of their best football under Graham. I was still working part-time for a local newspaper and doing some teaching.

Not long afterwards I sent another fax to the club. I sent it in the morning and later that same day my sister Alison, who was visiting my mother, answered the phone at home. I was in an upstairs room. I heard her say, 'Who is it, please?' Then: 'Jason, it's Gordon Graham.'

My fax had been addressed to 'George Graham, Manager's Office, Arsenal' – and now, within a few hours, calling from his car, was the manager himself, George, a.k.a. the Stroller, the Ringmaster, the Peacock, the Ayatollah, Gorgeous George, Beau Brummell of Bargeddie, and now, to my sister at least, just plain Gordon. The manager was calling me at home. He was waiting for me, *at the other end of the line*. Gordon. George. George Graham. 'Thank you for calling,' I said, my voice deepening as I strained for authority.

'Not a problem,' he said, in his unmistakable west-of-Scotland accent, softened by several decades in the English south. George, calling from his car. *It was really him*.

'How can I help?' he said.

I told him that I was writing an article for a football magazine about how well the club were doing under him (they were top of the League); that I'd recently interviewed Alan Smith ('I know,' he said, 'I told him to do it.'); and that in particular I wanted to ask about Anders Limpar, the Swedish winger who been delighting with his trickery and goals. It was as smooth and bland a conversation as I could have hoped for. I was nervous; George was controlled. He spoke of Rocastle 'needing to knuckle down to try to win his place back. It's good to have everyone competing for places. It generates the right kind of hunger.' The only point of contention was when I asked about O'Leary. He used the opportunity to praise Bould, who was keeping O'Leary out of the team.

'Yes, but what about O'Leary? How's he doing?'

'Steve Bould has been absolutely exceptional, first class. If he keeps up this level of performance he'll be in the England squad.'

Sending those faxes off to Arsenal and having the people I'd thought so much about, talked about, even dreamed about, call me back was as exciting as it was bewildering. It was at once a kind of escapism into the fantasies of fandom and a form of displacement activity: I had no proper job, no real pattern to my days or weeks. I was drifting, retreating back inside the cage. I understand now that those faxes I sent to Arsenal and the interviews that arose from them changed my life. They turned out to be the first articles I published in national publications. They helped me to find momentum, to believe; they opened the way for me to have a career in journalism.

The next fax I sent, a couple of weeks later, was to Michael Thomas. I'd heard he was unsettled at the club, that he wanted greater freedom to play in a style that was anathema to Graham the pragmatist, the hard-headed utilitarian. As the others had done, Thomas called me back – but not as promptly as Smith and Graham had. Still, there was no initial call from a protective press officer, as there would have been today, no formal expression of scepticism. I simply sent a fax to the club, on a whim, saying that I wrote for football magazines, and the player called back. No ID or photocopied press pass was asked for; no fax to be sent on official headed paper. It seemed too improbable to be true, as if I was the victim of some hoax or bluff. But I wasn't, since here was Thomas calling and expressing eagerness to speak and be questioned. Clearly all was not well for him at Highbury and he told me that his ambition was to play on the Continent. 'At Arsenal we play a fast two-touch style of football but I would love to play in Europe. I can't deny that I'm a keen admirer of that slower style of play, where there's more emphasis on skill and building patiently from the back. I remember watching the exciting Spurs side of Hoddle, Ardiles and Villa in the early eighties and loving their style – I called it Continental football – that great emphasis on skill and passing.'

Our conversation turned inevitably to that night at Anfield and to 'that goal', as he called it. 'Friends say that I've gone down in history for that goal. People in the street who didn't even support Arsenal began recognising me. But it's now time to stop looking back, don't you think? I must move on. Time can't stand still. There's still so much in the game I want to do.'

His tone was uncertain; it was as if he knew what lay ahead for him: that no matter what he achieved, where he went or what he did in the game, he would be forever afterwards be associated with that one goal, that one fortuitous, glorious culmination.

One cold, damp evening in February 1993, I heard on the radio that Bobby Moore had died, at the age of fifty-one, from cancer. I'd grown up in a household in which Moore was a revered figure. To my father he was a symbol of a certain kind of English innocence, the ball-player of unusual dignity and grace. One of my father's happiest stories was of the day he met Moore and his then wife, Tina, on a long flight back from Hong Kong. Moore was, like my father, returning from a business trip and had taken it on himself to act as a cocktail-fixer in the upper-deck bar of a jumbo jet; they got talking, establishing an easy rapport as they discovered a commonality of interest and background. Throughout the flight Moore called my father Tel. 'What are you having, Tel?' 'What's it you do again, Tel?' 'One more before we land, Tel?'

When my father assumed the role of Moore, speaking as if he *were* Moore, in the frequent retelling of this story, he would quicken his voice, as if he were a little breathless, as if in his role of Moore he were chivvying everyone along, like the good captain he was: *Come on, what are you having? Come on, Tel, only five minutes to go. We need one big push before we land, Tel, so what are you having . . .?*

My father had enjoyed being called Tel and he made no attempt to correct Moore throughout the flight. Maybe it showed him that he could be someone else, anyone he wanted to be: Tel, not Tony, the old actor's trick of inhabiting a role.

On the evening after Moore died I drove out to the East End, parked my car and mingled with the many hundreds of people who had turned up to lay down scarves and floral tributes outside the gates of the Upton Park stadium in respect of their former captain. Photographs and posters had been attached to the main gates; in one picture a young, blond-haired, red-shirted Moore is shown receiving the World Cup from the Queen on that July day in 1966, when it must have seemed as if the whole world was watching and admiring him. In another Moore is sitting on a white leather ball, his back to a goalpost. A team shirt, a faded, decades' old claret and blue, was one of several like it tied to the gates.

I tried not to think of the last photograph of Moore I'd seen, in which he'd been shown debilitated by an illness the seriousness of which he'd sought to conceal even from his closest friends. That night in the East End my father's and Moore's deaths seemed somehow to be linked in my mind: the end of two East End lives, yes, but something more besides, something to do with the end of a certain way of life, with the loss of a certain sense of old-fashioned duty and decorum. As young boys both men had been told by their mothers the same thing: to stand tall, to speak well, to be polite, to make the best of themselves.

When Bobby Moore retired from football, having played more than 1,000 games at senior level, it must have seemed to him as if he would have the chance to do whatever he wanted next. To prosper in coaching or management, or in business or as a well-paid media analyst. None of this happened. There were failed investments; dodgy deals and a divorce; rumour and tabloid scandals (did he or didn't he steal the jewel in Colombia?). The trajectory of his decline seemed powerfully to parallel that of the game itself as football was torn apart in the seventies by hooliganism and neglect. Moore's only attempts at management were humbling, at non-League Oxford City, from 1979 to 1981, and then at Southend United, from 1983 to 1986. The last years of his life, when he worked as 'sports editor' of the repulsive *Sunday Sport* and as a fast-talking, match-day summariser on Capital Gold, had a strange melancholy. He was never knighted.

'It's ridiculous that the FA didn't use Bobby, if only as a defensive coach,' says Jeff Powell, Moore's biographer and close friend (he was best man at his second wedding). 'Elton John at Watford asked me if I could set up a meeting with Bobby about his becoming manager but then he went with Graham Taylor in the end. Bobby went to Southend, where he had nothing to work with, and Oxford City – City, not United, mind. And yet he was one of the youngest-ever people to get his full coaching badge, while he was at West Ham. He was apparently brilliant when Allison and Venables brought him to work with the youngsters at Palace. Throughout he remained exactly the guy he'd always been: nothing changed him, not even being a World Cup-winning captain. He was from what you might call an upper-working-class family. He had natural intelligence, values.'

But wasn't he a poor communicator, too reserved and aloof? 'I'm not sure that's right,' Powell says. 'The attitude at

the FA was absurd. It was as if they saw footballers as mud-
died oafs, regarded them as an encumbrance. Bobby's
understanding of football was fantastic. As a player he had
no real pace, no left foot, wasn't great in the air, and yet he
had such knowledge and feel for the game.

'You must remember that football in the seventies
was very physical for a period on the pitch; it became a
ferocious game. The violence on the terraces had a psychological relationship with what was happening on the
pitch. You had Ron Harris, Peter Storey, Norman Hunter,
real hard-men, but Bobby rose above it all. He could be as
hard as anyone but in his own quiet, intelligent way. When
he played against Pele he didn't try to kick him; he took
him on in one of the great defender–forward duels of all
time, and the respect between them was mutual. If someone
kicked him during a game he would pick himself up, have
a look and say nothing. Twenty minutes later you'd see the
person who'd kicked Bobby lying on the pitch and ready for
an ambulance. The referee would be wondering how that
happened.'

Powell paused. 'We all still miss him terribly but he was
lost to the game long before he died.'

No one lives with the dread of measurement more acutely
than athletes. No other lives are so fiercely measured and
yet, perhaps, so dependent on luck and chance. Thomas
made a great run from deep that night at Anfield to collect
Smith's pass, just as he had done tirelessly throughout the
game, just as he did midway through the second half when
he collected Richardson's pass inside the box but shot
weakly at Grobbelaar. He was still lucky; at the last, the ball
broke for him just so. But according to Steve Nicol what happened was about more than simply luck or fate.

'*Things happen. That's the way it is in life and there's nothing you can do about it.*'

Standing outside Upton Park and mourning Bobby Moore, I decided to try to find the street where my father had once lived with his parents – Claude Road, E13. It was the setting for one of his poems about a VE Day street party, in which he wrote of long tables being pushed together on pavements, of women in 'factory turbans' serving mugs of tea, of the 'relief and joy etched' on their worn faces. I wondered where exactly I would the find the church where he'd won a Bible for good attendance. I drove slowly around the area of Upton Park, with its car-cluttered streets of terraced houses. Entire streets were now occupied by long-settled immigrant families from Bangladesh and Pakistan. They had made of the East End a place of their own, with its own mosques and specialist food and clothing stores, creating in the process their own community, their own extended and intimate networks of family and friends, just like the old East End had been.

Had I ever seen Moore playing for West Ham during his final mediocre months at the club? It was said that he was slow and clumsy towards the end, playing as if the boredom was very great. But that's not how my father remembered him – as slow and clumsy – or those who played with or against him. 'There should be a law against Bobby Moore,' Jock Stein once said. 'He knows what's happening twenty minutes before everyone else.'

It was starting to rain, making it even harder to read the street signs. And I was becoming annoyed at myself for continuing to brood on the old, unknown world of an East End past that had preoccupied my father so acutely during the last year of his life that it must have seemed more vivid to him than the daily routine of his working life. I'd always wanted my father to grapple more energetically with the present, to be with us, here and now. I thought back to what his mother had said: that once he'd left the East End he would never want to go back. She was wrong. At the end of his life it seemed as if the only place he wanted to be was back in the East End, but it was an East End that no longer existed, or if it existed it was merely a construct of lonely imagination and memory. And so he continued to re-imagine what in fact he'd already experienced, engaged in a long, private struggle against forgetting.

The sudden, unexpected death of a parent steals not only a sense of future possibility, of the life you might have led in different circumstances, the life you sometimes wonder about, a parallel, hypothetical shadow life in which that parent is still alive, but also some part of the past, and especially of a greater understanding of your own and that parent's past. There was still so much about my father I did not know. I did not know where he went to school; where exactly he had lived on Claude Road; what qualifications he had, if any; what he believed in, if anything. He was baptised as a Catholic, but I never once remember his going to church and, because he died intestate, and because he never spoke of such things, I had no idea as to whether he would have preferred to have been buried as a Catholic or not. In the event he was cremated, and his ashes were scattered in woodland at a crematorium in Harlow. His possessions – his books, business diaries and personal letters, including the love letters my mother had written to him – were packed into boxes and shut away in the attic, where they remained undisturbed for the next sixteen years until my mother decided one Sunday afternoon to start sorting through them (she found then, among many other curiosities, a letter my father had received from Ron Greenwood). But I still haven't looked in those boxes, and I'm not sure I ever will.

My father has no gravestone; there's no plot of land to visit or tend. It all happened so quickly and traumatically: the table-tennis match, his own last game; the ambulance; the shocks and discoveries of the days that followed. And then the nothingness of his ashes being scattered on the wind.

The night after Bobby Moore's death I decided to stop searching for my father. It was time simply to let be. He'd lived as best he could, in a way that enabled him to get by, to cope. I thought back to how he'd spoken about his determination one day to find himself younger than his old pal from the rag trade, John Tyler. I thought he'd been joking when he said that; he wasn't.

None of this mattered any more. I loved and respected him and I always would. My interests were his. All that mattered most to me in life, I'd learnt or taken from him. Parked up in a side street in East London, the wipers scraping across a windscreen blurred by rain, I remembered something my sister Alison had once said about our father – that he had what she'd called a 'real voice'. Ah, *that* voice. What was it about it, and in England where accent can be such a tiresome indicator of class and background? What I now think my sister meant was this: that there was nothing in how our father spoke, or in the manner in which he spoke, to place him geographically; nothing about his accent or diction to suggest that he'd grown up in the old East End. And yet he spoke without affectation or contrivance. He wasn't trying to sound posh, as were so many self-improving Tory MPs in the eighties, with their elocution lessons and faux mannerisms. He simply spoke as he spoke, in his own way – and consequently sounded like no one else, just himself. Just then there was no other voice in the world I'd rather have heard but his, even if it was to have heard him say only two words: 'Go home.'

Twelve: The Big Sleep

My third and most recent visit to Liverpool was in November 2007, twenty-three years after Crystal Day, and this time I was back in the city to watch football – a Sunday-afternoon Premier League match between Liverpool and Arsenal, which was being shown live on Sky Sports. The Premier League, Sky Sports: someone waking Rip Van Winkle-like from a deep sleep would scarcely be able to comprehend the changes that have occurred in English football over the last twenty years. The moneyed homogeneity that has overtaken the game at the highest level – the rapacity, the greed, the disconnectedness between fans and the players, the outrageous ticket prices, the astronomical wages – would astonish our contemporary Rip Van Winkle. How, for instance, would he respond to this headline, from the *Observer*, from the summer of 2008: 'Kaka set to become the world's first £1m per month player'?

Today English football is locked into the greatest, gaudiest spending spree in its history, and, in spite of the worldwide credit crunch in effect as I write, rising unemployment, falling house prices and recession in Britain and the rest of Europe, the spree goes on (the most recent Sky and Setanta deal for live TV rights for Premier League was worth

£1.7billion to the clubs over three years), with £100,000-per-week salaries for players in England becoming routine. The game is at the very centre of our thin-spun celebrity and entertainment culture: an engine of globalisation and cash generation, a symbol of aggressive meritocracy, and, in the shape of the small army of foreign players, managers and club owners, of a deracinated cosmopolitanism. The Premier League is the richest, most watched, admired, and imitated in the world. The League's leading players – Cristiano Ronaldo, Fernando Torres, Didier Drogba, Cesc Fàbregas, Deco, Steven Gerrard, Wayne Rooney – are among the most recognised and admired people on the planet. They are objects of fantasy and desire, their wealth stupendous. But their separation from the people who pay to watch them, the fans, is absolute.

Alan Smith retired from playing in the summer of 1995. It was hard for him, he says now, watching as some of his former team-mates played on for many years afterwards, including his old friend Lee Dixon, to whom he is no longer close.

'It was a hard time for me, after retirement,' he says. 'I had friends still there. There was a gradual upping of the salaries; £200,000 was the ceiling when I stopped playing. For me, it wasn't about money, but there were lads there of the same age enjoying football for another four or five years after I'd retired. Nowadays, the fans are much further away from the players, that distance is there . . . supporters can't relate to someone on a hundred grand a week. If you go to Old Trafford after a game, the players' cars – all blacked-out windows – are chauffeured around to an entrance and then the barricades go up and the players are off. There's more envy now on the part of the fans, and you can understand that. As soon as all-seater stadia came in, it was bound to get more corporate. The atmosphere was bound to go.'

In 2008 four English teams – Arsenal, Chelsea, Liverpool and Manchester United – reached the quarter-finals of the European Champions League, a record for the competition. Three of them went on to reach the semi-finals and two, Chelsea and Manchester United, the Final. But it was obviously a triumph for the clubs rather than for the national side, which had failed to qualify for the 2008 European Championship, or for English players, since so few of them are regulars at our best four teams.

Football was slow to embrace the unfettered free market. Throughout the eighties, through much of the social and economic convulsion of that decade, when the old industrial infrastructure of Britain was allowed to decay beyond usefulness and a new spirit of entrepreneurial capitalism was at large in the country, football had remained unreformed, distinctively apart from the rest of society. During the eighties discussions were held intermittently between the chairmen of the so-called Big Five clubs – Arsenal, Everton, Liverpool, Manchester United and Spurs – about the possibility of forming a new breakaway Premier Division. But these talks were motivated by commercial imperatives rather than by any disinterested attempt to remake the game for the common good.

Following protracted negotiations with England's leading clubs, the Football Association published, in 1991, a document supporting the establishment of a new elite division, autonomous of the Football League. The document was written by its technical director, Charles Hughes, who in the eighties had published dense, pseudo-intellectual and widely ridiculed papers offering theoretical justifications of the long-ball game. This latest report was called 'The Blueprint for the Future of Football', and one of its proposals was that the game should seek to attract 'more affluent middle-class consumers'. The era of the fan was coming to an end as football caught up with the rest of the country by becoming articulate in the language of market capitalism. We were all consumers now and, it was decided, we, the fans, were a 'captive market'.

There was another important era coming to an end as well – the era of Margaret Thatcher. Little did she know when she made her triumphalist speech at the Guildhall on 26 May 1989 that by the end of the following year she would no longer be prime minister, removed from office not at a general election but by an internal party coup. She had become too autocratic, her detractors within the party said; she had lost her instinct for reform; the punitive poll tax showed that she no longer understood the aspirations of ordinary families; she was becoming too Eurosceptic, too much of the self-serving monarch. She was succeeded in November 1990 by John Major, a former bus conductor from Brixton in South London and a life-long Chelsea supporter. Here was a politician who not only understood football but who also watched it – and who was sympathetic to Lord Chief Justice Taylor's recommendations.

On 27 May 1992 the twenty-two clubs comprising the old First Division officially broke away to establish their own Premier League, freeing themselves in the process from any formal obligation to share revenues with clubs in the rest of the Football League. The ethos of redistribution that had defined football since the foundation of the

League was at an end. As if in celebration, Rupert Murdoch's BSkyB won an auction to pay £305million for the exclusive TV rights to the new FA Carling Premiership (a second four-year deal worth £670million was signed in 1997). Football, in the language of the ad men, had just become a 'A Whole New Ball Game'.

What was obvious was that the game in England was modernising faster than most would have thought possible at the end of eighties. The Taylor Report had obligated clubs in the higher divisions to invest in stadium infrastructure, for which they received government subsidy through the Football Trust. The ownership structures of clubs were changing and some were preparing to follow Tottenham Hotspur in becoming publicly limited companies; a new generation of director-entrepreneurs, led by David Dein at Arsenal, were intent on taking control of clubs away from the old established family owners, such as the Hill-Woods, and using their positions to ingratiate themselves at the top of the game; the euphoria generated by England's performances at Italia '90, where Paul 'Gazza' Gascoigne had delighted a nation with his eccentricities and clownish, antic disposition, his talent and tears, was contributing to rising attendances.

The Premier League was the first major sports league in Europe to be developed by and for television, though Sky came close to losing the first auction for exclusive rights to ITV. Those first televised games on Sky were accompanied by extraordinary hype and fanfare: Monday-night 'live' specials; dancing girls and cheerleaders; half-time entertainment (I was once at a game at which two sumo warriors, dressed in team colours, engaged in combat); brash and frenetic title credits; garish graphics and multidimensional camera angles. So few of us subscribed to Sky Sports in the early weeks and months of football's new deal that scarcity quickly acquired special value. Something exciting was happening to televised football and I, like many fans, wanted to find out exactly what. No matter the game – a wet night at Ewood, a bore draw at the Dell – it felt like an event in those early weeks to be watching football live on Sky in a pub or bar. The launch of the Sky-endorsed Premier League was a triumph of marketing, in keeping with an era in which so much of the public discourse would come to turn on issues of media control, spin and presentation. Before long, ticket prices began to increase exponentially as the game sought to exclude one set of fans, the urban working class, as Hughes had implicitly advocated, while attracting another more affluent set, the prosperous middle classes. (It would soon become attractive beyond its own domestic market – to the international plutocracy.) The poor and the young were being priced out of the game. By 2004 the average cost of a Premiership ticket was £40 – four times the minimum at some German or Italian grounds. 'The Premier League is now the most commercially successful football venture of its type in the world,' says John Williams of Leicester University's Football Unit. 'It was held up by Tony Blair as a modernisation model for the rest of British industry to follow. It's a bust-to-boom economic, global entertainment miracle.'

That may be so, but there's still a powerful nostalgia among fans of my generation for a lost, less aggressively commercial era of football, when the game seemed less cynically concerned with exploiting the loyalty of those who pay to watch and with selling itself to a global audience. 'The whole game is ridiculous now,' says Jon Holmes, who was one of Britain's first sports agents and is a former chairman and chief executive of the European division of SFX Entertainments, the worldwide 'talent' agency that represents David Beckham, Michael Owen and Steven Gerrard, among many others. 'I can remember on the day of Hillsborough walking away from the other semi-final and thinking that football as I know it had probably died, that I wouldn't now be able to take my son to games. It's over. Then Italia '90 came along. The BBC did it well. The Italians staged it passionately. The football was on the whole dire but England were one of the better sides: there was drama against Cameroon, the last-minute goal against Belgium, the epic semi-final against Germany, when England were the better of two good sides. It was as if the whole nation stopped for that game: the M1 was deserted, Westminster deserted, twenty million-plus watching on TV. That game proved to Sky you could get a mass audience for football. Lineker was popular, a different type of footballer. There was the Gazza factor. Then the money was provided to rebuild stadiums. The game went upmarket on prices and this helped stop hooliganism. It's still there, of course, down in the lower divisions, where tickets are cheaper.'

I was sitting with Holmes in an office he shared with the PR company Bell Pottinger in Holborn, central London. He seemed uncomfortable as he sat at his desk in an open-plan part of the office, as if he wanted to be anywhere but in that overlit space, in the high gloss sheen of a media hub. 'Today the attendances are quite good, but I'm not sure about the involvement from the fans. Everyone seems to support the main teams, Arsenal, Chelsea, Man United, Liverpool. I don't think kids are going to the games, and so the relationship with the local side has gone. Too many people are buying foreigners. If England do badly, people will start to lose interest. England doing well at the World Cups in eighty-six and ninety was critical to the rebirth of football.'

Holmes conceded that as one of the first sports agents he had contributed to the inflation of players' salaries. 'Players were treated abysmally, sold down the river by their own union. Look, it's a ridiculous industry; everyone pays the wrong people. The PFA are paid by the employers, the agents are paid by the club. Whose interests do they represent if they are paid by the clubs? Players think that's clever if they're not paying the agents – but they are; it's their money.'

The role of the agent had changed since the late 1970s, when Holmes first began to represent a young Gary Lineker, then at Leicester City. 'Agents are no longer advisors; they are concierges, there to tell lies and get the players out of shit. It's useless now . . . Why should I go around lying and getting people out of jail? Newcastle have just paid five and a half million for a bloke [Joey Barton] who may soon be going to jail. [He did.] Lee Hughes is coming out of jail for killing someone [the former West Brom striker was convicted of manslaughter after a drink-driving incident]. There will be a clamour of clubs wanting to sign him. There's no sense of responsibility in the game, no moral compass. The FA is cowed by the big clubs.'

He glanced up at a TV screen showing footage of Joey Barton in action for Manchester City. He looked at the screen, at me, and then sighed. The culture of the young footballer today was so aggressively acquisitive, he said. 'The peer culture is so dominant. We had a player I looked after who had five cars on lease but he didn't know where three of them were; they'd gone in gambling debts. In the past, football was not seen as an end in itself. There will be tragedies in this generation as too many players are used to a standard of living that will collapse once they stop playing. A lot of them will have to stay connected to the game; they have no other skills, and a lot of them lose their money through gambling or bad investments.'

In the late eighties Holmes represented the two most successful players in England, Lineker and former England goalkeeper Peter Shilton. They were well paid, but not excessively so. 'When Lineker signed for Everton [in 1985] he was earning seventy grand a year – with bonuses, about one hundred thousand. Shilton was on about two hundred thousand but that all went in gambling. He was hopeless; he had five houses but about fifteen mortgages! When Lineker went to Barcelona [in 1986] he was on two hundred and fifty thousand a year; about three hundred and fifty thousand when he came back to Spurs [in 1989]. He was the top earner in the country at that point.'

I asked Holmes if he thought that today's high salaries were immoral. 'Of course there's no moral justification for what they get. But we don't earn because of morality. People who work with old and terminally ill people earn less than you and me. There's no moral justification for that. It's all about market forces. Compared to [Roman] Abramovich, what they earn is still quite minor. But it has an effect on people; it creates a culture and climate. How do they use their money? Are they doing good with it? Is it developing them as people? I'm not sure it is.'

And so he went on: enraged, amusing, appalled. Here was one of the game's most intelligent and influential agents estranged from a world that he and those who followed him had done so much to create.

As I left the Bell Pottinger offices I thought of a conversation I'd had recently with Jeff Powell, who, after many decades as a sportswriter, had seemed as frustrated and disengaged as Holmes. 'There's been a terrible distancing of the players,' he'd told me. 'They have an absurd sense of their own self-importance, living behind high-security fences, behind the barbed wire with guard dogs patrolling. They've lost touch with reality, with who they are. Most of them have a distorted self-opinion, and think they're better than they are. The players used to mix in the pubs after the game; they were left alone because fans were used to seeing them, they lived in the same local community. Now, they have this rock-star aura of attraction, and seem to want to live like that. But I think they're worse off for not having a dialogue with all sorts of people, including us, the sports journalists. This culture of separation we have now from the body politic of football is tragic.'

On arriving in Liverpool I'd booked a room at a boutique hotel on Hope Street, which connects the city's two great cathedrals: a link road between faiths, a route across the old sectarian divide. The area in and around Hope Street, with its restored Georgian buildings, has been revitalised, like so much of the city centre. I was in town for what turned out to be the first of four meetings between Arsenal and Liverpool in the 2007–08 season; towards the back end of the season, they played each other three times in eight days in the month of April, with the return League fixture at the Emirates being squeezed between the home and away legs of a Champions League quarter-final. Both teams had started the season well, and at this point remained unbeaten. After three years of transition, during which time

Chelsea had emerged as the country's best team, Arsenal were once more mounting a title challenge. The game was thrilling; Arsenal utterly overwhelmed Liverpool with the brilliance and rapidity of their passing and movement – late in the game the centre-backs Kolo Touré and William Gallas frequently joined the attack or turned up on the wings as structures and formations dissolved and everything became more open-ended, fluid and improvised, with players interchanging positions in a demonstration of what can only be described as total football. And yet the game finished 1–1.

The style of the two sides was a study in contrasts: Liverpool kept hitting high, hopeful balls from the back, in the style of Arsenal of old, seeking out the six-feet-seven striker Peter Crouch, who came on as a substitute early in the game. Every time a Liverpool player hit it long, the Arsenal fans shouted 'Hooof', an onomatopoeic chorus of derision.

There was no palpable hostility between the rival fans that November afternoon, none of the expressions of mockery or regional antagonisms of old. The atmosphere was completely benign, as if the rival groups of fans were indifferent to each other. North and south: the shame is for England. No more. England no longer feels like two nations: in broad caricature, a benighted, socialist north and an affluent, more individualistic Tory south. To speak of two nations you must first have a coherent understanding of the meaning of one nation – and England today scarcely feels like a unified nation at all, hence all the wider anxious self-questioning which has become so much part of the culture. What is Englishness? Whither the British state?

London may be the capital of the United Kingdom but it

feels increasingly like a quasi-independent city-state: heterogeneous, multicultural, complicated, polyglot, hugely unequal, teeming. A global city. *The* global city. To visit devolved Scotland, by contrast, is to find yourself at large in what feels like a foreign country: homogeneous, confident, self-contained, social-democratic, of Britain but increasingly apart from it.

With the light already fading, though it was not yet four in the afternoon, and as I waited for the players to come out and for the match to begin, I glimpsed something of what had been lost from our football culture and perhaps from society in general when most of those around me, men and women, boys and girls, rose from their seats to sing along to Gerry and the Pacemakers' 'You'll Never Walk Alone', which was being played over the public-address system. For a few transitory moments I did not feel lonely in that crowd, as I sometimes do on match days at the Emirates when the collective hush of 60,000 people watching football can be estranging. These supporters seemed to be unified in a mystic communion that transcended the inadequacies of the present Liverpool team. Theirs was a connection extending back to Shankly and the slums of Scottie Road. Then the music stopped. The singing ended. The scarves that were held aloft and stretched as tightly as cloth on tenterhooks were lowered. People sat down and began chatting. My incorrigible sentimentality was replaced by the hard-headed realism of fandom. There was a game to watch, a team to support. *Fuck off, Liverpool.*

That night I had a dream about my father and for hours afterwards I couldn't get back to sleep. I kept thinking about the dream, about how he'd appeared before me in this very hotel room on Hope Street, looking very much as he had the last time I'd seen him properly. Eventually I got up in the unquiet darkness and walked over to the window. My room was at the top of the hotel, quite high up. From there I could see right across the city and on, in my imagination, to the sweep of the waterfront, which had been declared a UNESCO World Heritage site in 2004. It had stopped raining and I stood at the window for a long time, looking out over the soft sodium glow of the damp city streets, so far removed from the conflict and blight of the eighties. Like most great cities, Liverpool, its old dock-side warehouses and wharves reclaimed and rebuilt, continues to be remade and reinvented; as the European City of Culture for 2008 it would be soon receiving all visitors with confidence. So much had been restored and renewed – including St George's Hall, which had been reopened on 23 April 2007 after the completion of a £23million restoration. I'd visited St George's just that afternoon, and spent time in the Great Hall, with its marbled columns, Minton-tiled floor, high vaulted ceiling and stained-glass windows.

Football had brought me back to the city and, as I stood at the window looking out over it, I wondered what my father would have made of all the changes in the game in the years since his death. What if he was our contemporary Rip Van Winkle, and hadn't died but had been in a long, deep, coma-like sleep? What would he now make of the game and how would I begin to explain the transformations to him without, also, first describing how much England itself had changed?

I booted up my laptop with the intention of doing some writing but instead, with the glow of the screen on my face, I clicked on the Google Earth icon. I wanted to return to some of the places I'd visited earlier in the day and to try to see them not just virtually but rather afresh, as if I were seeing them through my father's eyes, to see as he would have done had he woken from his big sleep. The Google globe was spinning on its axis on the screen, a whole blue world turning. I clicked on the screen and zoomed in over the north-west of England, over Liverpool, the picture shrinking and then enlarging. I swooped in low over St George's Hall, hovering over the surrounding rooftops, before I moved on to the site of the new super city-centre shopping-mall development which, when completed, would be the largest of its kind in Europe. From there, I went north to Anfield, where the streets of terraced houses around the stadium remained eerily familiar, essentially unchanged from when my father and I had first visited in the seventies: Baltic Street, Vienna Street, Venice Street, Bagnall Street, Gilman Street. The shops and pubs on those streets were, like many of the actual houses, neglected and run-down. Earlier in the afternoon, as I'd explored the area around the stadium, it had appeared as if some of the houses, indeed entire streets, had been requisitioned and were awaiting demolition. There was obviously still tremendous deprivation in the city, even if it wasn't really to be found in the centre, with all the ceaseless clatter and toil of all its bright new reconstruction. It was out in the periphery, on huge estates such as Netherley which were built following the slum clearances.

We were now on our way out to those peripheral zones but first we paused to sweep in low over Goodison Park. As we zoomed in I found myself wanting to explain to my father how, because so many Liverpool supporters now came from outside the city – from very far away, in fact – Everton had begun to call itself the 'people's club', the club supported by Liverpool people from Liverpool. I pulled back and hovered a while above Stanley Park, its flat greenness bordered by neat rows of mature trees. The landscape below, even that which might be called natural, was intensely cultivated, part of nature but also somehow artificial. We zoomed in on the site of what will one day soon be the new Liverpool stadium, when the club finally leaves Anfield: for now, just an empty field on a screen.

I imagined telling my father of how Liverpool had come to be owned by two American billionaires, Tom Hicks and George Gillet, who, in February 2007, had bought the club for £218.9million. 'We respect the heritage and legacy of this franchise,' George Gillet had said at the time. 'Our job is to be custodians of this franchise; and to add to the lustre, not detract from it.'

Both Hicks and Gillet own sports franchises, to use a favoured word, in North America – *We can visit*, I would say to my father. *Let's drop in and take a look at what else they've been doing with their money*. Hicks and Gillet had immense plans for Liverpool. They said that they would pay for the construction of a new stadium. They would respect the club's history. They would do nothing to damage its integrity. Both men had expanded their vast business empires through the expert manipulation of debt and leveraged buyouts. But how to explain that, little more than a year after their purchase, Gillet – who was no longer talking to the man now referred to as his former partner, namely Tom Hicks – was in discussions to sell his fifty per cent share of Liverpool at a considerable profit to Dubai International Capital, the so-called investment arm of the Dubai government, even though the club had been loaded with at least £350million worth of debt as the Americans had sought through various leverage deals to finance the building of the new 70,000-capacity stadium in Stanley Park? (The Florida-based Glazer family had also leveraged the buyout of Manchester United in May 2005, and now the club was paying interest of £62million a year on debt acquired during a 2006 refinancing arrangement.)

Former Liverpool chairman David Moores, of the Littlewoods dynasty, who had been Liverpool's largest shareholder before the sale to Hicks and Gillet, eventually spoke publicly of his dismay at how the integrity of the club was being compromised by the opportunism of the feuding American co-owners. 'It's heartbreaking,' he told the *Liverpool Echo*. 'I'm almost lost for words about the damage that's being done to the club at the present time. As a fan, and as someone who loves the club, it is totally unacceptable to see this being played out in the public arena. This is most certainly not what the club is about. In fact, I can't ever remember – even going back to when I was a supporter as a kid – stuff being played out in public like we have seen in the last six months. It is embarrassing and it is not an acceptable way of doing things. I've never known anything like it.'

One struggles to feel sympathy for Moores. If he cared so much about the club perhaps he shouldn't have sold his majority shareholding to the Americans in exchange for tens of millions of pounds.

For a time, before they were tentatively reconciled at the beginning of the 2008–09 season, Hicks and Gillet had continued to go their own way, asking before certain games to be sat apart, like two brothers who had thrown food at each other at a children's party. They may have been disunited in public but they were oddly united in their desire to court the affection of Liverpool fans. Banners had begun to appear on the Kop calling on the Americans to agree to sell the club to Dubai International Capital; this was Gillet's preferred option, but not Hicks's. Gillet could only sell his fifty per cent of the club with Hicks's agreement and vice versa. They were locked together by way of their co-ownership of the club into a position of mutual antagonism: each unable to act definitively without the approval of the other. When Hicks's son, who is also called Tom, went into a Liverpool pub to talk to fans about his father's plans for the club he was spat at and abused. Both Hicks and Gillet and their families in America have received death threats.

The mistake both Hicks and Gillet had made – perhaps Hicks more than Gillet, in the view of the fans – was to have publicly criticised Liverpool's Spanish manager, Rafael 'Rafa' Benítez and to have approached Jürgen Klinsmann about becoming a replacement. In November 2007 the fans marched in their thousands in support of Rafa, before a Champions League game against Porto. The tubby, cerebral Spaniard, with the goatee beard and fidgety, anxious manner – he was known as the 'loner with the laptop' when he first arrived at the club from Valencia – was in the process of becoming Liverpool's most popular manager since Shankly, after establishing a bond with the fans by winning the Champions League in his first season in 2005. (Liverpool were 3–0 down at half-time to AC Milan, yet eventually won the trophy following a penalty shoot-out.)

To outsiders it can seem an irrational bond. Yet in this deeply religious city and on the night of the march it was as if Benítez was being sanctified: banners bearing his image were held aloft by the marching fans, and if you didn't

know he was a football manager you could have been for-
given for thinking that he was a priest or some kind of
political martyr. Even odder was to hear Liverpool fans in
the weeks afterwards calling on their American billionaire
owners to sell the club – or *franchise*, as we must learn to
call it – to an investment fund belonging to the Dubai government, under the control of Sheikh Mohammad bin
Rashid Al Maktoum.

It's obvious why the Al Maktoum family would want to
take control of a club as famous and distinguished as
Liverpool. For Sheikh Mohammad, sport is one of the most
powerful engines of globalisation, a supreme instrument of
soft power. Dubai is in love with its putative self-identity,
with the idea of what it will become, once all the construction of skyscrapers, hotels, roads, apartment blocks and
sports stadiums is at an end, once its various sub-cities –
Sports City, Media City, the World, the Universe – are finished and complete.

With the globe spinning on its axis that night in my hotel
room, I pulled back from Liverpool, from England, from
Britain, from Europe, and at the click of a button travelled vast
distances, journeying across oceans and continents, until I
reached the vast yellow aridities of the Gulf states. Once
there I followed the coastline of the Persian Gulf before
dropping down among the luxury hotels, the preposterous
skyscrapers and construction sites of the Dubai city-state.
It's wondrous and disturbing, this attempt by the Al
Maktoums to create the perfect globalised city-state in the
desert, irrespective of the environmental consequences, a
city dedicated to boundless leisure and the business of
making serious money. Money and leisure: the defining
nexus of our modern sporting culture; and Dubai is the

ultimate contemporary sports-and-communications city. Its influence in sports extends far beyond the international tournaments it hosts. Its national airline, Emirates, is the sponsor of Arsenal football club, and that was where I intended to go next, following the lines of connection mapping the global game.

Back towards the United Kingdom. London came into view, first as a huge, grey incoherent sprawl, and then the image began to sharpen. I hovered over the street grids, rail lines and road networks of the urban conurbation, hovered above the Emirates stadium itself – the second-largest stadium in the Premier League, built at a cost of £430million, a shining symbol of all that Arsenal had become over the last decade. I would tell my father of how I'd sat in most parts of the ground, including once in the grandly named Diamond Club, where I was greeted with a glass of champagne and a handshake from celebrity chef Raymond Blanc, who supervises lunch there. Many of the people sitting around me in the Diamond Club (cost: £25,000 a year for a pair of tickets, with another £25,000 paid up front for the privilege of being a member) did not seem to be there for the football. Perhaps they were there for the food – seared scallops, pumpkin polenta, lamb shanks. It occurred to me after the game, as I was offered more champagne and canapés by white-coated waiters, that Arsenal have ceased to be an English club in any recognisable sense. They may be based in London but they are the leaders of the new footballing cosmopolitanism. 'We represent the future, national teams the past,' Wenger said once when asked about the absence of English players from his team. What he meant, I think, was that his Arsenal are a model of progressive internationalism, in which national identity plays a small part and nearly every player speaks in the same broken English, the Esperanto of the twenty-first century.

I would say that, for all its new wealth, the excellence of many of its foreign players and coaches, the ambition of its foreign club-owners and its worldwide prestige, English football's astounding recovery has come at the cost of part of its identity. It's much more comfortable and safer to go to games than it ever once was, but the experience of match day has, in the top division at least, become far too corporate and controlled, bleached of much of its local colour. The game has become too detached from its old class and cultural associations, its regional specificities.

Where are all the groups of young boys and teenagers? This my father would no doubt have asked. Where are the equivalent to the lads who used to stand with you on the North Bank? They don't come any more, I would have to tell him. The tickets are too expensive for them. They cannot afford to go.

Where are all the working men with their sons and daughters? Where are the pensioners? They don't come any more, either, I would have told him, because ticket prices in the top division have risen by more than 300 per cent since 1989; companies and corporations have bought up whole blocks of seats.

Most distressing, I would have told him, is that the Football Association has done nothing, in its weakness and capitulation to the power brokers of the Premier League, to prevent the foreign takeover of our elite clubs, by men such as Hicks and Gillett at Liverpool, or Thaksin Shinawatra, the former prime minister of Thailand who briefly owned Manchester City before selling out to Abu Dhabi United

Group, as the club was passed from one inscrutable autocrat to another. The government refuses to intervene or legislate to prevent this takeover. To do so would be to violate the free-market orthodoxies to which both main British political parties continue to adhere. It was once the case that FA rules prevented club directors from being paid: they were custodians of a club's wellbeing; clubs could form limited companies but they were not-for-profit. Directors and chairmen of football clubs may often have been notorious for their egoism, opportunism and capriciousness, but they were often fans and did not, until very recently, come into football to make money. 'Dead money' was how Peter Hill-Wood described David Dein's purchase of his stake in Arsenal in 1983, after all. Yet today, as the political writer and Cambridge academic David Runciman puts it, 'Awash with money, preyed on by robber barons, rife with dodgy accounting, lubricated by back-handers, English football increasingly resembles nothing so much as American business during one of its periods of excess: the Enron-crazed 1990s, say, or Wall Street in the 1920s before the crash.'

Liverpool are, as I write, one of nine Premier League clubs owned by foreign billionaires, with others, such as Arsenal – whose majority shareholder, with twenty-five per cent of the club, is the Uzbek billionaire Alisher Usmanov – vulnerable to hostile takeover. It's hard to conceive of great continental clubs such as Juventus, AC Milan, Real Madrid, Barcelona or Bayern Munich being permitted to fall under the ownership of Russian oligarchs whose wealth is of dubious origin or of oil-rich autocracies such as Dubai or Abu Dhabi, or a former prime minister of Thailand who faced corruption charges in his own country and who has been described by Amnesty International as a 'human-rights abuser of the worst kind'. In the European countries where these clubs are based there remains a residual sense of the intrinsic value of football, of its capacity to unite a nation in moments of grand public occasion, of its being, as David Conn has written, a 'distinct social and cultural activity with inherent values'. Not here, not now, when the Premier League has become a playground of competition for oligarchs.

In a moment of candour while speaking to the magazine *France Football*, even Arsène Wenger, a true global soul if there ever was one – born in the contested borderlands of France and Germany, a Frenchman with a German name, he has worked in the tax haven of Monaco, in Japan and, for the last twelve years, in London – expressed concern at the transformation of the game in England. 'Fans are the keeper of our football,' he said. 'But the first signs of danger are there to see. Stadiums are starting to empty, TV channels and radio stations are overcrowded with football. There is a kind of overdose looming. I'm sure that there is a limit to the amount of football people can take, on TV and also financially. Suddenly the English model has gone from owner-supporters to owner-businessmen. The danger wasn't there yesterday, but it's there today. Of course you can have business integrated into the sport while still respecting the values of football. However, perhaps it is time for people to worry. Before you had a young kid who could watch his Liverpool team from the stand and who, after succeeding in life, would dream of buying his club. Things have changed beyond recognition all of a sudden.'

It's certainly true that, as Tom Bower, author of *Broken Dreams: Vanity, Greed and the Souring of British Football*, says,

'No other country allows the crown jewels of their major sport to become the uncontrolled playthings of investors whose backgrounds remain untested. Premier League football is not played for English fans, but for one billion paying spectators on global television. Financially that might be rewarding for rich investors and for the players themselves, but the benefit for the fans and the national team is questionable. The English game, some believe, is facing a fatal blowback.'

One instance of this blowback was England's failure to qualify for the 2008 European Championship in Switzerland and Austria in the very season that four English clubs reached the quarter-final of the Champions League. England's abject campaign resulted in the dismissal of coach Steve McLaren. He was swiftly replaced not (as I think he should have been) by an exceptional British coach, such as Martin O'Neill, who my father would have remembered from his days as a player under Clough at Nottingham Forest, but by Fabio Capello, an Italian of hardened achievement but who, at the time of his appointment on a reported salary of £120,000 per week, could speak no more than a few sentences in English – at least, in public, at press conferences when he should have communicating his urgent vision for renewal. Listening to Capello at his first press conference, wrote Martin Samuel in *The Times*, the nature of the surrender was unequivocal. 'The appointment made by Brian Barwick, chief executive of the FA, was not a victory after all, not the triumph it had been painted, but a terrible, hollow defeat. England lost, Italy won – again. Lost the way, lost the plot, lost all knowledge of what had been invented within these shores, with no clue how to get it back.'

So much writing by those who follow and report on the England national team as well as in the fanzines and on fans' websites has this same tone of regret. Never before, it's true, have so many people been as repelled as they are by the ethos of football as represented by our rapacious leading clubs. Even the often-ridiculous Sepp Blatter, president of FIFA, complained in the run-up to the 2006 World Cup in Germany of football's 'Wild West style of capitalism' and of elite players earning 'pornographic amounts'. Within two years Blatter would live down to expectations, and reaffirm just how ridiculous he can be, by likening Cristiano Ronaldo of Manchester United, a young man of immense ability who is paid by his club as much as £130,000 per week, notwithstanding the vast sums he receives from sponsorship and advertising deals, and who was then involved in a protracted transfer dispute between United and Real Madrid, to a 'modern-day slave'. He was a slave, according to Blatter, because United were refusing to allow him to break a long-term contract he had only recently signed. Alex Ferguson's reply was as terse as it was admirable. 'These days footballers can earn five or six million pounds a year,' he said. 'I do not want to dignify this kind of statement with a response but when you consider the history of slavery, it was a very unfortunate statement.'

Multimillionaire superstars being referred to as slaves by the man who runs the world game; the capture or hostile takeover of our clubs by foreign plutocrats; the dominance each year of the Premier League by the same few 'brands and franchises'; the first million-pound per month player; prohibitively expensive ticket prices – one wants to give up on the game, to turn away from it and watch from a distance as it continues to eat itself, gorging greedily on the fat and flesh of the fans, its own 'captive market'. And yet something stops me from turning away altogether, stops me from declaring that I'm finished with football; something keeps me watching and reading about it, keeps me going to games even as I recoil at the excesses and the crass commercialism – and, I would have told my father, that something is to do with love; it's to do with the indelible bond formed in early childhood, a commitment that's as irrational as faith and for the true believer just as enduring.

Before switching off the computer I had one last place to visit. I keyed in a street name and postcode, the globe pivoted and spun, the screen blurred before sharp focus was regained and there before me photographed from the air on a day of radiant clarity was the quiet cul-de-sac where I once lived with my parents in Harlow. I felt as if I was looking down from the basket of a hot-air balloon, sweeping in low over a landscape that seemed so familiar and yet had all the unreality of an architect's model. There were cars and houses but no people. I felt as if I was returning home after a long absence only to find everyone in the street inexplicably gone; the props and stage set were in place but there were no actors. I zoomed in closer until I was looking directly into our old garden: now a large flat green-brown expanse of emptiness. Why did it look so empty? Then I realised: the weeping willow tree had been cut down and the uncultivated area of wasteland at the far side of the garden on which our goat once grazed had been smoothed into an extended lawn. I zoomed in closer still but, in my eagerness to see with

greater clarity, I crash-landed in the garden. The Earth flat-
tened out. I could see no more.

When I was at school in the late seventies there was a terrace legend at Highbury named Dainton Connell, a.k.a.
Denton or the Bear. He was an incomparably glamorous
figure: a kind of warrior leader of the terraces. He was a
fighter during a period when fighting and violence defined
many football fans. Those who knew him and fought
alongside him say that he had extraordinary strength and
courage and that he was never cruel or gratuitously violent.
Everyone I knew who stood on the North Bank or Clock
End at Highbury claimed to know or have met Denton. I
never met him but there were many times when I returned
from a match and said that I'd stood alongside him, joined
in the chants with him, charged with him. Denton was
unusual for a terrace leader of that time because he was
black – his parents were Jamaicans. It's said that during
the late seventies, when the National Front were infiltrat-
ing the terraces, Denton's presence and popularity at
Highbury – he was, in the argot, a 'main face' – helped to
repulse the racists. But the club he had supported with such
ferocious devotion (he followed them in Europe, turned up
for youth- and reserve-team games) refused to allow his
wake to be held at the Emirates stadium, even though Neil
Tennant of the Pet Shop Boys, for whom Denton worked,
had offered to pay for the cost of hiring a suite there. It
was as if the club wished not to be associated with the man
who the journalist Janet Street-Porter, who made a documentary about Denton in the late seventies, has called
'probably the most famous Arsenal fan ever'.

The tributes to Denton posted on websites were remarkable

for their sincerity, warmth, and candour. This, from 'Ralph', is characteristic: 'As Arsenal as Herbert Chapman. A true Gooner before it was fashionable. The term "larger than life" was never more relevant. Thanks for over thirty years of memories, and the help you offered me all those years ago. Never forgot it, mate. See you on the other side.'

If you look carefully at the crowd at the Anfield Road End as Winterburn runs towards them after Thomas has scored to win the title for Arsenal you will be able to see a big, bear-like man in a jester's hat, delirious with happiness. That man is Denton.

In later years he worked as a bouncer for and confidant of the Pet Shop Boys, and it was while on tour with the band in Moscow that he was killed in a car accident one wet October night in 2007; the car in which he was a passenger overturned and crashed into a river. He was forty-six, married, with two children. His funeral was an astounding event: a cross between an East End gangster's wake and the passing of a monarch. 'He had mellowed and a lot of his reputation was from another time,' one of his close friends said, attempting to explain why Denton was so loved and admired by fellow fans. 'He was just Arsenal through and through – and, if you were an Arsenal fan, he was a friend of you. He never hit a scarfer [an ordinary fan]. He looked out for the younger fans when the team were playing in the north.'

Out of curiosity and respect I went along to see the funeral parade, which attracted so many thousands of people that part of the Holloway Road had to be closed to accommodate the mourners as they walked from the Emirates stadium to the Mary Magdalene Church. The Pet Shop Boys were there; so were Ian Wright, Lee Dixon, the boxer Frank Bruno and the comedians Matt Lucas and David Walliams. But more fascinating than the celebrity mourners was seeing the scarred and battered faces of some of the hooligans of long ago who had turned out to say thank you and goodbye to their lost leader. These were men in middle or late-middle age who, in all probability, had been on the terraces for my first game at Highbury in 1975, when West Ham fans took control of the North Bank; men who were now openly weeping in the street.

What were they weeping for? They were of course weeping for Denton but I think they were also mourning a football culture that had gone forever, a life they'd once lived, the camaraderie they'd once shared. Denton, said his friend Dan Miller, addressing the congregation at the funeral, was the first black skinhead. 'He got bigger but he mellowed and a nicer person you couldn't hope to meet. He was cuddly, warm and humble, always skint. Everywhere he went – christenings, weddings, funerals, West Ham away – D made good days great days with his hilarious antics. He never took sides among his own.

'Now he's gone, it's the end of an era.'

Epilogue: At the Emirates

'The closer you come to the end, the more there is to say. The end is only imaginary, a destination you invent to keep yourself going, but a point comes when you realise you will never get there. You might have to stop, but that is only because you have run out of time. You stop but that does not mean you have come to the end.'

Paul Auster, *The Country of Last Things*

On the morning of Christmas Eve 2007 my wife and I visited my mother's eldest sister – Connie Scott – at home in Harlow. She'd been living in the same brick-built, end-of-terrace house for more than fifty years, on what was once one of the town's new model council estates. For me it was a house of fond memories; it was there that I sometimes used to go as a young boy when my parents were at work, passing the hours by juggling a football in the garden as Connie prepared dinner, and it was there that Connie had brought up her three daughters. She now lived in the house alone – her husband, Bert, having died some years before – but as the family matriarch she was seldom alone. She was very soon to become a great-grandmother, and was always being visited by her daughters and their children and, I hope, in time, if time allows, she will be visited by their children's children: the continuity and folk memory of family life.

As we sat at the kitchen table, watching Connie make mince pies – the sleeves of her sweater were rolled up and she worked the flour-whitened pastry into irregular wedges – I looked out into the long, narrow garden, thickly hedged in on one side by hawthorn. At the bottom of the garden there was a paved area where a children's swing used to be, and beyond that the area where Bert used to park his caravan. I thought about some of those family Christmases past, when so many of us had gathered at Connie's house on Christmas Day, when several tables were pushed together in her rectangular-shaped living-room. We all sat around them, adults and children together: my grandfather Edgar at the head of the table, content in the company of his three adult daughters and their husbands, each with their own children. I have no idea how Connie was able to prepare a traditional Christmas roast-turkey lunch for so many, with only one oven, long before the advent and ubiquity of the microwave and dishwasher.

The next morning, Boxing Day, some of us would go off in a convoy of cars to football, invariably – this being a West Ham family – to Upton Park, if the Hammers were at home. It would usually be the men and the boys who went, though on one occasion my sister Alison came along too; she was always a stern moralist and she was appalled to discover so many young boys on the terraces smoking. She even rebuked several of them, urging them to give up. They just laughed.

That morning with Connie we got talking about football; I'd recently left my job as editor of the *Observer Sport Monthly* magazine, and she asked if I was missing working in and around sport. She began to speak about Arsenal. I knew she'd become interested in football over the past ten years but I'd no idea just how interested: she told me she watched the highlights of the Premier League on BBC1's *Match of the Day* on Saturday nights, then woke early the next morning, 'to have a quick bath', so that she was ready to watch the same programme again when it was repeated. She then watched BBC2's *Match of the Day 2* on Sunday night – that's a lot of football, in one weekend, for anyone. She knew the names of all the Arsenal players, spoke of her admiration for Wenger, and of how regretful she was that there were so few English players in the squad, let alone the team. 'I hope Walcott comes through. He seems such a nice lad.'

Football offered a sense of continuity in her life: narratives, a cast of strong characters to get to know and care about, ever-changing storylines, drama, a sense of an ending, and the inevitability of resolution. There was always something to look forward to – the next match, a new signing, the emerging pattern of another season. 'Do you know one of the things I'd dearly love to do before I die, Jay,' she said, 'and that's to go to a match at the Emirates.'

'I'll sort that,' I said.

But it was not as easy to buy a pair of tickets for an Arsenal game as I'd expected. Nowadays, every home game is a sell-out, with at least two thirds of the tickets taken by season-ticket holders. It's often impossible to buy a ticket on match day. After much scrambling around I was promised a pair of tickets for Arsenal versus Aston Villa on Saturday 1 March 2008 – £100 each, in Club Level – by a friend of a friend. I rang Connie and told her that we were on; I'd sorted it.

A few days before the game I received a text from this friend of a friend: he'd been arrested, or so he claimed, for 'touting'. He'd been accused of using an independent fans' association for selling season tickets at more than cost price, something he denied. His tickets had been confiscated, he said. What to do? The thought of disappointing Connie so close to the Saturday of the game was too painful. After a series of increasingly desperate emails and phone calls (including to the two friends who each had a pair of season tickets and with whom I usually went to games at the Emirates but who so late in the week could not help) I managed with relief to buy a pair of tickets, for the upper tier.

Connie and I travelled to north London by train from Harlow town station, a short ride of about fifteen minutes. I'd not lived in the town since 1983, and it must have been at least twenty-five years since I'd set off for a game from this station. The last time would probably have been with my friend, the West Ham fan who ended up in prison after a riot on a cross-Channel ferry.

In the car on the way from Connie's house to the station we passed the site of Harlow Sportcentre, and Connie told me how she had paid an extra penny on her rent in the late fifties to contribute to the cost of its building. 'The charge was optional,' she told me, 'but I thought it would be a good thing for the town to have.'

When I visited Harlow in the summer of 2003 to write about the town following the publication of a report by

ML E

MPs into urban blight in many former new towns, I was dismayed to discover that the Water Gardens had been demolished and that the Henry Moore statue called *The Family* was missing. 'I'm afraid one of the heads was knocked off it and stolen,' the local MP told me.

Now, Harlow was once more in the process of being redeveloped and even the missing head from Moore's *The Family* had been found and replaced, with the statue once more occupying public space. But so much of what I'd enjoyed as a boy – all those sports facilities in the town – had been closed down, demolished or relocated. Harlow Town's football stadium, where those thrilling FA Cup matches were played in the late seventies, was a building site, with a Barratt Homes development sprawling across what was once the pitch. The dry-ski centre had been pulled down, with flats built on its former site. The town swimming pool was still standing but was an empty shell of disuse, its Olympic-sized swimming lanes drained. The skating rink in the town park had been abandoned many years before. The Sportcentre itself was soon to be relocated, to be replaced by hundreds of so-called eco-homes. So much spoiled promise and tarnished idealism.

We arrived at Arsenal tube station about forty-five minutes before kick-off. The Emirates Stadium, which opened in July 2006, is built on the former Ashburton Grove industrial site, and is a short walk from Arsenal tube station. From the street you go up some steep steps and then cross a bridge which takes you over the Northern City railway line. I was at both the last League game at Highbury and the first at the Emirates, and I still can't say I love the new stadium as I did the old one. It's impressive in all its grandeur and gleaming efficiency, but it's in no way love-able. As you wait to buy a pre-match drink in the inner-stadium you could be in an airport terminal any-where in the developed world, so starkly impersonal is the setting, with its high, cavernous ceilings, muzak, TV screens and imposing glass and metal walls.

Then, from our position high on the bridge over the rail-way track, we saw the stadium, this vast concrete and glass bowl constructed on the site of a former rubbish dump, the words 'Emirates Stadium' emboldened in huge red characters above the Arsenal club badge. Connie gasped and for a moment it was as if she were lost in wonder. I tried to see the stadium as she did, as if for the first time, and there indeed it was shining before us, such a bold statement of ambition and of architectural gigan-tism.

We walked round to the front of the stadium, and bought a programme from a seller positioned alongside the two bronze cannons that stand outside the main entrance. Someone had laid down a portrait of Denton and some flowers on the pavement beside the guns. 'Who's that man?' Connie asked, pointing at the portrait. And I told her.

Once we were inside the stadium and in our seats, Connie asked about the final game at Highbury, on 7 May 2006. It had been at once a celebration and a long goodbye; after the final whistle there had been a performance on the pitch from the Who frontman Roger Daltry; a parade by former players from different eras; a return of the march-ing band that used to play before matches in the fifties, sixties and seventies; there were fireworks, which were pale and insipid against the late-afternoon spring sky. No one seemed to be living more intensely through those last moments at the venerable stadium than Wenger. Knowing that his team had to win to have any chance of finishing fourth and thus securing a place in the next season's Champions League, he was unusually hyperactive, especially early on when Arsenal were losing, continuously on his feet and gesturing in manic agitation.

After the match, with Arsenal's place in the Champions League secure following a frenetic 4–2 win, Wenger joined his players on a languorous walk around the pitch. I've never before seen him so relaxed or animated as he signed autographs and touched hands with some of those reaching out for him. When he was interviewed on a podium erected in the centre of the pitch, Wenger reflected on the 'special qualities' he'd discovered at Arsenal, and on how his teams had always played with spirit, togetherness and 'yes, even sometimes art'.

If the owner of a football club is wealthy enough, success can be bought; you can even buy the Premier League, as Blackburn did in 1995 and Abramovich's Chelsea have done most recently. But it's far better, surely, to achieve consistent success without having to pay grotesquely inflated transfer fees for ready-made superstars, as Chelsea have done; to achieve success and respect, as Arsenal have under Wenger, through the discovery and nurturing of exceptional young individuals, from all over the world, and making of them, through the collective expression of the team, something remarkable, lasting and true. Arsenal are today one of the superpowers of the European game, with 60,000 spectators at every home game and a growing worldwide fanbase. In spite of his inscrutability and reserve, and his at times baffling expressions of self-righteous indignation – his sense that Arsenal are uniquely persecuted by referees and other teams, repeatedly fouled and unfairly cheated – Arsène Wenger has effected a glorious revolution during a period when it has been said that the Premier League is not an English league any more; England simply 'hosts' the world league. At their best his Arsenal have shown us not only how the game can and should be played – 'yes, even sometimes art' – but also how young men of different races, religions and nationalities can work together harmoniously to create a moral example and vision of the cosmopolitan good life. 'Football,' Wenger has said, 'must be about values and morals, always.'

For a long time after the end of the game, Connie and I remained in our seats, watching the highlights of Arsenal's scrambled draw on the electronic screen. We watched the patient procession of fans making their way to the exit gates and then, in our imaginations, we followed them as they made their way down the hard stone stairs or in the lifts to ground level and out on to the streets, where they might have gathered for a while, chatting about what had been, the relief of such a late equaliser, before heading off to one of the nearby tube stations or their cars, leaving behind them in the returning normality and near-silence of the streets the debris of match day: the scattered cans and cartons, the discarded burger wrappers, newspapers, plastic bottles, ticket stubs, cigarette packets, sweet wrappers.

In April Connie would be eighty, and as we sat in our seats she spoke of how her trip to the Emirates would be the start of a 'lucky year' for her. She's small, not much more than five feet tall, with pale-blue eyes and white-blonde hair. She has huge vitality.

'I hope you didn't mind all the swearing,' I said.

'I only hear what I want to,' she replied, smiling.

Removed from the rarefied enclave of the Club Level seats where I usually sat, in the company of all the new Gooners who'd been drawn to the club since the turn of the century, even I'd been mildly surprised by the ferocity of the language in the upper tier. There'd been no singing or optimistic chanting, as one would have hoped and liked; most of the singing and scarf-waving takes place in the lower tier. With Arsenal a goal behind for much of the game, and struggling, there was only, increasingly, exasperatedly, shouted expressions of anger and frustration, much of it aimed at the ref. I thought again of how irrational fandom can be. So many of the fans around me did not seem to be enjoying their afternoon; the experience of being there seemed much more about endurance and managing disappointment: the disappointment of Arsenal's erratic passing; of the excellence of Aston Villa, so well organised by Martin O'Neill; of the news from elsewhere, where rivals Manchester United and Chelsea were both winning easily.

When Arsenal equalised deep into injury time, in the final seconds of the match, there was an ecstatic outpouring of relief. 'It was as if everyone rose as one,' Connie said. 'It was magnificent.'

Suddenly, with the match ending in a draw, and with Arsenal one point clear at the top of the table with ten games remaining, strangers were shaking hands and slapping one another across the back and shoulders. Most importantly, they were smiling again. There was even a smartly syncopated chant of old: *We are top-o-th-league/We are top-o-th-league.*

Hearing the chant returned me to that long-ago Saturday afternoon in April 1989, when Arsenal beat Newcastle 1–0 at Highbury but elsewhere in England fans had been crushed to death at an FA Cup semi-final, in the centenary season of the Football League. So much since then had changed about the game, for better and worse. For better, because of the diminishment of hooliganism, the absence, on the whole, of racism, and the improved facilities for fans inside stadiums. (So benign has watching football become, at least at the highest level in England, that my eighty-year-old aunt can feel comfortable about attending a match and describe it to me as a 'truly beautiful experience'.)

For worse, because football has ceased to be the people's game, in any meaningful sense. It's become a game defined by egoism, rapacity and greed, and by a grotesque mercantile, neoliberal winner-takes-all ethos.

'I'm a people's man,' said Bill Shankly, 'only the people matter.'

The new project to play an international round of matches 'recognises the truly global appeal of the Barclays Premier League whilst understanding that the traditions of the English game have always underpinned our success,' said Richard Scudamore, chief executive of the Premier League, in February 2008. 'It is an idea whose time has come.'

With the ground all but empty of fans Connie and I finally left our seats, but not before she paused to have one last lingering look. I followed her gaze across the pitch, which, on arrival, she'd described as being 'as smooth and perfect as a carpet'. I wanted to tell her about the end of the

1988–89 season, when the pitch could not have been less like a carpet: it was as pitted and rutted as a battlefield. Instead, I waited as she absorbed all that she could of the now-emptied, four-tier bowl-shaped stadium and then pointed up at a plane passing high above. 'I wonder if they're looking down at us inside the stadium,' she said.

Outside there were many hundreds of people still massing around the entrance to Arsenal tube station, funnelled into lines by police on horseback – still police on horseback, after all these years. The atmosphere was orderly and quiet. All around people were hard at work, dismantling the stalls and tables that had been erected before the game in the small front gardens of some of the Victorian terraces, from where programmes, fanzines, scarves, hats, badges, flags, sweets and burgers had been sold. Emerging from the station, rather than being intimidated, Connie had allowed herself to be swept along by the match-day bustle, the hustle of the touts, the shouts of the guys selling fanzines – *Get yer latest Gooner here!* Now the mood was different, much more subdued. People just wanted to get home.

Rather than taking our place in the queue outside the station we walked along Gillespie Road, where I pointed out one of the former entrances to Highbury, the entrance outside which my father and I were caught up in a crush all those years ago. Arsenal first played at Highbury in September 1913, when they left their old base south of the river in Woolwich to move north, but now the old stadium was a vast construction site. Huge cranes leered bearing the name Sir Robert McAlpine, darkening the skyline. The North Bank and Clock End had long since been demolished but the structures of the old West Stand and the listed East Stand with its Art Deco facade remained. The marble entrance halls were in the process of being transformed into million-pound apartments, with the space once occupied by the pitch serving as a communal garden.

I hadn't wanted Arsenal to move from Highbury, from that wonderfully small, intimate jewel of a football stadium, enclosed as it was by those Victorian terraced streets. I didn't want the club to sell naming rights of the new stadium to a Dubai-based airline, or for there to be flashing electronic adverts at the side of the pitch during play, their garish flicker a terrible distraction, or for the club to have no local-born English players in the team, or for an Uzbek billionaire to use his outrageous wealth and power stealthily to mount a hostile takeover. But if you're not to be enfeebled by sentiment, if you're not to become resentful, you've got to move on, to let go, to live in the present, to love your club for what it is, not for what it could or used to be. You cannot keep trying to hold on to something over which you have no control. Perhaps one of the hardest lessons of life is this: when things are gone they're gone, as one of the cowboys puts it in Cormac McCarthy's great novel *Cities of the Plain*. They ain't comin' back.

'You're looking cold, Jay,' Connie said as we stood outside what was once Highbury. 'I think we should go.'

And then: 'We left it late, didn't we!'

She was right – I was feeling cold as well as a little despondent as I stared up at the crane-darkened skyline, and we'd certainly left it late.

'Leaving it late,' I said, 'is an Arsenal tradition.'

She smiled and we turned to head off in the direction of Finsbury Park station. As we walked, my thoughts returned to another day when we'd left it late, so very late: 26 May 1989, and the last game of the last season of the eighties, the last season of its kind there ever was to be. *One minute to go. Just one minute.*

I closed my eyes and, fleetingly, there he was again, as he was at Anfield and has been in the ongoing present through all the years since, Michael Thomas, free, and lost to the moment. He must know the defenders are closing on him, must feel the hot rush and strain of their exertion. He has the ball and is moving towards the penalty spot. The goalkeeper is coming towards him, narrowing the space. Thomas has the ball. He's waiting for the goalkeeper to commit. *I was just waiting for him.*

Thomas, right at the end.

Tony, Frank and Jason Cowley in 1989.

Author's Note

This book is broadly the story of one celebrated football match and of the world as I found it at the end of the 1980s. I name all my sources in the text or in the acknowledgements section which follows, with the exception of one person who spoke to me on the condition of anonymity. I have changed the name of one person who features in the narrative.

I would like to thank all those who spoke to me in the preparation of this book as well as those who replied to emails and letters and phone calls. I would like especially to thank all my family, living and dead. Special thanks to Sarah Cowley – I'll never forget the first time I saw you; to Oliver Price, friend, researcher, former colleague, Gooner; to Ernest Hecht for all those trips to Highbury and the Emirates and much more; to Kevin Conroy Scott for his unstinting commitment; to Andrew Gordon for your initial enthusiasm; to Mike Jones for your calm and expertise; to Monica O'Connell, Laura Barber, Rory Scarfe and Roy Robins for your brilliant close readings.

Thanks also to: Alan Smith, David O'Leary, Lee Dixon, Paul Davis, Kevin Richardson, Michael Thomas, Theo Foley, Dave

Hutchinson, Jim Rosenthal, Kate Hoey, Peter Hill-Wood, Peter Robinson, Kenny Dalglish, Steve McMahon, Ian Rush, Gary Ablett, Steve Nicol, Phil Scraton, Tom Bower, David Conn, David Renton, John Williams, Jeff Powell, Jon Holmes, Roger Alton, Nick Greenslade, David Luxton, Andrew Hussey, John Belchem, Matthew Jennings, Michael Barrett, Jonathan Bumstead, Henry Sheen, Simon Chapman, Stuart Burrows, James Corbett, Jamie Jackson, Colin Randall and Nick Randall.

Bibliography

Tony Adams with Ian Ridley, *Addicted*

John Aldridge, *The Autobiography*

John Barnes, *The Autobiography*

David Conn, *The Beautiful Game: Searching for the Soul of Football*

George Graham, *The Glory and the Grief*

Phil Scraton, *Hillsborough: The Truth*

Perry Groves, *We ALL Live in a Perry Groves World*

Jasper Rees, *Wenger: The Making of a Legend*

Xavier Rivoire, *Arsene Wenger: The Biography*

Ray Pallet, *Goodnight Sweetheart: Life and Times of Al Bowlly*